You can't wait to use the applications in this book?

Order your *MIDI Programming for the Macintosh* disk today!

All of the programs in this book are available on a Macintosh disk with full source code and compiled applications and resource files. You'll find a complete set of tools for MIDI programming, such as applications that demonstrate processing MIDI data in real-time, applications that give examples of processing System Exclusive MIDI data, and much more. All the source code is ready to run or can be extracted module by module for use in other programs. Source code examples are in Lightspeed™ Pascal and Microsoft QuickBASIC™ and use MIDIBASIC™ and MidiPascal™ libraries.

To order, return this postage-paid self-mailer with your payment of $20, plus sales tax if you are a California resident, to: M&T Books, 501 Galveston Drive, Redwood City, CA 94063. Or, call toll-free 800-533-4372 (In CA 800-356-2002). Ask for **Item #023-0**.

YES! Please send me the *MIDI Programming for the Macintosh* programs disk for $20 _____

California residents add applicable sales tax _____% _____

TOTAL _____

_____ Check enclosed. Make payable to M&T Books.

Charge my _____ VISA _____ MasterCard _____ American Express

Card # _____ Exp. date _____

Name _____

Address _____

City _____ State _____ Zip _____

7018

MIDI Programming
for
the Macintosh

M&T BOOKS

MIDI Programming
for
the Macintosh

Steve De Furia
and
Joe Scacciaferro

Ferro Technologies

M&T Publishing, Inc.
Redwood City, CA

M&T Books
A Division of M&T Publishing, Inc.
501 Galveston Drive
Redwood City, CA 94063

M&T Books
General Manager, Ellen Ablow
Editorial Project Manager, Michelle Hudun
Editor, Dave Rosenthal
Cover Designer, Michael Hollister
Cover Photographer, Michael Carr

Ferro Technologies
Software Design, Steve De Furia
Editor, Barbara Williams
Design and Production, everon enterprises
Illustrator, Steve De Furia

Library of Congress Cataloging-in-Publication Data

De Furia, Steve.
    MIDI programming for the Macintosh

    Includes index.
    1. MIDI (Standard)   2. Computer sound processing.
3. Macintosh (Computer) -- Programming.   I. Scacciaferro,
Joe. II. Title.
MT723.D4   1988   789.9'9   88-13801
ISBN   1-55851-021-4 (book)
ISBN   1-55851-022-2 (book/disk)
ISBN   1-55851-023-0 (disk)

91   90   89   88   4   3   2   1

Limits of Liability and
Disclaimer of Warranty

How to Order the
Accompanying Disk

All of the programs in this book are available on a Macintosh disk with full source code and compiled applications and resource files. You'll find a complete set of tools for MIDI programming, such as applications that give examples of processing System Exclusive MIDI data, and much more. All the source code is ready to run or can be extracted module by module for use in other programs. Source code examples are Lightspeed™ Pascal and Microsoft QuickBASIC™ and use MIDIBASIC™ and MIDIPascal™ libraries.

The disk price is $20.00. California residents must add the appropriate sales tax. Order by sending a check, or credit card number and expiration date, to:

MIDI Programming for the Macintosh Disk
M&T Books
501 Galveston Drive
Redwood City, CA 94063

Or, you may order by calling our toll-free number between 8:00 A.M. and 5:00 P.M. Pacific Standard Time: 800/533-4372 (800/356-2002 in California). Ask for *Item #023-0.*

Acknowledgments

The authors wish to thank Allen Marsalis of Altech Systems, Diana Bury, John McEnerney, and David Neal of THINK Technologies, and Jerry Kovarsky of Casio for their enthusiastic assistance and encouragement throughout this project.

Trademark Acknowledgments

All terms mentioned in this book that are known to be trademarks or service marks are listed below. In addition, terms suspected of being trademarks or service marks have been appropriately capitalized. M&T Books cannot attest to the accuracy of this information. Use of a term in this book should not be regarded as affecting the validity of any trademark or service mark.

Macintosh is a trademark of Apple Computer Inc.
MIDIBASIC and MIDIPascal are trademarks of Altech Systems
Lightspeed Pascal and Lightspeed C are trademarks of THINK Technology
Turbo Pascal is a trademark of Borland International
QuickBASIC is a trademark of Microsoft Corp.
ZBASIC is a trademark of Zedcor Inc.
CZ-1, CZ-230s, CZ-1000, CZ-5000, MT-540 are trademarks of Casio Inc.
DX7 and TX 802 are trademarks of Yamaha Music Corp.
LXP-1 is a trademark of Lexicon Inc.
MSB+ is a trademark of J.L. Cooper Electronics
JamBox 4 is a trademark of Southworth Music Systems Inc.

Foreword

Why would a computer programmer want to learn how to write MIDI programs?

As a programmer with little music ability, I know why a programmer would want to write music programs. No other form of programming, except for graphics, is as stimulating.

When choosing my first computer, back in 1979, I purchased an Apple II for its superior graphics and sound capabilities. Making sounds and graphics were all I expected to do with it. There was no printer, and no disk drive. My first music application (loaded from a cassette tape) took over a minute just to load the program! The first program I wrote that made any sound was written in Applesoft Basic. It wasn't phenomenal, but I beamed at the fact that my very own computer was capable of making graphics and sounds.

Within a few months, I changed my major to computer sciences and got a job at the local Apple dealer. Sounds and graphics held my interest in computers through the dark and dreary days of endless programming classes involving the most boring computers. Waiting in line to sign on to a keypunch machine was a real drag, but having a "graphic sound system" at home tied into my stereo was pretty cool. Now that MIDI has made it possible to communicate with virtually any electronic musical instrument available, it's easy to see why a programmer might grab the chance to write a MIDI application—its hot, rad, hep, and, yes, totally tubular. In other words, it's stimulating. Not often do you get to shake the rafters with a few GOSUBs.

Why would a musician want to learn how to write MIDI programs?

A number of programming languages now exist for the Mac and other personal computers—MIDIBASIC and MIDIPascal have been out for over a year. The way is well-paved for anyone wanting to write MIDI programs, but why would a dedicated musician want to learn computer programming just to write a MIDI application? I would venture to guess it would be in order to achieve total control over the equipment—to know and to do everything—and who better to write music software than musicians? Every talented musician I've talked to can shoot holes through most commercial software.

Even though there seems to be a shortage, there are many computer programmers in this world. There are even more musicians, but there are precious few musician/programmers. In all honesty, I am not one of them . . . not yet. Maybe you are , and I hope my programming talents and this book will provide something useful to those who can best put it to work.

Allen Marsalis

Author of MIDIBASIC and MIDIPascal

Contents

Part One

What's in it for You

Part 1

What's in it for You

In this book we'll show you how to write your own Macintosh music software using MIDI (Musical Instrument Digital Interface) conventions. **MIDI Programming for the Macintosh** was designed to be useful to people with varying levels of programming and MIDI experience. In writing the book we made the following assumptions:

- You want to write your own MIDI programs for the Apple Macintosh computer.

- You want your programs to have the features that make Macintosh programs easy to learn and easy to use, namely menus, the mouse, dialogs, etc.

- You are familiar with Pascal or BASIC programming, or you are using this book in conjunction with Pascal or BASIC manuals.

We don't assume that you're a veteran Macintosh programmer.

We don't assume that you understand what MIDI devices like synthesizers, sequencers, and drum machines are.

We don't assume that you know how these devices are used in a MIDI system, or how they can be accessed by a computer.

You may be a super-hacker or MIDI wizard looking for some light reading. You may be experienced with computers, but unfamiliar with MIDI and therefore unsure of what a MIDI program could be used for. Perhaps you already have your own MIDI studio and you want to do things that no one has written the software for. In any case, we hope you'll find what you're looking for in this book.

The book doesn't have to be read from start to finish. Depending on your experience, you may want to skip right to the section that interests you most.

If MIDI is new to you. . .

You may be an experienced programmer looking for new application areas to explore. MIDI makes it possible to connect all sorts of musical instruments and sound processing devices to your computer. To the computer, any of these MIDI music machines is just another peripheral, like a printer, modem, or joystick. Experienced programmers will quickly recognize that this new class of peripherals will require new software applications. However, without a solid understanding of MIDI concepts, those programmers will find themselves "all dressed up with no place to go."

Part 2 will tell you what MIDI is and will familiarize you with the types of MIDI devices and functions that are in common use. It will bring you up to speed in understanding the basic concepts of a MIDI system, and give you some insight into the application possibilities MIDI makes available to you as a programmer. Part 2 also includes a complete MIDI programmer's reference with detailed summaries for every message and data format defined by the current MIDI 1.0 Specification. This quick reference will be an invaluable aid when you begin to create your own programs.

If you are already an old hand at writing Macintosh software, you can skip ahead to parts 4 and 5 for examples of how to make the most of what MIDI has to offer, once you've gotten your MIDI basics together.

If Macintosh programming is new to you. . .

Creating programs with the features we take for granted when using our Macintoshes—the mouse, pull-down menus, dialogs with buttons and check boxes, quick screen graphics, windows, etc.—is not a trivial task. These features are built into Mac programs by calling the Mac's ROM-based *Toolbox routines*. Learning to use the Mac Toolbox is like learning an additional programming language. Although this book is not intended to be a complete Toolbox programming reference, or a "bible" for commercial program development, it will present the basics of Toolbox programming, while giving you a set of software tools that you can use and expand upon in any Macintosh application. Our Pascal program example demonstrates many of the fundamentals of programming with the Mac Toolbox; our BASIC program example will demonstrate many of QuickBASIC's built-in Macintosh commands that allow you to create Mac software without using the Toolbox. Both of these programs will show you how to create an event-driven application "shell" that uses menus, dialogs, the mouse, resource files, and more.

In Part 3 we'll explain the flow of a typical event-driven Macintosh program, and provide you with tips and references for Toolbox programming. The two application examples in parts 4 and 5 will demonstrate many uses of Macintosh as well as MIDI routines.

If programming is new to you. . .

You may be a musician who uses the Mac to run commercial MIDI software every day, but is new to computer programming. You're intrigued by the MIDI tools you're already using, and can think of many other things you wish you could do with your MIDI software. You are in the opposite position of the seasoned programmer who's new to MIDI. Rather than being all dressed up with no place to go, you know where you want to go, you're just not sure how to get there from here! Until recently, programs for practical MIDI applications like those presented here would have been beyond the scope of a beginner's book. This was largely due to the need to write assembly code to handle communication between the computer and the MIDI interface. None of our programming examples use assembly language routines to access the MIDI interface. Instead, we use a set of *library commands* developed by Altech Systems. These excellent MIDI programming tools are available in BASIC and Pascal versions, MIDIBASIC and MIDIPascal. They allow us to present powerful MIDI programming examples without having to resort to any assembly language. Although this book isn't meant to stand alone as a how-to programming book, we have taken great care to develop and present our examples in a manner that will be instructive to the beginner. The programs are developed as a series of short modules (subroutines, functions, and procedures). Each module focuses on a specific task within the overall application. The use of short, single-purpose modules allows us to identify, isolate, and demonstrate numerous MIDI and Macintosh programming concepts.

In Part 3 we present guidelines for creating your own software as well as a list of references for more information. We take a look at how to specify and design a simple interface testing program, and then present a working version in BASIC and Pascal. Part 3 also contains an overview of Macintosh programming techniques, as well as complete command references for MIDIBASIC and MIDIPascal.

The application examples (source code, resource files, and compiled versions) are included on the disk that accompanies this book. These examples are mainly made up of procedures and subroutines that you can transfer into your own programs. Feel free to modify them or use them as is.

What you need to get started. . .

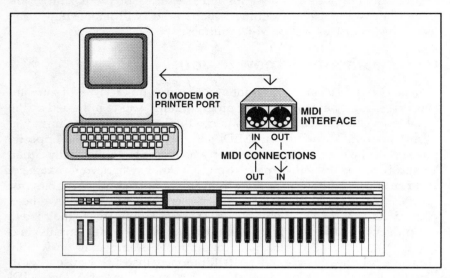

You'll need the following hardware and software to create and run the program examples in this book.

- Macintosh Plus, SE, or Macintosh II with the latest system file (version 6.0 as of this printing)

- two 800K disk drives, or one 800K disk drive and a hard disk (highly recommended)

- ResEdit, Apple's resource editing utility

- MIDIPascal by Altech Systems and a Pascal compiler. We used Lightspeed Pascal by THINK Technologies for our Pascal examples and highly recommend it.

or MIDIBASIC by Altech Sytems and QuickBASIC by Microsoft (interpreter and compiler)

For information on using other Pascal implementations or C, and ProLog, be sure to read "Other Languages" on page 8.

- any Macintosh compatible MIDI interface and a pair of MIDI cables

- any MIDI instrument that has a keyboard or other controller, and that makes sounds, such as a synthesizer, sampler, or digital piano

If you don't already own any MIDI gear and you're looking for a starter system, check out Casio's CZ-230S and MT-540. Both are excellent low-priced MIDI "peripherals." Each offers a wide variety of excellent sounds (the CZ-230 uses PD synthesis to create sound, and the MT-540 uses PCM samples). They both have built-in MIDI drum machines as well. These units are entirely self-contained, complete with built-in speakers, and are small and lightweight.

About ResEdit. . .

Apple has a developer's programming utility called ResEdit. It is a graphic-based resource editor. With it you can create new resource files or edit existing ones. ResEdit can be downloaded from most Apple on-line SIGs (Special Interest Groups) or it can be obtained by contacting Apple directly. You will need ResEdit if you want to compile stand-alone versions of MIDIBASIC programs, or if you want to alter any of the dialogs we've created for our programs.

You can also create resource files with any text editor and then use a *resource compiler* (RMaker, Rez) to convert it into a resource file. However, you'll find that the syntax for creating resources is very rigid (more like assembly code than BASIC or Pascal).

ResEdit allows you to work with resources by manipulating windows, control locations, text strings, etc., with the mouse. When you're done editing a resource file, ResEdit will compile it and create an object code version that can be linked to your program. Check the documentation for your programming language for information on how to link resources to your programs. Be aware that ResEdit has gone through several revisions and some of the earlier versions were a bit quirky. As of this writing, the current version of ResEdit is V1.2b1. If you don't have this (or a later) version, be sure to update.

Resources used by programs in this book. . .

Our Pascal program example uses a resource file to hold various dialog boxes (resource type DLOG), alerts (resource type ALRT), and dialog item lists (resource type DITL). The resource file is included on the source code disk that is available with this book. If you purchased the book without the disk and would like to obtain it, please see the disk order form in the front of this book.

About programming languages. . .

LightSpeed Pascal

The Pascal programs in this book were written with THINK Technologies Lightspeed Pascal Version 2. Lightspeed Pascal is an excellent program-development system for the Macintosh. It features a very powerful compiler and a unique Mac-style environment for managing programming projects. All of the "housekeeping" normally associated with development systems is handled by Lightspeed's *project manager*. It takes care of such chores as building and linking, managing object files, etc. You can compile and run your programs under a very powerful, interactive debugger. Compiled Lightspeed Pascal programs run fast enough to handle complex real-time processing of MIDI data (as demonstrated in our *Real-Time MIDI Lab* application).

Microsoft QuickBASIC

The BASIC programs in this book were written with Microsoft's QuickBASIC. QuickBASIC is an implementation that includes both a BASIC interpreter and compiler. You can build and test your programs interactively using the interpreter and compile them as stand-alone applications when your project is complete. Although compiled QuickBASIC programs are faster than interpreted ones, they generally do not execute quickly enough to support complex real-time MIDI applications. QuickBASIC is certainly fast enough to handle simple real-time applications and non-real-time applications like System Exclusive editors and librarians. We've included BASIC examples in this book because so many people are already familiar with BASIC programming. If you're one of those who already knows a little BASIC, you might be pleasantly surprised at how quickly and easily you can have your own MIDI programs up and running.

Other Languages

As this book goes to print, MIDIBASIC and MIDIPascal can also be used with a number of other languages. MIDIBASIC is supplied in two versions, one for Microsoft QuickBASIC and its older BASIC, the other for Zedcor's ZBASIC.

MIDIPascal is supplied in both Lightspeed format and the standard Macintosh REL format. MIDIPascal can be adapted for use with Lightspeed C, Turbo Pascal, and Prolog. For information on how to interface the MIDIPascal library with these and other languages, contact Altech Systems, 831 Kings Highway, Shreveport, LA 71104.

Part Two

A Programmer's Introduction to MIDI

Part 2

A Programmer's Introduction to MIDI

Overview of MIDI

MIDI is a communication standard, developed and adopted by the manufacturers of electronic musical instruments. Although it is essentially only a set of specifications to ensure compatibility of equipment, its adoption as an industry standard has contributed to a technology explosion in the field of music. The widespread use of microprocessor-driven sound generating devices, and the ability to connect them via MIDI, allows computers to analyze and regenerate sound, and to control, monitor, edit, and store musical events. The proliferation of MIDI gear has not only revolutionized the art of music, but has created new opportunities for programmers as computers become an integral part of MIDI systems.

In this section we will take a look at MIDI basics, review the simple hardware requirements that define a MIDI device, and the data format that comprises the bulk of the MIDI Spec.

MIDI Hardware

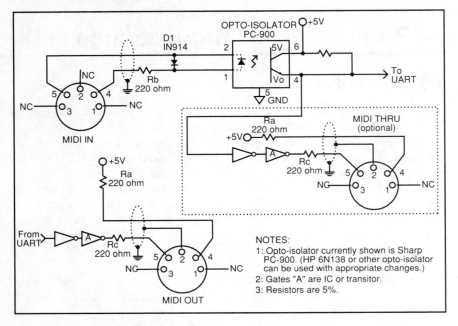

MIDI is a simple serial communication bus, similar to the computer industry's RS-232 or SCSI bus. Instead of this information being used to control a printer or a modem, the MIDI bus carries information pertinent to music composition, performance, and production.

The hardware portion of the MIDI standard specifies the type of cable and connector used for signal transmission, as well as the signal used to transmit MIDI data.

The MIDI signal is a serial voltage transmission, standardized at the rate of 31,250 bits per second. MIDI messages are comprised of bytes encoded to define the type of message being sent (*status bytes*) and those which convey information relevant to the preceding status byte (*data bytes*).

A MIDI cable is simply a shielded, twisted-pair cable with a 5-pin DIN plug at either end. Pins 4 and 5 are connected to the twisted pair of wires and carry the MIDI signal. Pins 3 and 5 are currently unused, but are available for future expansion of the MIDI Spec. Pin 2 is grounded when attached to a MIDI *port* —the 5-pin DIN socket provided on MIDI devices to receive the MIDI cable plug.

There are three types of MIDI ports: IN, OUT, and THRU. MIDI messages travel in only one direction over the cable, so each MIDI port function is restricted to its single designated use. The MIDI IN port allows a device to *receive* messages for its microprocessor via the MIDI cable. The MIDI OUT port allows a device to *transmit* signals via the MIDI cable from the device's microprocessor to another device. The MIDI THRU port allows a device to *pass* messages through to another device without acting on those messages itself.

Not all MIDI devices are equipped with all three ports (and some are provided with several of each type). Most have at least one MIDI IN and one MIDI OUT port. The THRU port is not essential for transmission or receipt of messages and is not available on all devices.

Any microprocessor-based device such as a synthesizer, sampler, sequencer, drum machine, effects processor, lighting board, computer, etc., can use these MIDI ports to send and receive MIDI data. The information exchange can be as simple as denoting which key on a synthesizer was pressed or was sophisticated enough to simulate an entire multi-track recording studio.

MIDI provides not only the means for information exchange among linked devices, but also a means by which they can interactively control each other. The instrument sending information is said to be the *master*, an instrument receiving information is said to be the *slave*. Because MIDI devices are equipped with input ports as well as output ports, they can be both master and slave, as needed.

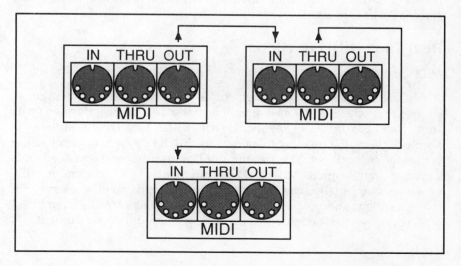

Understanding the Elements of a MIDI System

All MIDI instruments, like synthesizers, drum machines, and sequencers, have built-in MIDI ports. They can be connected directly with a MIDI cable. Connecting a Macintosh into a MIDI system requires a Mac/MIDI interface. One side of the interface connects to one of the Mac's serial ports (SCSI), the other side of the interface has two standard MIDI connectors for IN and OUT. Some interfaces have multiple IN and OUT ports. Mac/MIDI interfaces run at one of three clock rates: .5MHz, 1MHz, or 2MHz. The most commonly used is 1MHz. Once your Mac is equipped with a MIDI interface, it can be incorporated into any MIDI system.

MIDI Devices (Hardware and Software)

In the world of MIDI it is sometimes hard to distinguish the peripherals from the controllers. In the computer industry a printer could never control a computer's operation except for a minor handshaking wait or ready command. In a MIDI system it is not uncommon for a synthesizer to be merely a sound generator for the computer in one application and then to become the master controller using the computer just as a display or storage device.

It is easier, therefore, to consider the functions that MIDI devices perform rather than detailing specific devices. In the following section we have divided these functions into two major categories: real-time and non-real-time. Real-time, in this context, is concerned with the generation of sounds and the actions performed on these sounds (including recording), *as they are played*. Non-real-time functions are those which occur *after the performance*, such as editing, playback, etc.

Real-Time MIDI Functions

MIDI Controllers

A MIDI controller can be thought of as a MIDI message generator. A controller produces MIDI messages in response to actions performed on its front panel controls (i.e., keyboard, switches, sliders, etc.). A simple example of this is the pressing of a note on a MIDI keyboard controller. The controller recognizes that a specific key has been pressed and sends this information through its MIDI OUT port to the rest of the system. A MIDI controller can usually send information for the movement of a variety of wheels, sliders, knobs, and switches. MIDI controllers are often combined with sound sources and a sequencer in a single multitask instrument.

MIDI Sound Sources

There are a large number of devices that fall into the general category of sound sources. The one thing they all have in common is the ability to produce some type of audio signal. This signal can be as simple as a single sinewave, or as complex as a chord by a 10-piece orchestra, as long as the sound device can understand and alter its sounds in accordance with the MIDI message it is receiving. A sound source, unless combined with a controller or an event recorder, will always be a slave device.

MIDI Processors

MIDI processors cannot generate a MIDI message without first receiving one. They cannot produce sound, but they can affect many aspects of the MIDI system. Although this may sound like a severe limitation, these devices comprise one of the largest categories of MIDI equipment. MIDI processors are used to enhance other MIDI devices. One example is a MIDI channel filter. This device is used in conjunction with a sound source that is designed to respond to all MIDI channels. The channel filter can be set to a selected channel and will only pass information that arrives on that channel to the sound source, thus enhancing the sound source to be channel-selective. Another example of a popular MIDI processor is the MIDI *delay*. This device, inserted between a MIDI sound source and a keyboard, will delay and repeat MIDI Note On and Note Off messages to add an echo effect to the sound.

MIDI Sequencers

A MIDI event recorder can be any device that is capable of storing MIDI performance information in the sequence and tempo in which the event was received. This information can then be edited or played back exactly as it was originally performed. The most common type of MIDI event processor is the MIDI *sequencer*. A sequencer can be incorporated into a synthesizer, but is also available as a stand-alone device or a software package for a computer. In all cases, the MIDI sequencer simply records digital MIDI information. In order to hear the results of this information you must send this data to a MIDI sound source.

The illustration on the following page shows an example of a typical sequencer display.

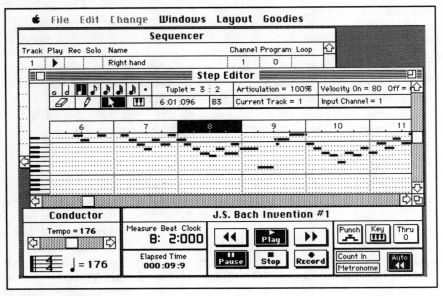

Sequencer Screen

Multitask MIDI Devices

Devices that incorporate a controller, internal sound voices, and in some cases a sequencer, are known as compound, or multitask, MIDI devices. One of the most popular of these is the synthesizer. Another example of a multitask device is the drum machine. A drum machine is simply a sequencer combined with a sound source that produces only drum sounds. Multitask devices have become increasingly popular and are readily available from many manufacturers. The obvious advantage of these devices is their flexibility. In one application they can be a controller and, with little or no adjustment, they can then perform as a complete sound source. Although each function within a multitask instrument will not have all of the features a dedicated device might contain, they provide an economical and versatile alternative to the use of an array of specialized devices.

Non-Real-Time MIDI Functions

Librarians

Inside each sound source there are hundreds of stored parameters that define each sound the instrument is capable of generating. The number of different sounds, or programs, the instrument has is limited by its memory capacity. Librarians allow you to off-load these sounds to a computer. Once in the computer they can be stored to disk. This gives you virtually unlimited sound source program storage. The ability to move your programs on- and off-line also allows sounds to be arranged in any order that suits your specific needs. A studio synthesist, for example, might want to have only brass sounds on one disk for easy access; a live performer might arrange programs so that they can be loaded in the order that they will be used in a performance.

Librarian Screen

Editors

Once the parameter information is captured inside your computer, you may want to display this information on the screen and modify some of the parameters. Some very clever screen editors actually emulate a visual control for each parameter or groups of parameters. This technique of screen editing has become very popular because many sound source manufacturers do not provide single parameter controls. Instead, they nest all the parameters and only provide access through a single value control. Screen editors are also used with sampling devices. Since a sampled sound is a collection of digital values, those values can be plotted and displayed on a screen, and then modified at will.

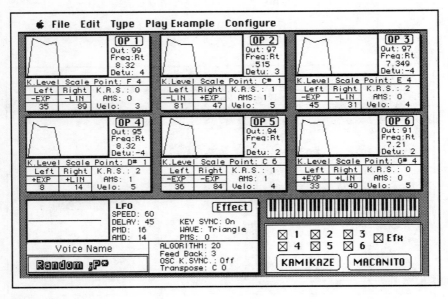

Editor Screen

It is important to remember that all of the information stored in the computer is only a simulation of the audio signal, comprised of the data that represents the value of each parameter. Without a sound source to interpret this data and produce an audio signal, there would be no sound, just digital information. Without sound the computer is like a flight simulator. It can make it seem like you're flying, but until you add sound, you can never really get off the ground.

Overview of the MIDI 1.0 Specification

At the end of this section is a MIDI quick reference guide that details the formats and values used for each message currently defined by the MIDI Spec. The complete specification, along with explanatory material, is contained in our book, **The MIDI Resource Book** (Hal Leonard Books). The MIDI 1.0 specification can also be purchased from the International MIDI Association, 11857 Hartsook Street, North Hollywood, CA 91607.

Except for its simple hardware requirements, the MIDI 1.0 Specification is primarily a software spec. There are five specific types of MIDI messages which can be grouped under two broad categories: *channel messages* and *system messages.* Channel messages allow selective transmission and reception of data; system messages make information available to the entire MIDI system simultaneously.

Channel Messages

Channel Voice and *Channel Mode* messages are the most commonly communicated mesages on the MIDI bus. Information in the message status byte identifies one of sixteen MIDI channels. This channel number alerts devices in the MIDI system that this message is only for those devices that have been set to the same channel.

MIDI channel assignments allow information transmitted throughout a group of linked devices to be acted upon by only those devices set to receive messages on that channel number. In this respect, it is similar to the transmission of cable TV signals. Most cable stations today send at least 32 different signals simultaneously. You can choose which station you will watch by selecting a specific channel on your TV. Even though all 32 signals are present at your TV's cable wire, only the channel you have selected is read by your TV. This information is then processed by your TV and placed onto your screen and into your speaker. If the cable wire in your house is connected to three different TVs, each set can be tuned to a different station simultaneously without affecting the reception on any other set.

Channel Voice Messages

Channel Voice messages are generated by manipulating the on-board performance controls of a MIDI instrument. For example, specific Channel Voice messages are transmitted by the instrument whenever you push a key, move the modulation wheel, or step on a foot switch. Instruments receiving Channel Voice messages will respond to them as though their own on-board controls are being manipulated. This makes it possible to control one MIDI device from another, or from a computer.

> NOTE: Not all MIDI devices transmit or respond to every message defined by the MIDI Spec. If a device receives a message that it doesn't recognize, it simply ignores it. A *MIDI Implementation Chart* detailing which messages the device transmits and recognizes is included in the owners manual of every MIDI device.

Each Channel Voice message is made up of two or more bytes. The first byte is a status byte that identifies the specific message type, and the MIDI channel on which it is transmitted. The status byte is followed by one or two data bytes, depending on the type of message. Following is a brief description of each of the Channel Voice messages.

Note On

These messages are generated every time a key is pressed on a MIDI keyboard. The Note On message contains the MIDI channel number (0-15), the key number (0-127), and a velocity value (0-127). If the keyboard is capable of transmitting dynamics, the velocity value reflects how quickly the key pushed down. A value of 1 represents the lowest velocity, 127 the highest. If the keyboard is not capable of transmitting dynamics, a velocity value of 64 is transmitted. A value of 0 is used to indicate that a key has been released. (This is an alternative to the Note Off message.)

Note Off

These messages are generated every time a key is released on a MIDI keyboard. The Note Off message contains the MIDI channel number (0-15), the key number (0-127), and a velocity value (0-127). If the keyboard is capable of transmitting dynamics, the velocity value reflects how quickly the key released. A value of 1 represents the lowest velocity, 127 the highest. If the keyboard is not capable of transmitting dynamics, a velocity value of 0 is transmitted.

Polyphonic Key Pressure

A keyboard with pressure sensitivity for each key will transmit these messages whenever the player applies pressure to the keys as they are held down. A separate message is generated for each key to which pressure is applied. The message contains the MIDI channel number (0-15), the key number (0-127), and a pressure value that corresponds to the amount of force applied to the key (0 is minimum pressure, 127 is maximum).

Control Change

These messages are generated whenever a MIDI controller (modulation wheel, foot pedal, foot switch, breath controller, etc.) is moved by the player. The message contains the MIDI channel number (0-15), the controller ID number (0-97), and a controller value (0-127). The controller value represents the current position within the overall range of continuous controllers like knobs, pedals, and sliders. As a continuous controller is moved from its minimum position to its maximum postion, the controller value will increment from 0 through 127. For switch controllers, 0 indicates that the switch is off, 127 that it is on.

Program Change

These messages are generated whenever the player selects a new sound from the instrument's front panel. The message contains the MIDI channel number (0-15) and the ID number of the selected sound (0-127). On many instruments, the transmission/reception of these messages can be selectively enabled or disabled by the user.

Channel Pressure

A keyboard that is pressure-sensitive will transmit these messages whenever the player applies extra force to any of the keys as they are held down (often referred to as *After Touch*). Unlike Polyphonic Key Pressure, a single message is generated regardless of the number of keys held down. This message contains the MIDI channel number (0-15) and a pressure value that corresponds to the amount of pressure applied to all keys (0 is minimum pressure, 127 is maximum).

Pitch Wheel Change

This message is transmitted whenver the intrument's pitch bender (usually a wheel) is moved. The message contains the MIDI channel number (0-15), a low-resolution position value (0-127), and a high resolution position value (0-127). The low-resolution value represents the position of the bender, with 64 representing the centered position, 0 representing maximum flat, and 127 representing maximum sharp. The use of a high resolution value is optional. If it is not used, its value is set to 0. (The value must be transmitted even if it isn't used.)

Channel Mode Messages

Channel Mode messages determine whether or not an instrument will respond to all channels or to only a selected one. These messages also determine whether an instrument will assign incoming Channel Voice messages to its internal voices *polyphonically* (more than one note per MIDI channel) or *monophonically* (one note per MIDI channel). There are four MIDI Modes:

- OMNI On/Poly-Mode 1
- OMNI On/Mono-Mode 2
- OMNI Off/Poly-Mode 3
- OMNI Off/Mono-Mode 4

OMNI On

When set to OMNI On, an instrument will try to respond to all messages it receives (via MIDI IN) without regard to channel number. All messages the instrument transmits (via MIDI OUT) will be assigned to one channel. Any instrument not capable of channel assignment must be set to channel 1, otherwise assignment can be to any of the sixteen MIDI channels. It is common practice to set the transmit channel and the receive channel to the same number.

OMNI Off

When set to OMNI Off, the instrument can be assigned to a specific MIDI channel. It will only respond to messages on the assigned channel(s), ignoring messages on any other channel, and it will transmit voice messages only on the assigned channel(s). It is common practice to assign both the transmit and receive channels to the same number.

Poly

When set to Poly, the instrument assigns incoming Channel Voice messages polyphonically to its internal voices. This makes it possible to transmit and receive chords (more than one note at the same time) on a single MIDI channel.

Mono

When set to Mono, the instrument assigns incoming Channel Voice messages monophonically to its internal voices. The instrument will play only one note per MIDI channel. This makes it possible to play several different sounds at once. (Each sound is assigned to a different channel.)

System Messages

System messages, unlike Channel Voice and Channel Mode messages, are available to all devices connected to the MIDI system. The information that they carry will be seen simultaneously by every connected device. If this information is irrelevant to a particular device, it will be ignored. If, for example, you are sending MIDI Clock messages from your computer to the MIDI system, only those devices that recognize MIDI Clock will respond.

There are three different types of system messages: *System Common, System Real-Time,* and *System Exclusive.*

System Common Messages

Quarter Frame
This message is only used by instruments that transmit or recognize MIDI Time Code (MTC). Each of eight message variations acts as a timing pulse for the system, and defines a unique location in SMPTE time code. Eight Quarter Frame messages are required to completely define the SMPTE time (two each for hours, minutes, seconds, and frames).

Song Position
This message is used to indicate a location within a MIDI sequence. The location is given as the number of 16th notes from the start of the sequence.

Song Select
This message is used to select a specific sequence or drum pattern from a sequencer or drum machine.

Tune Request
When an instrument receives this message, it will perform its on-board tuning routine (if it has one).

Real-Time Messages

MIDI Clock
This message is used as a timing pulse by MIDI sequencers and drum machines. It is transmitted twenty-four times per quarter note.

Start
This message is generated whenever the *play* or *start* button of a sequencer or drum machine is pushed. When received by a sequencer or drum machine, the sequence or drum pattern will start at its beginning.

Stop

This message is generated whenever the *stop* button of a sequencer or drum machine is pushed. When received, any sequencer or drum machine that is currently playing will stop.

Continue

This message is generated whenever the *continue* button of a sequencer or drum machine is pushed. When received, a sequencer or drum machine will begin playing again from the point in the sequence at which the last *stop* command was received.

Active Sensing

This message is sent every 300 ms. whenever the instrument is idle (not being played) to confirm that the MIDI connection has not been broken. Not all instruments use Active Sensing, and only those that do can generate and/or recognize these messages.

System Reset

When this message is received, an instrument will return to its default settings (those that are active when it is first powered up). Not all instruments recognize this message.

System Exclusive Messages

For programmers and designers the system exclusive message is one of the most exciting features of MIDI. This message was originally specified to allow manufacturers the freedom of sending and receiving any amount of information they felt necessary. The only restriction is that, to avoid confusing other brands of equipment that might be connected via MIDI, each system exclusive message must carry a manufacturer ID that is only recognized by their own equipment. Due to the unrestricted size of this message, manufacturers began sending complete dumps of their equipment's parameter settings. Programs were then developed to not only save these dumps to mass storage, but to allow retrieval, display, and editing of these settings on any computer. Recently, the System Exclusive message format has been expanded to include three new formats: *Sample Dump Standard*, *MIDI Time Code*, and *MIDI Files Standard*.

Sample Dump Standard

The Sample Dump Standard (SDS) allows the transfer of digital sample information among machines. Because this information is nonexclusive, it provides expanded information sharing among brands of equipment. For example, it allows you to record a sample sound on one instrument, display and edit the waveform on a computer, and then play the altered version back on a completely different unit.

MIDI Time Code

MIDI Time Code (MTC) is a series of formatted messages that are incremented at regular intervals to precisely indicate the passage of time. MIDI devices capable of reading MTC can use these signals to incorporate timing references as an integral part of recorded events. This makes it possible to search for, and sync to, specific locations on stored material. Because MTC is compatible with (in fact, it is based upon) a widely used audiovisual timing standard (SMPTE Time Code), it provides new possibilities of communication and control between MIDI devices and non-MIDI devices such as audio- and videotape machines. The potential of MTC as a synchronization tool for computers, video, film, and music has just begun to be explored.

MIDI Files Standard

The MIDI Files Standard provides a standardized format for storing sequence data files on disk. This makes is possible to exchange data files between dissimilar software applications and/or hardware. For example, a data file written to disk by a Macintosh sequencer application can be read by an IBM sequencer application. The MIDI Files Standard defines only how data is stored in a disk file—it does not define a standard for transmitting data files via MIDI.

MIDI Quick Reference

MIDI Hardware

Transmission
- 31.25 kBaud
- Asynchronous
- Start bit/8 data bits/Stop bit

Circuit
- 5 mA current loop
- Logic 0 is current ON
- One output shall drive one input only
- Input opto-isolated
- Input requires less than 5 mA to turn on

Connectors
- DIN 5 pin, female, panel mount
- Pins 1 & 3 not used and left unconnected
- Labeled: MIDI IN and MIDI OUT

Cables
- Maximum length: 50 feet
- Ends terminate with DIN 5 pin, male
- Shielded, twisted pair.

MIDI THRU
- Optional
- Direct copy of MIDI IN data
- Labeled: MIDI THRU

MIDI Messages

Data Formats:

Status Bytes:　　Bit 7 is always 1　　　**1 x x x n n n n**

The four low-order bits (nnnn) of Channel Message Status bytes are used to identify one of sixteen channels. Bits 4, 5, and 6 specify one of seven Channel Message Status types.

The four high-order bits of System Message Status bytes are always set (binary 1). The four low-order bits specify one of sixteen System Status bytes (eleven are currently defined).

Data Bytes:　　Bit 7 is always 0　　　**0 x x x x x x x**

Since bit 7 must always be reset to 0 in a MIDI Data byte, the maximum range of values conveyed by a single byte is 0-127 (00-7FH). Messages that require a larger range of values convey the value's MSB and LSB in two or more MIDI Data bytes.

Message Formats:

Each MIDI message consists of a single Status byte followed by 0 or more data bytes. The basic formats for the different types of messages are outlined here. The specific hex codes for every defined message are given in the Hex Message Summaries.

Channel Voice, Channel Mode, and System Common Formats:

Status	Data 1	Data 2

The number of Data bytes in the message is defined by the particular Status byte.

System Real-Time Format:

Status

Each message consists of a single Status byte.

System Exclusive Formats:

SysEx	ID	Data	EOX

The basic format for all System Exclusive messages is the same. A message must start with the System Exclusive Status byte followed by a System Exclusive ID code. Any number of Data bytes may follow the ID code. The last byte of a System Exclusive message must always be the End Of Exclusive Status byte.

Manufacturer System Exclusive Format:

SysEx	ID:Mfr	Data	EOX

The Manufacturer System Exclusive message consists of the System Exclusive Status byte, Manufacturer ID, and any number of Data bytes followed by the End Of Exclusive Status byte. Details of the formats used must be published by the manufacturer.

Universal Non-Real-Time System Exclusive Format:

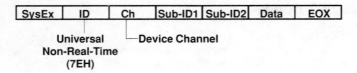

In a Universal Non-Real-Time System Exclusive message, the Universal Non-Real-Time identifier follows the System Exclusive Status byte. Next is a Device Channel number, used to identify which device(s) in the system the message is intended for. Up to 127 devices may be independently addressed. The value 127 (7FH) is used to indicate that the message is intended for all devices in the system. The Sub-IDs identify the specific message. Any number of Data Bytes may follow, depending on the particular Sub-IDs. The final byte in the message is the End Of Exclusive Status byte.

Universal Real-Time System Exclusive Format:

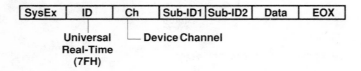

The basic format for Universal Real-Time System Exclusive messages is the same as used for Non-Real-Time messages. Any number of data bytes may follow the Sub-IDs (dependent on the particular message they define). The final byte in the message is the End Of Exclusive Status byte.

Universal Noncommercial System Exclusive Format:

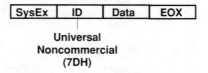

The basic format for Universal Noncommercial System Exclusive messages consists of the System Exclusive Status byte, the Universal Noncommericial Identifier, and any number of Data bytes. The final byte of the message is the End Of Exclusive Status byte. Noncommercial SysEx formats are for research purposes only, and are not to be used on any products made available to the public.

MIDI Mode Summaries

OMNI ON/POLY   [Mode 1]

Received: Voice Messages are recognized from all channels and are assigned to voices polyphonically.

Transmitted: Voice Messages for all voices are transmitted on the assigned Basic Channel.

OMNI ON/MONO   [Mode 2]

Received: Voice messages are recognized from all channels and are assigned to one monophonic voice.

Transmitted: Voice Messages for a single voice are transmitted on the assigned Basic Channel.

OMNI OFF/POLY   [Mode 3]

Received: Voice Messages are recognized from the assigned Basic Channel and are assigned to all voices polyphonically.

Transmitted: Voice Messages for all voices are transmitted on the assigned Basic Channel.

OMNI OFF/MONO   [Mode 4]

Received: Voice Messages are recognized on the assigned Basic Channel through (Basic Channel + M) -1 and are assigned monophonically to voices 1 through M, respectively. The number of voices assigned (M) is specified by the value of the second byte of the MONO MODE ON message (see Mode Message Summaries).

Transmitted: Voice Messages for voices 1 through M are transmitted, one voice per channel, the assigned Basic Channel through (Basic Channel + M) -1, respectively.

Channel Message Hex Summaries

Channel Voice Messages

NOTE OFF

8n	kk	vv
n = Ch# 0-F	k = key # 00-7F	v = velocity 00-7F

NOTE ON

9n	kk	vv
n = Ch# 0-F	k = key# 00-7F	v = velocity 01-7F [00=NOTE OFF]

POLYPHONIC KEY PRESSURE

An	kk	vv
n = Ch# 0-F	k = key# 00-7F	v = Pressure Value 00-7F

CONTROL CHANGE

Bn	cc	vv
n = Ch# 0-F	c = Ctrl# 00-79	v = Ctrl Value 00-7F

PROGRAM CHANGE

Cn	pp
n = Ch# 0-F	p = Pgm# 00-7F

CHANNEL PRESSURE

Dn	vv
n = Ch# 0-F	v = Pressure Value 00-7F

PITCH WHEEL CHANGE

En	ll	hh
n = Ch# 0-F	l = MSB 00-7F	h = LSB 00-7F

Channel Mode Messages

LOCAL CONTROL OFF

Bn	7A	00
n = Ch#r 0-F		

LOCAL CONTROL ON

Bn	7A	7F
n = Ch#r 0-F		

ALL NOTES OFF

Bn	7B	00
n = Ch# 0-F		

OMNI MODE OFF
(ALL NOTES OFF)

Bn	7C	00
n = Ch# 0-F		

OMNI MODE ON
(ALL NOTES ON)

Bn	7D	00
n = Ch# 0-F		

MONO MODE ON
(ALL NOTES OFF)

Bn	7E	mm
n = Chl# 0-F		m = # of MONO Channels 01-10 [if mm= 00, # of ch = # of rcvr voices]

POLY MODE ON
(ALL NOTES OFF)

Bn	7F	00
n = Ch# 0-F		

System Message Hex Summaries

System Common Messages

QUARTER FRAME

F1	nd
	n = Msg Type 0-7
	d = Msg Data 0-F

SONG POSITION POINTER

F2	ll	hh
	l = Song PosPt r	h = Song Pos Ptr
	LSB 00-7F	MSB 00-7F

SONG SELECT

F3	ss
	s = Song#
	00-7F

TUNE REQUEST

F6

EOX

F7

System Real-Time Messages

TIMING CLOCK

F8

START

FA

CONTINUE

FB

STOP

FC

ACTIVE SENSING

FE

SYSTEM RESET

FF

System Exclusive Message Hex Summaries

SAMPLE DUMP HEADER

F0	7E	cc	01	ss	ss	ee	ff	ff	ff	gg	gg	gg	hh	hh	hh	ii	ii	ii	jj	F7

cc = Channel Number 00-7F
ss ss = Sample # (LSB first)
ee = Sample Format 08-1C
ff ff ff = Sample Period (LSB first)
gg gg gg = Sample Length (LSB first)
hh hh hh = Sustain Loop Start Point (LSB first)
ii ii ii = Sustain Loop End Point (LSB first)
jj = Loop Type [00 = fwd only] [01 = bckwd/fwd]

SAMPLE DUMP DATA PACKET

F0	7E	cc	02	kk	sample data	ll	F7
		Ch# 00-7F		Running Packet Count 00-7F	120 bytes of sample data 00-7F	Checksum	

DUMP REQUEST

F0	7E	cc	03	ss	ss	F7
		Ch # 00-7F		Sample Number (LSB first)		

SET UP

F0	7E	cc	04	st	hr	mn	sc	fr	ff	sl	sm	ai	F7

cc = Channel Number 00-7F
st = Set-up Type:
    00 = Special
    01 = Punch In Points
    02 = Punch Out Points
    03 = Delete Punch In Points
    04 = Delete Punch Out Points
    05 = Event Start Points
    06 = Event Stop Points
    07 = Event Start Points with additional information
    08 = Event Stop Points with additional information
    09 = Delete Event Start Point
    0A = Delete Event Stop Point
    0B = Cue Points
    0C = Cue Points with additional info
    0D = Delete Cue Point
    0E = Event Name in additional info
hr = Hour and Type (bit fields :0 yy zzzzz)
    yy = Type: 00 = 24 Frames/Second
    01 = 25 Frames/Second
    10 = 30 Frames /Second (drop frame)
    11 = 30 Frames/Second (nondrop frame)
    zzzzz = Hours: 00-17
mn = Minutes 00-3B
sc = Seconds 00-3B
fr = Frames 00-1D
ff = Fractional Frames 00-63
sl = Event Number (Special Type when Set-up Type is 00) LSB 00-7F
sm = Event Number (Special Type when Set-up Type is 00) MSB 00-7F
ai = additional info: Event specific data bytes 00-7F

LOOP POINT TRANSMISSION

F0	7E	ch	05	01	ss	ss	bb	bb	cc	dd	dd	dd	ee	ee	ee	F7

ch = Channel Number
ss ss = Sample Number (LSB first)
bb bb = Loop Number (LSB first; 7F 7F = Delete all loops)
cc = Loop Type
    00 = Forwards only (unidirectional)
    01 = Backwards/Forwards (bidirectional)
    7F = Off
dd dd dd = Loop Start Address (in samples; LSB first)
ee ee ee = Loop End Address (in samples; LSB first)

LOOP POINTS REQUEST

F0	7E	ch	05	02	ss	ss	bb	bb	F7

ch = Channel Number
ss ss = Sample Number (LSB first)
bb bb = Loop Number (LSB first; 7F 7F = Request all loops)

DEVICE INQUIRY

F0	7E	cc	06	01	F7

cc = Channel Number
06 = General Information
 (sub-ID#1)
01 = Device Inquiry Message
 (sub-ID#2)

DEVICE ID

F0	7E	cc	06	02	mm	ff	ff	dd	dd	ss	ss	ss	ss	F7

cc = Channel Number
06 = General Information (sub-ID#1)
02 = Device ID Message (sub-ID#2)
mm = Manufacturers System Exclusive ID Code
ff ff = Device Family Code (14 bits, LSB first)
dd dd = Device Family Member Code (14 bits, LSB first)
ss ss ss ss = Software Revision Level: Format Device Specific

WAIT

F0	7E	cc	7C	pp	F7
		Ch# 00-7F		Packet# 00-7F	

CANCEL

F0	7E	cc	7D	pp	F7
		Ch# 00-7F		Packet# 00-7F	

37

NAK

F0	7E	cc	7E	pp	F7
		Ch# 00-7F		Packet# 00-7F	

ACK

F0	7E	cc	7F	pp	F7
		Ch# 00-7F		Packet# 00-7F	

FULL-TIME CODE MESSAGE

F0	7F	7F	01	01	hr	mn	sc	fr	F7

hr = Hour &Type (bit fields:0 yy zzzzz)
    yy = Type: 00= 24 Frames/Second
    01=25 Frames/Sec
    10=30 Frames /Sec (drop frame)
    11=30 Frames/Sec (non-drop)
    zzzzz = Hours: 00-17
mn = Minutes 00-3B
sc = Seconds 00-3B
fr = Frames 00-1D

USER BITS

F0	7F	7F	01	02	$0u_1$	$0u_2$	$0u_3$	$0u_4$	$0u_5$	$0u_6$	$0u_7$	$0u_8$	$0u_9$	F7

These 4-bit fields decode in an 8-bit format:
$<u_1u_2>$ $<u_3u_4>$ $<u_5u_6>$ $<u_7 u_8>$
u_9 = Format Code (bit field: 00ii)

Part Three

Introduction to Macintosh Programming

Part 3

Introduction to Macintosh Programming

In this section, we'll go over the basics of programming in general, as well as programming the Macintosh. If this is new to you, take the time to go over the following material before moving on to the MIDI code examples. Although this book isn't intended to be a complete how-to manual on writing Mac programs, this chapter will get you pointed in the right direction. Before we go any further, here is a list of books we recommend for more information on the specifics of Macintosh programming.

- **Inside Macintosh**: volumes I through V—Addison-Wesley (*the* definitive Macintosh reference)

- **How to Write Macintosh Programs**, Scott Knaster—Addison-Wesley

- **Macintosh Programming Secrets,** Scott Knaster—Addison-Wesley

- **Macintosh Revealed**: volumes One and Two, Stephen Chernicoff—Hayden Books

If you are new to programming, be sure to get hold of one or more of these books. For more details on the software side of MIDI we also recommend the following books:

- **MMA Detailed Addendum To The MIDI 1.0 Spec**—International MIDI Association

- **The MIDI Resource Book**, Steve De Furia and Joe Scacciaferro—Hal Leonard Books

- **The MIDI System Exclusive Book**, Steve De Furia and Joe Scacciaferro—Hal Leonard Books

Programming the Macintosh User Interface

Note to experienced programmers: If you're already a veteran Macintosh programmer, you might want to skip ahead to parts 4 and 5—Building MIDI Applications.

The Macintosh is well-known for its easy-to-learn, easy-to-use software. Much of this reputation is based on its unique user interface, which allows (among other things) programs to be controlled by selecting choices with a mouse. The very features that make the Macintosh such a dream to use—the mouse, pull-down menus, dialogs, multiple windows, etc.—can make it a nightmare to write software for unless you've studied up on the Macintosh ROM-based Toolbox routines or QuickBASIC's built-in Macintosh commands. Of course, you can write your programs without taking advantage of these features. It's relatively easy to create a *command-line* style program using BASIC's PRINT and INPUT statements or Pascal's *writeln* and *readln* statements. However, if you're a novice Mac programmer, you were probably drawn to the Macintosh in the first place because of its elegant interface, and we assume you'd like your own programs to behave with the same kind of elegance. Our programs behave in a Mac-like manner because we take advantage of Toolbox routines and Macintosh commands in our examples. If Mac programming is new to you, you'll find examples of how to set up and use many of the Macintosh's most popular features. We cannot, within the scope of this book, tell you all you need to know to write full-blown Macintosh programs; our emphasis here is on how to design and write MIDI programs. We have tried to place our examples within the context of the Mac's user interface without overwhelming a novice programmer with all of the details that go into a completed commercial application. Be sure to study *Inside Macintosh* and any of the other Macintosh programmer's references we listed earlier if you want to tap the full potential of the Toolbox.

Event-Driven vs. Command-Line Programs

Before the Mac, most programs were command-line programs. While the program was running, prompts would appear on a command line whenever input was desired from the user. The program forced the user to conform to a one-step-at-a-time approach to using the program. This makes it relatively simple for the programmer to design the user interface. The program determines how control flows from task to task. At any given moment, the user's options are restricted to responding to the current command-line prompt. From the user's point of view, however, this is often an awkward way to work.

Mac programs are *event-driven*. The user can select any one of many options at any time while the program is running. This is a more natural working environment for most of us since we don't often approach a task in the rigid structure imposed by command-line driven programs. The programmer's job of defining the user interface is no longer simple. A program must be able to detect a number of user actions, or events, and respond appropriately to them. There is no way of telling in advance which events will occur, or in what order they will occur.

To show you the difference between the two approaches, let's look at how the same program operation could be written using command-line and event-driven techniques. For example, all MIDI programs require the Macintosh to be "configured" to the MIDI interface. The configuration consists of telling the program which serial port the interface is connected to (modem or printer), and what clock rate the interface uses (.5MHz, 1MHz, or 2 MHz).

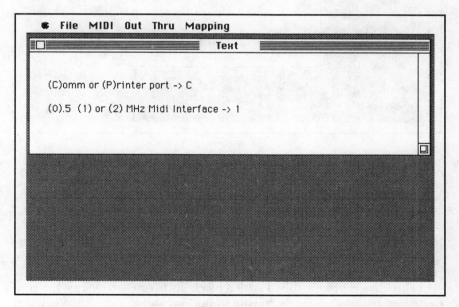

Command-line prompts and responses to the configure portion of a MIDI program

The previous illustration shows the user interface for a sample command-line configuration routine. First, you are prompted for the interface speed. You type in a code for the correct speed. Next, you are prompted for the clock rate and again you respond by typing in a code. For a simple routine that requires only *two* data values, this may not seem too awkward, but consider what a command-line interface would be like for an operation that required *eight* values.

The following figure shows the user interface of an event-driven routine to configure the Mac. (It's taken from our Real-Time MIDI Lab application.)

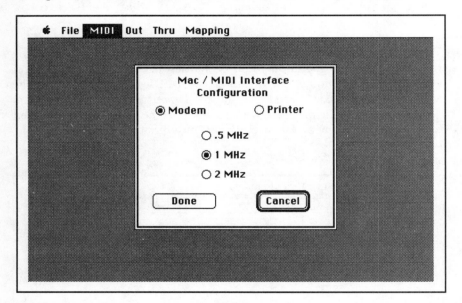

Configure dialog

You can set and reset the configuration values at any time while the program is running by selecting the "configuration" item from the "MIDI" menu. Once selected, the dialog window shown in the illustration appears. In the window are five small "radio buttons" and two larger push buttons. Each radio button is labeled with a configuration parameter: modem, printer, .5 MHz, 1 MHz, and 2 MHz. The buttons indicating the currently set values are "lighted" (filled with a black dot). You can change the configuration settings by simply "pushing" buttons with the mouse. When you push a new button, it is lit and the previously lit button is unlit. The program doesn't require you to push the buttons in any order. In fact, you can reset the buttons as many times as you wish. The settings don't become active until you "dismiss" the dialog window by pushing the done button. If you want to move on without storing any of the changes that you've made, you can push the cancel button instead. From the user's point of view, the event-driven version is much easier to use than the command-line version. From the programmer's point of view, however, the event-driven version requires many more lines of code and a working knowledge of the Macintosh Toolbox. Let's examine the code required for these two approaches to setting configuration values.

```
PROCEDURE DoConfigure;
{ command-line procedure to get configuration settings from user }
BEGIN
   WRITELNLN;
   WRITELNLN;

   WRITELN('(C)omm or (P)rinter port ->');
   READ(s);
   WRITELNLN;

   IF (s = 'C') OR (s = 'c') THEN
      MidiPort(3);

   IF (s = 'P') OR (s = 'p') THEN
      MidiPort(4)

   WRITELN('(0).5  (1)  or  (2) MHz Midi Interface ->');
   READ(n);
   WRITELNLN;

   IF (n >= 0) AND (n <= 2) THEN
      MidiPort(n)
END;
```

The code for the command-line configuration procedure is quite straightforward and relatively simple to write. It consists mainly of a series of WRITELN and READ statements. The WRITELN statements prompt the user for a code. The READ statements get the code value from the user.

Compare the code for the event-driven version of the configure routine which is shown on the following pages. The code is considerably more involved since it is the programmer's responsibility to handle and respond to any of the user's actions, including such details as detecting menu choices, displaying the dialog window and its buttons, lighting up the current selections, responding to new button pushes and relighting buttons if necessary, resetting the values and returning to the main program if done is pushed, etc. Also, the dialog window and all of the items it contains (text and controls) must have been previously defined in the program or a resource file. The Toolbox provides the means for doing all of the low-level work. For example, when you want to light or unlight a button, you use the Toolbox's *SetCntrlValue* procedure. (You have to write the code that determines which button and whether to light or unlight it.) In our example, four separate procedures are used to handle the configuration operation of the program. *DoConfiguration* is the high-level routine. It calls *ShowResDlog* to display the configuration dialog window and *ResetDlogContrl* to light up the currently selected values. Next it waits for, and reacts to, user actions. Radio button pushes are handled by *ResetRadioList*. If the done or cancel buttons are pushed, *DoConfiguration* cleans up the display (and if done is pushed, stores the new values). The Toolbox routines are highlighted in bold type and you can see that these procedures rely heavily on the use of the ToolBox.

```
PROCEDURE DoConfigureDlog;
   {event-driven procedure to get congifuration settings from user}
   VAR
      DlogItem, DlogType, whichSCSI, clockRate, ItemListOffset: integer;
      DlogRect: rect;
      DlogHandle: handle;

BEGIN
   ItemListOffset := 5;
   whichSCSI := theSCSI;
   clockRate := clockMhz;
   ShowResDialog(MIDISetupDlogID);

   ResetDlogCntrl(ModemDlogItem, theSCSI, commPort);
   ResetDlogCntrl(PrinterDlogItem, theSCSI, printerPort);
   ResetDlogCntrl(halfMegDlogItem, clockMhz, halfMeg);
   ResetDlogCntrl(oneMegDlogItem, clockMhz, oneMeg);
   ResetDlogCntrl(twoMegDlogItem, clockMhz, twoMeg);
   REPEAT
      BEGIN
         ModalDialog(NIL, DlogItem);
         CASE DlogItem OF
            ModemDlogItem, PrinterDlogItem:
               BEGIN
                  ResetRadioList(ModemDlogItem, PrinterDlogItem, DlogItem);
                  whichSCSI := DlogItem ;
               END;

            HalfMegDlogItem, OneMegDlogItem, TwoMegDlogItem:
               BEGIN
                  ResetRadioList(HalfMegDlogItem, TwoMegDlogItem, DlogItem);
                  clockRate := DlogItem - ItemListOffset;
               END;

            OTHERWISE
               ; {do nothing}
         END {CaseDlogItem}
      END; {repeat}

   UNTIL (DlogItem = DoneDlogItem) OR (DlogItem = CancelDlogItem);
   IF DlogItem = DoneDlogItem THEN
      BEGIN
         anyChanges := TRUE;
         theSCSI := whichSCSI;
         ClockMhz := clockRate;
      END

   ELSE
      anyChanges := False;
   DisposDialog(TheDialog);
END;{DoConfigureDlog}
```

```
PROCEDURE ShowResDialog;{DLOGID}
  {display a resource dialog window}
BEGIN
  TheDialog := GetNewDialog(DLOGID, NIL, WindowPtr(-1));
  SetPort(TheDialog);
  DrawDialog(TheDialog);
END; {ShowResDialog}


PROCEDURE ResetDlogCntrl (theDlogItem, theParameter, theValue: integer);
  {set radio buttons and check boxes}
  VAR
    DlogType: integer;
    DlogRect: rect;
    DlogHandle: handle;
    cntrlHandle: controlHandle;

BEGIN
  GetDItem(theDialog, theDlogItem, Dlogtype, DlogHandle, DlogRect);
  cntrlHandle := ControlHandle(DlogHandle);
  IF theParameter = theValue THEN
    SetCtlValue(cntrlHandle, 1)
  ELSE
    SetCtlValue(cntrlHandle, 0);
END; {ResetDlogCntrl}


PROCEDURE ResetRadioList (lowButton, hiButton, selectedButton: integer);
  {turn on selected radio button, turn others off}
  VAR
    DlogSelection, DlogType, theButton: integer;
    DlogRect: rect;
    DlogHandle: handle;
    cntrlHandle: controlHandle;

BEGIN
  DlogSelection := selectedButton;
  FOR theButton := lowButton TO hiButton DO
    BEGIN
      GetDItem(theDialog, theButton, Dlogtype, DlogHandle, DlogRect);
      cntrlHandle := ControlHandle(DlogHandle);
      IF theButton = selectedButton THEN
        SetCtlValue(cntrlHandle, 1)
      ELSE
        SetCtlValue(cntrlHandle, 0);
    END;{for count}
END; {ResetRadioList}
```

Structure of Event-Driven Programs

With the Macintosh, the user initiates program commands by some action, like pointing and selecting with the mouse or typing a command key combination. Most (if not all) of the program's options can be accessed directly by such actions. Any user action—hitting or releasing the mouse button, or pushing keys on the keyboard—generates an *event*. In some cases, events can be generated by the computer—for example, when a disk is ejected or inserted. The main body of most Macintosh programs consists of an *event loop*. The purpose of the event loop is to *trap* any event that occurs. Once the event is trapped, the program must identify the type of event and decide either to ignore it or to process it further. The following seven screens trace the chronology of events that occur, starting with the selection of a menu item and ending with the execution of the program operation indicated by the menu choice.

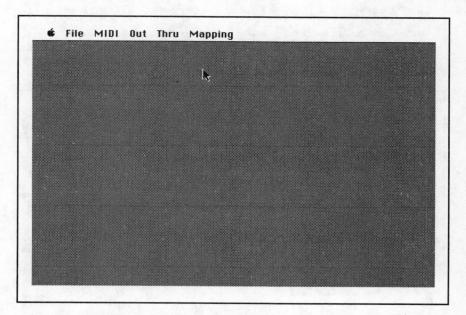

1. Event loop waiting for event

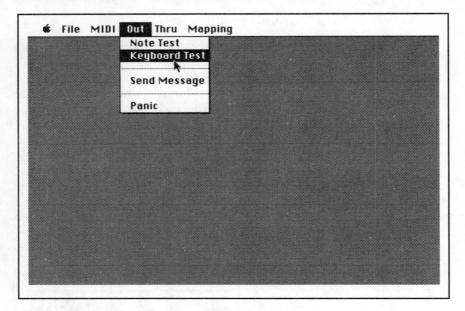

2. Keyboard Test item chosen from Out menu

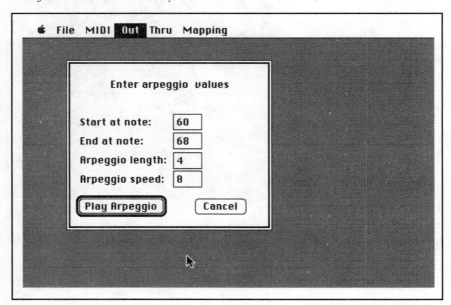

3. Arpeggio dialog window displayed

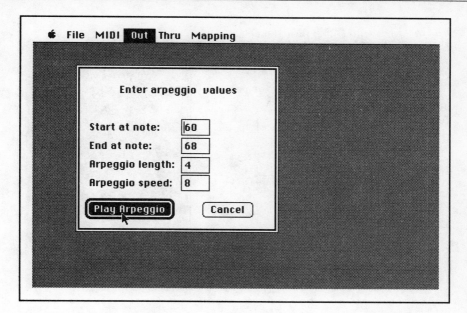

4. Play Arpeggio button selected

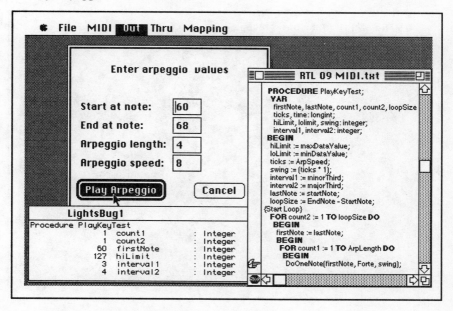

5. PlayKeyTest procedures executed

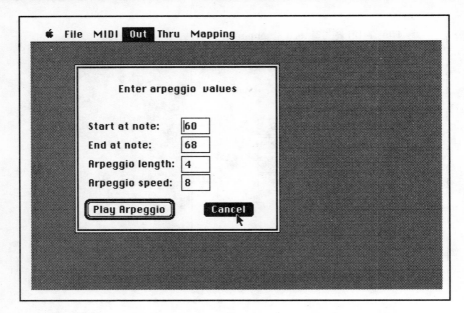

6. Cancel button selected

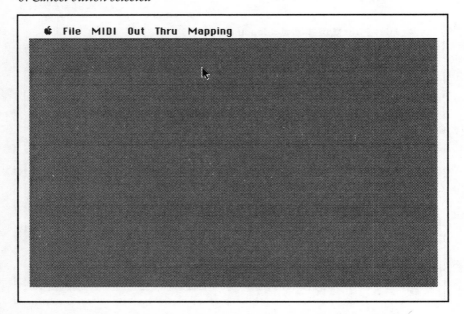

7. Event loop waiting for event

Most Macintosh programs use the same general structure, or *shell*, regardless of the application. The shell is structured in levels. The highest level handles the major, general blocks of the application (*initialize, run, stop*). Below this level are routines that handle the operations for each block. Below this there are additional levels, each one handling more specific tasks until an operation is completed. Here is a graphic map of a typical Macintosh application shell.

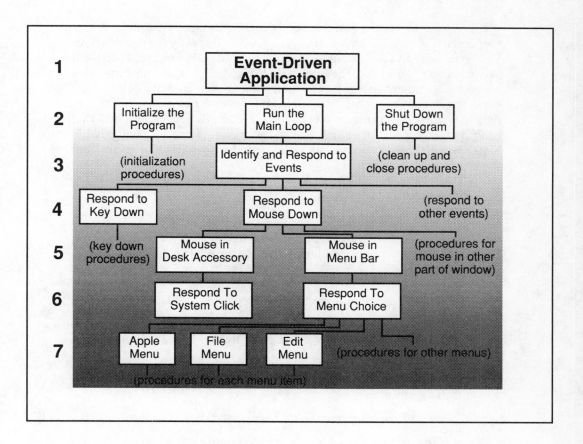

Overview of Program Creation

There are several steps to creating a good program. First of all, you must have a clear understanding of exactly what you want the program to do. Once you know what you want to accomplish, you can design a logical set of steps to perform the required task(s). When you are satisfied that the design will satisfy your needs, you can translate your design into the programming language of your choice. Finally, you can run and test your program.

We'll try to teach you the basics of good program design by example. Before we present the code for a program or routine, we'll specify the problems we want it to solve and define our logical solutions in plain English. Then we'll give you code examples of the solution in BASIC or Pascal. The approach we take here is similar but less formal than the methods used in a commercial development environment. Although it might seem a bit rigorous if you're new to writing programs, or you like to code "on the fly," you'll find that careful planning and attention to detail *before* you start coding will pay off. Not only will the programs be quicker to write, but they'll run correctly from the beginning.

Specification Guidelines

Before you can design a program or write any code, you need a complete understanding of what the program should do. The *specification* is a concise, English description of the problems to be addressed. Here are some things to keep in mind when you define the problem:

- Define the problem as completely as possible. Consider such details as:

  Where will the program's data come from (keyboard input, MIDI input, etc.)

  Where will the program's output go (text window, graphic window, MIDI output, etc.)

  How will the program handle unexpected data or events?

- Write out the specification in simple English.

- List the variables that you'll need and their allowable range.

- List a set of sample data values that will be used to test the program.

Design Guidelines

Using the specification as your guide, design a solution in plain English. This will allow you to create an effective solution to the problem without having to worry about the syntax of a particular programming language. The design will serve as your blueprint when you translate your ideas into the language you choose. The design will also be a good source of documentation should you decide to update the program at a future date or rewrite the program in a different language.

Design your program in levels. The top level contains the major, overall logic of the program. In the case of Macintosh programs, the top level usually contains the event loop; the lower levels describe how the details are handled. Your initial concern should be to design a logical solution to the *general* points of the problem. Don't move on to design a lower level until you are satisfied that the previous level has been completed.

Coding Guidelines

Don't start writing code until you're satisfied with your design. Develop your code using the same top-down approach. Create a module, or set of modules, for each level of your design. Each module should be completed before you move on to lower-level modules. Use "dummy" code as a temporary measure. This will allow you to run the program as it is being written. You will be able to verify the overall logic of your solution on the first pass, and you can test the handling of finer details as you go along.

Use procedures, subroutines, and functions effectively. Each procedure should handle one specific task. Avoid complicated control structures, like heavily nested *IF* statements. The code for any program module should generally be one page or less in length. Modules that are larger than a page or two can almost always be broken into smaller code blocks (*procedures, functions,* or *subroutines*).

Testing Guidelines

At each level of development, test your program completely. Be sure to check unexpected, as well as expected, situations. For example, if your program requires the user to input a positive integer value at some point, what happens if the user inputs a character or negative value?

Test MIDI Interface: An Example

Here is an example of how we'll present program specifications, designs, and code for the two applications in this book. First, we'll present an English specification that defines the problems. Next, we'll show solutions, also in English. Finally, we'll "translate" our solution to executable source code—QuickBASIC or Lightspeed Pascal.

Specification

Description

Create a simple command-line program to test the Macintosh/MIDI interface hardware. The program should test the interface as a closed system (no other devices connected in the MIDI loop). To do this, a single cable is connected between the OUT and IN ports of the interface. The test will simply confirm that MIDI data is transmitted and received with no error introduced by the hardware. The following points should be addressed:

- The test consists of sending an 8-bit byte of data value to the OUT port and then checking the data after it has arrived at the IN port. If the interface is working correctly, the value of the two bytes should match exactly. Notify the user if the values don't match (that is, something is wrong with interface, connections, or MIDI initialization).

- The MIDI interface will be connected to the modem port

- The MIDI interface clock runs at 1 MHz

- The value of the test byte is entered by the user from the Mac keyboard

- The user can specify how many times to repeat each test, up to some defined limit

- Display both the output and input data

- Notify the user of failures

- Tests with new data values can be run after the current set of test repetitions is completed

- The program is stopped by hitting the mouse button

Constants

Minimum 8-bit value is 0; maximum 8-bit value is 255; maximum limit for repetitions is 100.

Variables

Testbyte holds an 8-bit test value; inbyte holds an 8-bit value from input buffer; limit holds the number of repetitions.

Design

Level 1 Design

```
initialize MIDI parameters
while waiting for the mouse to be hit
        test interface
        if mouse is hit stop program
```

The top level of the design is the blueprint for the main program loop when you begin coding. At the top level of the design only the major logic points are considered. This design covers all of the program actions without getting into any details. We don't worry about how to initialize MIDI parameters or how the actual test will be performed. Instead, we consider when they will take place.

Level 2 Design

```
initialize MIDI parameters:
        initialize MIDI library routines
        set serial port
        set interface speed
        enable MIDI buffers
        clear MIDI buffers

test interface:
        ask user to enter valid test data
        check to see if test data is in range (0-255)
        if test data is out of range then
                ask user to enter valid test data

        ask user for valid limit for the number of test repetitions (1-100)
        check to see if limit is within range
        if limit is out of range then
                ask user for valid limit for the number of test repetitions
        for 1 to the limit value
        do test
```

At this level, we start to consider some specifics. These design modules will become subroutines (or procedures) that are called from the main program loop. Initializing MIDI parameters is simply a matter of several steps. Testing the interface is somewhat more complicated. Values must be entered by the user before the actual test can be performed. The test itself may be executed any number of times (up to 100) as specified by the user. Since the actual test will involve a number of steps, it isn't defined here. This way we can see if the test is performed in a logical place, without worrying about the details of the test itself.

Level 3 Design

```
do test:
        clear MIDI buffers
        transmit test byte to MIDI out
        get input byte from MIDI in
        display current counter value, test byte and input byte
        If test byte and input byte don't match then
                display error message
```

Modules at this level are called from the subroutines and procedures from the previous level. At the lowest level of this design, we describe the fine details of the actual test. At this point, it's relatively simple to put our design into the format of a formal programming language.

Code

Following are source code examples of our Test Interface design. You can see how closely both the Pascal and BASIC versions follow the English design.

BASIC Source Code

```
'program: Test MIDI Interface

LIBRARY "MIDIBASIC"

    clearInput% = 5
    clearOutput% = 6
    bufferSize = 400
    resetMIDI% = 0
    commPort% = 3
    oneMeg% = 1
    minData% = 0
    maxData% = 255
    minLimit% = 1
    maxLimit%= 100
    OnOffFlag = 0

'<<<<<main program>>>>>
MOUSE ON
GOSUB InitMIDIParameters

WHILE OnOffFlag  = 0
    GOSUB TestInterface
WEND

LIBRARY CLOSE
END


'<<<<<sub routines>>>>>
InitMIDIParameters:
    MIDIOpen 400,400
    MIDI resetMIDI%
    MIDIPort commPort%
    MIDIPort oneMeg%
RETURN 'InitMIDIInterface

DoTest:
    MIDI clearInput
    MIDI clearOutput
    MIDIOut testByte%
    MIDIIn inByte%
    LOCATE 10,1
    PRINT"Test #",counter,": testByte = ",testByte%,"inByte = ",inByte%
    IF testByte% <> inByte% THEN
        PRINT "ERROR!: values do not match"
    END IF
RETURN 'DoTest
```

```
TestInterface:
  testByte% = -1
  inByte% = 1
  limit% = -1

  WHILE testByte% < minData% OR testByte% >maxData%
    INPUT "Enter value between 0-255 to transmit",testByte%
  WEND

  WHILE limit% < 0 OR limit%> 100
    INPUT "Enter number of times to run test",limit%
  WEND
  IF limit% = 0 THEN
    OnOffFlag = 1
    PRINT "Program stopped by entering zero."
    RETURN
  END IF

  CLS
  FOR counter = 1 TO limit%
    GOSUB DoTest
    OnOffFlag = MOUSE(0)
    IF OnOffFlag <> 0 THEN
      counter = limit%
      PRINT "Program stopped by mouse click."
    END IF
  NEXT
RETURN 'TestInterface
```

Pascal Source Code

```
PROGRAM TestInterface;
{$I+}
  USES
    MIDIPascal;

  CONST
    buffersize = 800;
    minData = 0;
    maxData = 255;
    minLimit = 0;
    maxLimit = 100;

  VAR
    OnOffFlag: boolean;

  PROCEDURE InitMIDIParameters;
  {initialize MIDIPascal and MIDI interface parameters}
  BEGIN
    InitMIDI(buffersize, buffersize);
    MIDI(resetMIDI);
    MIDIPort(commPort);
    MIDIPort(oneMeg);
  END;{InitMIDIParameters}

  PROCEDURE displayText;
  {show default text window}
    VAR
      txtRect: rect;

  BEGIN
    txtRect.top := 50;
    txtrect.bottom := 400;
    txtRect.left := 25;
    txtRect.right := 475;

    SetTextRect(txtRect);
    ShowText;
    writeln('This is InterfaceTest.');
    writeln;
  END;{display text}
```

```
PROCEDURE DoTest (testByte, inByte, testCount: integer);
{comparison test of IN and OUT buffers}
BEGIN
   MIDI(clearInput);
   MIDI(clearOutput);
   MIDIOut(testByte);
   write('* ');                       { this is needed to slow down Mac IIs, otherwise the In buffer }
                                       { is read before the MIDI data can get to it! }
   MIDIIn(inByte);
   moveTo(10,1);
   writeln('Test #', testCount, ': testByte = ', testByte, 'inByte = ', inByte);
   IF testByte <> inByte THEN
      Writeln('ERROR!: values do not match ');
END;{DoTest}

PROCEDURE TestInterface;
   {get test value, number of tests and test the interface}
   VAR
      testByte, inByte, testCount, limit: integer;

BEGIN
   testByte := -1;
   limit := -1;

   WHILE (testByte < minData) OR (testByte > maxData) DO
      BEGIN
         writeln('Enter value for test data (0-255)');
         {  use RETURN key not ENTER key}
         readln(testByte)
      END;

   WHILE (limit < minLimit) OR (limit > maxLimit) DO
      BEGIN
         writeln('Enter number of times to run the test');
         {  use RETURN key not ENTER key}
         readln(limit);
         IF limit = 0 THEN
            BEGIN
               OnOffFlag := true;
               writeln('Program stopped by entering zero.');
            END;
      END;

   FOR testCount := 1 TO limit DO
      BEGIN
         DoTest(testByte, InByte, testCount);
         IF button THEN
            BEGIN
               OnOffFlag := true;
               testCount := limit;
               writeln('Program stopped by mouse click.');
            END;
      END; {for counter loop}
END;{TestInterface}
```

```
BEGIN
{ main program}
  OnOffFlag := false;
  InitMIDIParameters;
  DisplayText;

  WHILE OnOffFlag = false DO
    BEGIN

      TestInterface;

    END;

  quitMIDI;
END.
```

MIDI Library Commands

The major stumbling block to writing MIDI software is writing code that can access the MIDI interface. The programming skill and experience necessary to write MIDI driver software is beyond that of most beginning programmers. Fortunately, you don't need that skill to write your own powerful MIDI programs. The examples in this book use a custom "CODE" resource created by Altech Systems. Both MIDIPascal and MIDIBASIC are machine language code libraries that handle MIDI housekeeping chores. Each library consists of about a dozen commands that can be called from within BASIC, Pascal, C, and Prolog programs. Below, we've included a command reference for both MIDIPascal and MIDIBASIC.

Altech MIDIPascal Command Reference

MIDIPascal is a code library of eleven routines. It comes in two formats, one for inclusion in LightSpeed Pascal programs as a library file and one as an MDS ".REL" file that can be linked with other compilers. Compiled Pascal programs that use MIDIPascal routines execute quickly enough to process MIDI data in real-time. Almost any MIDI application, short of sophisticated sequencing, can be handled by MIDIPascal programs. The examples in this book were written using LightSpeed Pascal. To include MIDIPascal in LightSpeed code, simply insert a "uses MIDIPascal" statement in your code, and include the MIDIPascal interface file and MIDIPascal.lib in the project's "build file."

> **Programmer's Note:** Code resources for MIDIPascal routines called by your program will be included in the program's resources when it is compiled. This makes it possible to create true, stand-alone Macintosh/MIDI applications.

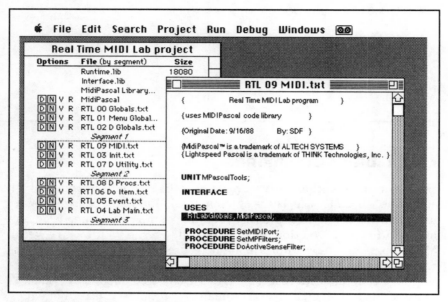

Real-Time MIDI Lab Project Menu

MIDIPascal Constants

The MIDIPascal interface file contains declarations for a number of global constants to use with your programs. Using symbolic constants is, of course, strongly preferred to using numeric values. (The meaning of a statement such as "MIDI(outputDisable);" is clear enough that it doesn't need comments to explain its use, while the meaning "MIDI(4);" is not immediately apparent. In the command reference that follows, we've listed the global constants for each MIDIPascal statement. Whenever applicable, we use these constants in our code examples.

InitMIDI (InSize, OutSize: integer);

```
const
   maxSize = 32767
```

InitMIDI initializes the communication buffers used by MIDIPascal routines. InSize and OutSize are the size, in bytes, of the buffers. They are passed by value. The maximum buffer size is 32767 bytes. InitMIDI must be the first MIDIPascal call in a program. Once it has been called, QuitMIDI must be executed before ending your program. The MIDI buffers are FIFO (first in, first out) stacks.

MIDIIn (byte: integer);

MIDIIn returns a single byte value from the input buffer. Its argument is passed by reference (no constants or expressions). Each call to MIDIIn permanently removes one byte from the input buffer. If your program needs to know the number of bytes waiting in the buffer, call Incount before calling MIDIIn. MIDIIn returns a value of -1 if the buffer is empty.

MIDIOut (byte: integer);

MIDIOut sends a single byte value to the output buffer. Its argument is passed by value (constants or expressions can be used).

GetMIDI (theString: string, mode,count, result: integer);

```
const
   normalMode = 0
   nibbleMode1 = 1
   nibbleMode2 = 2
   stringFull = 0
   timeOut = 1
   badNibble = 2
   badString = 3
```

GetMIDI returns a string of data from the input buffer. The number of bytes returned is determined by the logical length of "theString." To set the length of the string use and assignment statement ("theString := 'abc';"). GetMIDI's string variable is passed by reference. It may not be a string expression or literal. theString must be initialized before it can be used with GetMIDI.

The mode variable is used to specify the format of data bytes received in the buffer. Some MIDI devices transmit data in 2-byte nibbles. GetMIDI will reformat 2-byte data formats by combining the low-order bits of two adjacent bytes. The order (normal, low-high, or high-low) is set with the mode variable as follows:

0 = normal mode: 8-bit data bytes

1 = nibble mode 1: one 4-bit nibble per byte in low-nibble, high-nibble order

2 = nibble mode 2: one 4-bit nibble per byte in high-nibble, low-nibble order

Mode is passed by value and may be a variable, constant, or expression. The count variable returns the number of bytes taken out of the buffer and put into theString. Count is passed by reference. The result variable returns a result code for the operation. The codes are:

0 = string full

1 = timed out for 1.5 seconds

2 = nibble out of range (0-15), last value in string

3 = zero length string, return with zero count

Result is passed by reference.

SendMIDI (theString: string, mode: integer);

```
const
  normalMode = 0
  nibbleMode1 = 1
  nibbleMode2 = 2
```

SendMIDI sends theString to the output buffer. The string variable is passed by reference. The mode variable is passed by value. The mode variable is used to specify the format of data bytes sent out via the MIDI interface. Some MIDI devices expect to receive data formatted as 2-byte nibbles. SendMIDI will reformat single-byte data in theString by transmitting the low-order and high-order bits as the low-order bits of consecutive bytes. The order (normal, low-high, or high-low) is set with the mode variable as follows:

0 = normal mode: 8-bit data bytes

1 = nibble mode 1: one 4-bit nibble per byte in low-nibble, high-nibble order

2 = nibble mode 2: one 4-bit nibble per byte in high-nibble, low-nibble order

InCount (byteCount: integer)

InCount returns the number of bytes currently in the input buffer. "byteCount" is passed by reference.

OutCount (byteCount: integer)

OutCount returns the number of bytes currently in the output buffer. "byteCount" is passed by reference.

MIDI (bufferStatus: integer);

```
const
    resetMIDI = 0
    inputEnable = 1
    inputDisable = 2
    outputEnable = 3
    outputDisable = 4
    clearInput = 5
    clearOutput = 6
```

MIDI sets the operational status of the MIDI buffers. "bufferStatus" is passed by value. The buffer status is set as follows:

0 = reset: clear and enable input and output buffers

1 = enable input buffer

2 = disable input buffer

3 = enable output buffer

4 = disable output buffer

5 = clear input buffer

6 = clear output buffer

When MIDIPascal is first opened with InitMIDI, both buffers are cleared and enabled.

MIDIPort (parameterValue: integer);

```
const
    halfMeg = 0
    oneMeg  = 1
    twoMeg = 2
    commPort = 3
    printerPort = 4
```

MIDIPort is used to select between serial ports and set the interface speed. "parameterValue" is passed by value.

0 = 0.5 MHz clock frequency

1 = 1 MHz clock frequency

2 = 2 MHz clock frequency

3 = communications port

4 = printer port

MIDIFilter (filterID, lower, upper, skipCount: integer);

```
const
    resetFilters = 0
    filter1 = 1
    filter2 = 2
    filter3 = 3
    filter4 =4
    filter5 = 5
    filter6 = 6
    filter7 = 7
    filter8 = 8
```

The MIDIFilter statement is used to filter data from the input buffer. This makes it possible to ignore unwanted MIDI data and eliminates the overhead needed to process it. Any one of eight separate filters can be specified with the filterID variable. The range of data to be filtered is set with the variables "lower" and "upper." MIDIFilter filters all data between these two values (inclusive). The skipCount variable is used to specify a number of additional bytes to skip following a byte that is within the filter's range. (Note that this is not an effective means of filtering MIDI data sent under running status.)

QuitMIDI;

QuitMIDI should always be called to disable MIDIPascal before exiting a program.

Altech MIDIBASIC Command Reference

MIDIBASIC is a code library of ten routines. It comes in two formats, a MicroSoft BASIC library file for use with MS BASIC and MS QuickBASIC, and a source program for Zedcor's Z BASIC. The examples in this book are written in QuickBASIC. MIDIBASIC routines are not automatically included as resources when your QuickBASIC programs are compiled as stand-alone applications. They must be inserted using ResEdit.

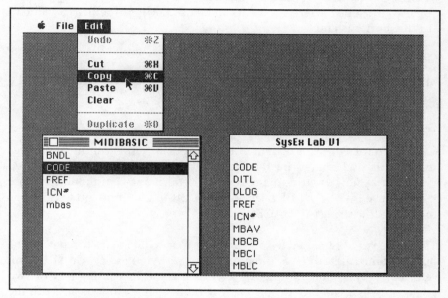

Use ResEdit to copy CODE resources from MIDIBASIC to SysEx MIDI Lab

Programmer's Note: As this book goes to print, there is a conflict between the CODE IDs used by QuickBASIC and MIDIBASIC. You can use the renumbering utility, *renumberCodes*, to resolve the conflict, or renumber the MIDIBASIC CODE IDs with ResEdit.

MIDIOpen InSize, OutSize

MIDIOpen initializes the communication buffers used by MIDIBASIC routines. InSize and OutSize are the size, in bytes, of the buffers. These may be real or integer, variables, constants or expressions. Variables and expressions are converted to 16-bit signed integers. The maximum buffer size is 32767 bytes. MIDIOpen must be the first MIDIBASIC call in a program. Once it has been called, a "Library Close" statement must be executed before ending your program. The MIDI buffers are FIFO stacks.

MIDIIn byte%

MIDIIn returns a single-byte value from the input buffer. Each call to MIDIIn permanently removes one byte from the buffer. The variable "byte%" must be declared *before* it can be used. MIDIIn returns a value of -1 if the buffer is empty.

MIDIOut byte%

MIDIOut sends a single-byte value to the output buffer. "byte%" must be an integer variable or expression.

GetMIDI theString$, mode%, count%, result

GetMIDI returns a string of data from the input buffer. The number of bytes returned is determined by the length of "theString." GetMIDI's string variable may not be a string expression or literal. It must be initialized before it can be used with GetMIDI. Use BASIC's SPACE$ command to initialize the string (theString$ = SPACE$(3), etc.).

The mode variable is used to specify the format of data bytes received in the buffer. Some MIDI devices transmit data in 2-byte nibbles. GetMIDI will reformat 2-byte data formats by combining the low-order bits of two adjacent bytes. The order (normal, low-high, or high-low) is set with the mode variable as follows:

  0 = normal mode: 8-bit data bytes

  1 = nibble mode 1: one 4-bit nibble per byte in low-nibble, high-nibble
     order

  2 = nibble mode 2: one 4-bit nibble per byte in high-nibble, low-nibble
     order

Mode% may be real or integer, variable, constant or expression.

The count% variable returns the number of bytes taken out of the buffer and put into theString$. It must be an integer variable. The result% variable returns a result code for the operation. It must be an integer variable. The codes are:

0 = string full

1 = timed out for 1.5 seconds

2 = nibble out of range (0-15), last value in string

3 = zero length string, return with zero count

SendMIDI theString$, mode%

SendMIDI sends theString$ to the output buffer. The string must be a variable or expression. The mode% may be real or integer, constant, variable or expression. The mode% argument is used to specify the the format of data bytes sent out via the MIDI interface. Some MIDI devices expect to receive data formatted as 2-byte nibbles. SendMIDI will reformat single-byte data in theString$ by transmitting the low-order and high-order bits as the low-order bits of consecutive bytes. The order (normal, low-high, or high-low) is set with mode% as follows:

0 = normal mode : 8-bit data bytes

1 = nibble mode 1: one 4-bit nibble per byte in low-nibble, high-nibble order

2 = nibble mode 2: one 4-bit nibble per byte in high-nibble, low-nibble order

InCount byteCount%

Incount returns the number of bytes currently in the input buffer. Its argument must be an integer variable.

OutCount byteCount%

OutCount returns the number of bytes currently in the output buffer. Its argument must be an integer variable.

MIDI bufferStatus%

MIDI sets the operational status of the MIDI buffers. Its argument may be real or integer, variable, constant or expression. The buffer status is set as follows:

0 = reset: clear and enable input and output buffers

1 = enable input buffer

2 = disable input buffer

3 = enable output buffer

4 = disable output buffer

5 = clear input buffer

6 = clear output buffer

When MIDIBASIC is first opened with MIDIOpen, both buffers are cleared and enabled.

MIDIPort ParameterValue

MIDIPort is used to select between serial ports and set the interface speed. Its argument may be real or integer, variable, constant or expression.

0 = 0.5 MHz clock frequency

1 = 1 MHz clock frequency

2 = 2 MHz clock frequency

3 = communications port

4 = printer port

MIDIFilter filterID$, lower%, upper%, skipCount%

The MIDIFilter statement is used to filter data from the input buffer. This makes it possible to ignore unwanted MIDI data, and eliminates the overhead needed to process it. Any one of eight separate filters can be specified with the filterID% argument. The range of data to be filtered is set with the arguments "lower%" and "upper%." MIDIFilter filters all data between these two values (inclusive). The skipCount% argument is used to specify a number of additional bytes to skip following a byte that is within the filter's range. (Note that this is not an effective means of filtering MIDI data sent under running status.)

Part Four

Building a Pascal MIDI Application

Part 4

Building a Pascal MIDI Application

Application 1: Real-Time MIDI Lab

Real-Time MIDI Lab (RTL) is an interactive "laboratory" for exploring real-time MIDI programming techniques. It demonstrates MIDI concepts on two levels. It will show the programmer how to write MIDI code in Pascal with MIDIPascal, and, at the same time, show examples of practical real-time MIDI applications. Here are the major elements of MIDI programming demonstrated by Real-Time MIDI Lab:

- How to configure the Macintosh to work with any MIDI interface

- How to use MIDIPascal's built-in *MIDIFilter* functions

- How to transmit any MIDI *Channel Voice* message: Note On/Off, Program Change, Control Change, etc.

- How to transmit MIDI messages over any channel

- How to transmit MIDI messages using *Running Status* format

- How to use the Macintosh to "play" complex sequences of notes on any MIDI instrument

- How to detect, read, and identify any MIDI data received via the MIDI interface's IN port

- How to display status and data values of incoming MIDI data

- How to construct *Running Status filters* that allow your program to ignore selected data transmitted to the Macintosh under Running Status

- How to *process* MIDI note, velocity, and control change data in real-time with procedures for auto harmonization, velocity scaling and inversion, and controller scaling and inversion

- How to reassign incoming MIDI data to any MIDI channel in real-time

- How to reassign (*map*) MIDI controllers, program numbers, and notes (keyboard zones)

RTL also provides examples of several Macintosh programming techniques:

- How to use Macintosh ToolBox Routines
- How to develop small, generalized procedures and functions that can be used as "tools" by other higher level procedures.
- How to set up an event-driven application that uses the mouse to choose program operations from pull-down menus
- How to display dialog windows and manipulate their controls
- How to use dialogs to get data from the user
- How to use a resource file
- How to draw in a window with QuickDraw routines

Specification of Real-Time MIDI Lab

Here is the basic specification we used to design Real-Time MIDI Lab:

Specifications of the User Interface

- All program operations are accessed via menu choices selected with the mouse
- No command-line style input operations (WRITELN, READ) will be used to get input from the user
- Any information given to the user by RTL will be displayed in dialog windows
- Any user input will be obtained through dialog controls, buttons, check boxes, and text boxes

Specifications of the Program Operations

Each program operation is linked to a separate menu item. Here are the specifications for RTL operations listed in the order that they appear on the menus. For each program operation there is a *description* of what the operation should do. When appropriate, the description is followed by a list indicating the *variables* that will be used by the operation, a description of the *range* of each variable, and a list of the *initialized* value of each variable.

This specification served as the "bible" for the design and coding phases of the program's development. The dialog windows for RTL were designed directly from these specifications *before* any code was written. They were created with ResEdit (Apple's resource editor). The variables identified in the specifications were written into the code using the same name (shown here in italics).

Apple menu

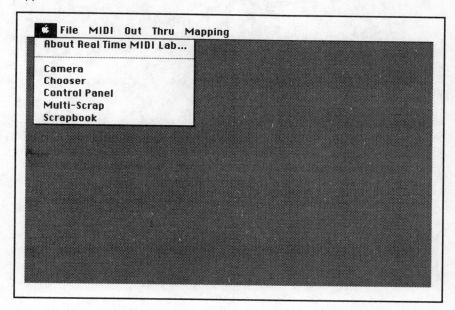

About Real-Time MIDI Lab. . .

Description
When selected, display an *alert box* that displays the program name and author. Dismiss the alert with a *default button*.

Quit
When selected, shut down the program and return to the Macintosh Finder. If a desk accessory is open, close the desk accessory, not RTL.

MIDI menu

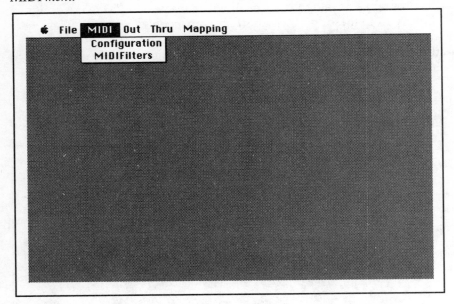

Configuration

Description
When selected, display a dialog window with controls that allow the user to set the port and clock-rate parameters of the MIDI interface. Settings are made by clicking on *radio buttons* with the mouse. The user may dismiss the dialog with either done or cancel. Done resets the interface configuration with changes made by the user; cancel dismisses the dialog without changing the previous settings.

Variables
theSCSI holds the currently selected port, modem or printer. *ClockMhz* holds the currently selected clock rate: .5 MHz, 1 MHz, or 2 MHz.

Initialized Values
The interface is set to the modem port and to a clock rate of 1 MHz on startup.

MIDIFilters

Description
When selected, display a dialog window with controls that allow the user to set up to eight preset data filters using MIDIPascal's built-in *MIDIFilter* function. Settings are made by clicking on/off radio buttons for each filter. Filters will be preset for the following types of MIDI messages: Active Sensing, MIDI Clock, MIDI Clock and clock commands, Program Change, After Touch, Control Change, Pitch Bender, and System Exclusive. The user may dismiss the dialog with either done or cancel. Done resets the interface configuration with changes made by the user; cancel dismisses the dialog without changing the previous settings.

Variables
The on/off status of the eight filters is held in an array called *MPFilters*.

Initialized Values
The Active Sensing filter is set to on when the program starts, the other filters are set to off.

MIDIOut menu

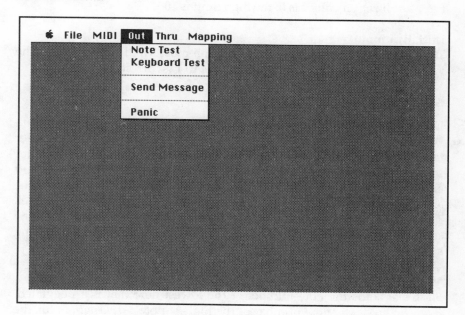

Note Test

Description

When selected, display a dialog window with controls that allow the user to transmit a message to play any note on a MIDI instrument by turning it on (Note On), waiting a short period of time, then turning it off (Note Off). The messages are transmitted on MIDI channel 1. The user can enter any valid note number or velocity value. The user can also enter a duration value that determines how long the program waits before turning the note off. A duration value of 0 suppresses the transmission of the Note Off message. The note, velocity, and duration values of the current message are displayed in the dialog window and played whenever a Play Note button is pushed. The dialog is dismissed by pushing a cancel button. Changes made to the note values are retained.

Variables

theNote holds the note number. *theVelocity* holds the velocity value. *theDuration* holds the duration value.

Range

The low limit for note and velocity values is 0, the high limit is 127. The low limit for duration values is 0, the high limit is 100.

Initialization

The note number is set to 60 (middle C on most MIDI instruments). The velocity value is set to 127. Duration is set to 1 (shortest duration).

Keyboard Test

Description

When selected, display a dialog window with controls that allow the user to transmit a series of note on/off messages that arpeggiate a series of notes on a MIDI instrument connected to the Macintosh. The starting note and ending note of the arpeggio can be set, as well as the number of notes in the arpeggio pattern. The speed at which the arpeggio is played can also be set. The values can be reset and the arpeggio can be replayed with the new settings as long as the dialog is active. The dialog is dismissed by pushing a cancel button. Changes made to the arpeggio values are retained.

Variables

StartNote holds the note number of the lowest note that is arpeggiated. *EndNote* holds the note number of the highest note. *ArpLength* holds the number of notes in the arpeggio. *ArpSpeed* holds the rate at which the arpeggio is played.

Range

The low limit for note numbers is 0. The high limit for note numbers is 127. The low limit for the arpeggio length is 0, the high limit is 8. The speed range is 1-15.

Initialization

The starting note value is set to 60 (middle C). The ending note value is set to 84 (two octaves higher). The arpeggio length is set to 4, the arpeggio speed is set to 1 (the fastest speed).

Send Message

Description

When selected, a dialog window with controls that allows the user to select, edit, and transmit several types of MIDI messages is displayed. The messages are: Note On, Note Off, Control Change, Program Change, Song Select, Tune Request, Start, Stop, and Continue. The message type is selected by pushing a radio button. Once a type is selected, its status and (if appropriate) data values are displayed in editable text boxes. The user changes these by entering any valid status or data values into the appropriate box(es). The message is sent by pushing a transmit button. The dialog remains active—additional messages can be edited and sent, until the cancel button is pushed. Changes made to message values are not retained when the dialog is dismissed.

Variables

SendList holds the status and data bytes for each message in the fields of an array of Pascal records.

Range

Status values must be between 128 and 255. Data values must be within 0 and 127.

Initialization

The initial values for each message type are listed in the following table.

Message	Status	Data1	Data 2
Note On	144	60	127
Note Off	128	60	0
Control Change	176	1	127
Program Change	192	0	-
Song Select	243	0	-
Tune Request	246	-	-
Start	250	-	-
Stop	252	-	-
Continue	251	-	-

Panic

Description

When selected, this operation transmits an All Notes Off and individual Note Off messages for all MIDI notes (0-127) for each MIDI channel (1-16). A dialog window is displayed showing the channel number on which the messages are currently being transmitted. The transmission cycles continuously through all MIDI channels until the dialog is dismissed by clicking the mouse.

MIDIThru menu

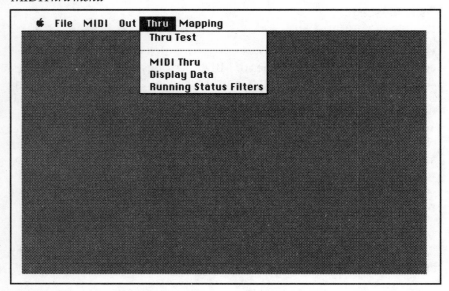

Thru Test

Description

When selected, display a dialog window with controls that allow the user to test the continuity of the MIDI interface. The test is the same one specified earlier in Part 3. The user can enter any 8-bit value for the test byte, as well as a delay value. The delay value inserts a pause between the transmission of the test byte and the comparison of the test byte and the data arriving in the MIDI IN port. The test is started by pushing a run test button. Once pushed, a new window is displayed and the value of both the test byte and result byte are drawn there for each test. An error message is displayed if the two bytes are not the same value. The test will run continuously until the mouse is clicked. Once clicked, the test window disappears and the user may enter new values into the Thru test dialog window and re-run the test. The dialog is dismissed when the cancel button is pushed. Changes to the byte or delay values are not retained.

Variables
testByte holds the value of the test byte. *repeatCount* holds the delay value.

Range
Test byte values may be from 0 to 255. Delay values may be from 0 to 100.

Initialization
The test byte value is set to 247 (MIDI Clock); the delay value is set to 10.

MIDI Thru

Description
When selected, this activates a real-time MIDI processing routine. (There is no dialog window associated with this operation.) The routine takes data from the MIDI IN port and modifies it in various ways depending on the type of MIDI data and the active settings of other RTL operations. The modified data is sent to the MIDI OUT port. Here is a summary of how MIDI data is modified by the MIDI Thru operation:

- Running Status filters can selectively remove any or all of the following messages from the MIDI data stream: Note On/Off, Polyphonic Key Pressure, Control Change, After Touch, or Pitch Bender

- Messages coming in on any of the sixteen MIDI channels may be reassigned to any other channel(s)

- Messages coming in from any of the ninety-seven MIDI controllers may be re-assigned to any other controller(s)

- The data values for all controller messages may be offset by a fixed value

- The data values for all controller messages may be scaled by a user-entered scaling factor

- The data values for all controller messages may be inverted.

- Program Change messages for any of the 127 MIDI programs can be reassigned to any program number(s)

- Velocity values may be replaced with a user-entered, fixed velocity value

- Velocity values may be scaled by a user-entered scaling factor
- Velocity values may be inverted
- Incoming note numbers for any range of keys can be transposed up to two octaves sharp or flat

Variables

theByte holds the current byte taken from the MIDI IN port. *RunningStatus* holds the current Running Status.

The values for the variables used by MIDI Thru are set with other RTL operations.

RSFilters is an array that holds the currently selected running status filters.

ChanMaps is an array that holds the channel reassignments for MIDI channels 1-16.

ControlMaps is an array that holds the channel reassignments for MIDI controllers 1-97. *CntrlInvertFlag* and *CntrlScaleFlag* hold the On/Off state for the controller data routines. *CntrlOffset* holds the offset value for controller data. *CntrolSFactor* holds the scaling factor value for the controller data.

ProgramMaps is an array that holds the program number reassignments for MIDI program numbers 0-127.

VInvertFlag, VScaleFlag, and *VFixedFlagCntrlInvertFlag* hold the on/off state for the controller data routines. *VOffset* holds the fixed offset value and *VSFactor* holds the scaling factor for velocity data.

NoteMap is an array that holds the note number reassignments for MIDI notes 0-127.

Initialization

MIDI Thru uses the current values set by Configuration, MIDIFilters, Running Status Filters, Channel, Controller, Program Change, Velocity, and Note Map operations. On start-up it uses the modem port (clock rate 1 MHz), and filters out Active Sensing. All other MIDI data is passed through unchanged unless new settings are entered via menu choices.

Data Display

Description
When selected, a MIDI Thru window is displayed. The window allows the user to view MIDI data as it flows through the Mac. Messages are displayed with the status name (Note On, Pitch Bend, etc.) followed by the data values. Data Display must be able to keep track of Running Status transmission (status bytes not re-sent with messages of the same type).

Running Status Filters

Description
When selected, display a dialog window with controls that allow the user to set Running Status filters for Note On/Off, Polyphonic Key Pressure, Control Change, After Touch, and Pitch Bender messages. Filters are selected by clicking a check box for each filter. These settings are used by the MIDI Thru routines. The user may dismiss the dialog with either done or cancel. Done resets the Running Status filter array with the changes made by the user; cancel dismisses the dialog without changing the previous settings.

Variables
RSFilters is an array that holds the currently selected Running Status filters.

MIDI Mapping menu

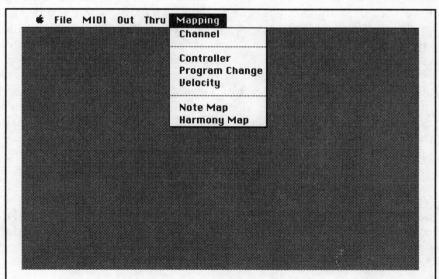

Channel

Description

When selected, display a dialog window with controls that allow the user to set channel reassignments for each of the sixteen MIDI channels. When the user enters a source channel value, the current reassignment for that channel is displayed. A new reassignment value can then be entered. A clear button can be pushed to reset the channel reassignment(s) (channel 1 to channel 1 .... channel 16 to channel 16). The user may dismiss the dialog with either done or cancel. Done resets the channel map with changes made by the user; cancel dismisses the dialog without changing the previous settings.

Variables

ChanMaps is an array that holds the channel reassignments for MIDI.

Range

Channel values may be between 1-16.

Initialization

On start-up, channel values are not reassigned.

Controller

Description

When selected, display a dialog window with controls that allow the user to set controller number reassignments for each of the 97 MIDI controller numbers. When the user enters a source controller number value, the current reassignment for that controller number is displayed. A new reassignment value can then be entered. Check boxes are used to select invert and/or scale processing of controller data. The user may enter a data offset value as well as a scale factor. A clear button can be pushed to reset the controller number assignments (controller number 1 to controller number 1 .... controller number 97 to controller number 97). The user may dismiss the dialog with either done or cancel. Done resets the controller map with changes made by the user; cancel dismisses the dialog without changing the previous settings.

Variables

ControlMaps is an array that holds the channel reassignments for MIDI controllers. *CntrlInvertFlag* and *CntrlScaleFlag* hold the on/off state for the controller data routines. *CntrlOffset* holds the offset value for controller data. *CntrolSFactor* holds the scaling factor value for the controller data.

Range

Controller values may be from 1-97. (Mod Wheel through Data Decrement — see MIDI specification information for controller ID numbers.) Controller offset values may be from 0-127. Scale factor values may be from 1-10.

Initialization

On start-up, controller values are not reassigned, invert and scale processing is off, data offset is 0, and scale factor is 1.

Program Change

Description

When selected, display a dialog window with controls that allow the user to set program number reassignments for each of the 127 MIDI program numbers. When the user enters a source program value, the current reassignment for that program is displayed. A new reassignment value can then be entered. A clear button can be pushed to reset the program assignments (program 1 to program 1 .... program 127 to program 127). The user may dismiss the dialog with either done or cancel. Done resets the program map with changes made by the user; cancel dismisses the dialog without changing the previous settings.

Variables

ProgramMaps is an array that holds the program number reassignments for MIDI program numbers 0-127.

Range

Program number values may be from 0-127.

Initialization

On start-up, program number values are not reassigned.

Velocity

Description

When selected, display a dialog window with controls that allow the user to set velocity processing for Note On velocity data. Check boxes are used to select invert, fixed, or scale processing. The user may enter a data offset value as well as a scale factor. If the fixed box is checked, the offset value will replace the original value. If the scale box is checked, the velocity data is scaled by multiplying it with the scale factor. If the invert box is checked, the velocity data is inverted. The user may dismiss the dialog with either done or cancel. Done resets the interface configuration with changes made by the user; cancel dismisses the dialog without changing the previous settings.

VInvertFlag, *VScaleFlag*, and *VFixedFlagCntrlInvertFlag* hold the on/off state for the controller data routines. *VOffset* holds the fixed offset value and *VSFactor* holds the scaling factor for velocity data.

Range
Velocity offset values may be from 0-127. Scale factor values may be from 1-10.

Initialization
On start-up, invert, scale, and fixed processing are off, data offset is 0, and scale factor is 1.

Note Map

Description
When selected, display a dialog window that allows the user to enter the limits to a key range and a transpose value by which to shift the note within the range. The user may enter these values in any order. If a range limit that conflicts with the current transpose interval is entered, the transpose interval is automatically recalculated. If a transpose interval that conflicts with a range limit is entered, the range limit is recalculated. (It is possible to set up multiple keyboard zones by repeatedly changing limits and transposing intervals.) A clear button can be pushed to reset the transposition (note 0 to note 0 .... note 127 to note 127). The user may dismiss the dialog with either done or cancel. Done resets the note map with changes made by the user; cancel dismisses the dialog without changing the previous settings.

Variables
NoteMap is an array that holds the note number reassignments for MIDI notes. *HiTransposeNote* holds the high note in the range, *LoTransposeNote* holds the low note in the range, and *KeyTranspose* holds the transpose interval value.

Range
Note values may be from 0-127. Transpose intervals may be from -24 to +24 (up or down two octaves).

Initialization
On start-up, note numbers are not transposed. Transpose interval is 0. The high note is 84 , and the low note is 60.

Harmony Map

Description

When selected, display a dialog window that allows the user to enter the limits to a key range and polyphony value. This operation processes incoming MIDI data by harmonizing notes played within the key range with a user-defined scale. The polyphony value determines how many notes are added to each note played. The scale is defined by pushing a new scale Button. When this button is pushed, an additional scale-map dialog window is displayed. This window has twelve text boxes arranged like the keys of a one-octave piano keyboard. The user may enter a harmony interval for each note in the octave, as well as rename the scale. A clear button can be pushed to reset the harmony intervals for each note to the intitialized values. The user may dismiss the scale map dialog with either done or cancel. Done resets the scale map with changes made by the user; cancel dismisses the dialog without changing the previous settings. When the scale-map dialog window is dismissed, the original harmony dialog becomes active again. If the scale-map name was changed, the new name is now shown in the window. The user can reset the note limits or polyphony values, or activate the harmony routines, by pushing a harmonize button. Once the button has been pushed, the harmony routines remain active until the mouse button is clicked.

Variables

ScaleMap is an array that holds the harmony intervals. *HiTransposeNote* holds the high note in the range, *LoTransposeNote* holds the low note in the range, *HarmonySize* holds the polyphony value, and *ScaleName* holds the name of the scale.

Range

Note values may be from 0 to 127. Harmony intervals may be from -24 to +24 (up or down two octaves). The polyphony values must be from 1 to 4; the scale name can be any string of up to 255 characters.

Initialization

On start-up, the high note is set to 84, the low note is set to 60, the polyphony value is set to 2, and all of the harmony intervals are set to 4 (major thirds). The scale name is set to Major Thirds.

Building the Shell for Real-Time MIDI Lab

The following illustration shows the level structure, or *shell*, of the Real-Time MIDI Lab program.

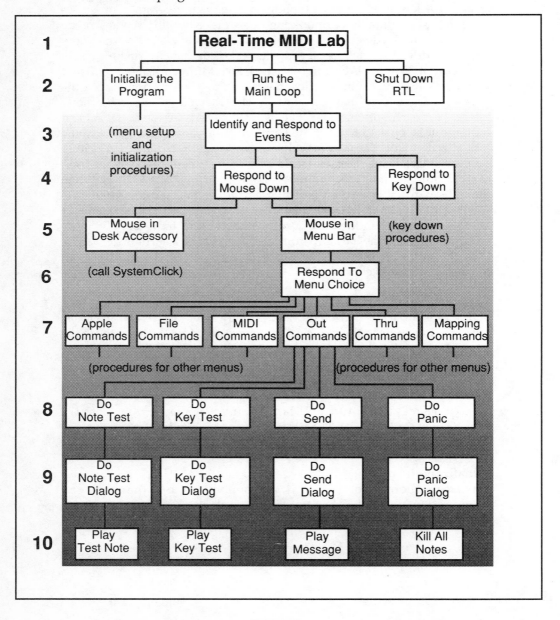

The program was designed in levels. The main program, level 1, performs the most general details of the overall design. It calls on procedures in level 2 to carry out more specific details. The level 2 procedures call on procedures in level 3, and so on, until an operation is completely executed. Many of the operations in the Out, Thru, and Mapping menus pass through nine levels before the operation is executed. As we mentioned in Part 3, by designing in levels and deferring the small details to the lowest levels, you can build your program from the top down, and test the overall logic of the design as you go. The first phase of building RTL is to create an empty shell that displays all of the menus and can process selections with the mouse. In this section we'll look at how the shell was designed and built. When we've finished with the shell, we'll look at the design and code for each of the program operations.

Level 1

Using the specification as our guide, here's the design we came up with for level 1.

Main Program

```
Main Program:
        initialize the program's variables

        until the user quits:
                run the main loop

        when the user is finished:
                shut down the program
```

Here is the Pascal code for Level 1. It consists of three procedure calls. *InitRTLab* calls on procedures that will initialize the variables we'll need (we've already defined them in the specification). *MainLoop* will call the event-handling procedure to process user actions. *DoShutDown* will clean up and close the application. MainLoop is inside of a Pascal routine; it will be called continuously until the user selects done.

The global variables *Finished* and *Quitting* are flags that we'll use to stop the execution of the REPEAT . . . UNTIL loop when they are set to true. *theEvent* is a record we'll access to find out what kind of events have occurred.

```
PROGRAM RTLab;
{$I+}
  USES
    InitProcedures, RTEventProcedures, RTLabGlobals;


VAR
    Quitting, Finished: boolean;
    theEvent: EventRecord;

BEGIN {main RT Lab}

  InitRTLab;

  REPEAT

    MainLoop

  UNTIL Finished;

  DoShutDown;
END. {main RT Lab}
```

Level 2 Procedures

On the next level we must design and build three procedures, one for initialization, one for the main loop, and one to shut down the program.

Initialize All Variables

```
initialize the program's variables:

        set the flags

        initialize the Mac's cursor

        initialize RTL's variables

        initialize MIDIPascal

        set up and display RTL's menus
```

Initializing the flags is done with assignment statements. The Mac cursor is set to the standard arrow pointer by calling *InitCursor*. Since each of the remaining initialization tasks require a series of steps, at this level we design a procedure that calls a separate procedure to handle each initialization separately.

```
PROCEDURE InitRTLab;
BEGIN
   Quitting := False;
   Finished := False;

   InitCursor;

   InitParameters;

   MIDIInit;

   SetUpMenus;

END;{InitRTLab}
```

Main Loop

```
run the main loop:

        identify and respond to any events
```

Since RTL is an event-driven program, it must be able to process Mac events mouse clicks, keys down, etc. This procedure calls the event handling procedure which, in turn, does the work of processing events.

```
PROCEDURE MainLoop;
BEGIN
   DoEvent;
END;{MainLoop}
```

Shut Down Program

```
shut down the program:

    shut down MIDIPascal
```

The only clean up that we need to do before quitting RTL is to clear MIDIPascal. This is done by calling the MIDIPascal command *QuitMIDI*. The *DoShutDown* procedure does just that.

```
PROCEDURE DoShutDown;
BEGIN
  QuitMIDI;
END;
```

Level 3 Procedures

Initialize RTL's Variables

```
initialize RTL's variables:
         initialize anyChanges flag
         initialize error list
         initialize configuration variables
         initialize MIDIPascal filter variables
         initialize Note Test variables
         initialize keyboard Test variables
         initialize Send Message variables
         initialize Thru Test variables
         initialize Running Status Filters variables
         initialize Channel Maps variables
         initialize Controller Maps variables
         initialize Program Change Maps variables
         initialize Velocity variables
         initialize Auto Harmony variables
         initialize Scale Map variables
         initialize Transpose variables
```

```
PROCEDURE InitParameters;
BEGIN
  {global variables for initializing  MIDI routines}
  anyChanges := False;
  InitErrorList;
  InitConfiguration;
  InitMPFilters;
  InitNoteTest;
  InitKeyboardTest;
  InitSendMessage;
  InitThruTest;
  InitRSFilters;
  InitChannelMaps;
  InitControllerMaps;
  InitPrgrmChangeMaps;
  InitVelocity;
  InitAutoHarmony;
  InitScaleMap;
  InitTranspose;
END;{InitParameters}
```

InitParameters calls procedures that initialize the variables used by each of RTL's program operations.

Initialize MIDIPascal

```
initialize MIDIPascal:

        set the in and out buffer sizes

        filter out Active Sensing messages

        set the MIDI port parameters
```

We have to add some new globals to the program. *Insize* and *Outsize* are used to set the size (in bytes) of MIDIPascal's input and output buffers.

```
CONST
    InSize = 1900;
    OutSize = 1900;

  PROCEDURE MIDIInit;
  BEGIN
    InitMidi(InSize, OutSize);        {initialize MIDIPascal}
    DoActiveSenseFilter;              {filter out Active Sensing}
    SetMIDIPort;                         {set to theSCSI and ClockMhz, clear and enable in and out buffers}
  END; {MIDIInit}
```

Since we've come to our first MIDI routine, let's follow it through so we can see the complete MIDI initialization process in context. After setting the size of the in and out buffers, we call two of our own MIDI "tools," *DoActiveSenseFilter* and *SetMIDIPort*. Here is the relevant code for DoActiveSense.

> Active Sensing messages are transmitted continuously by some instruments (Yamaha) when they are idle. We can eliminate a lot of extra overhead in our programs if we don't have to process these messages, so we set RTL to start up ready to filter these messages out of the MIDI data stream.

Active Sensing Filter

```
  CONST
{From MIDIPascal interface file}
     resetFilters = 0;                    {MidiFilter filter constants}
     filter1 = 1;
     filter2 = 2;
     filter3 = 3;
     filter4 = 4;
     filter5 = 5;
     filter6 = 6;
     filter7 = 7;
     filter8 = 8;


{From RTL Global file}
     ActiveSense = $FE;              {Status byte value}

  TYPE
     MPFilterArray = ARRAY[0..8] OF integer;

  VAR
{From RTL Init file}
     MPFilters: MPFilterArray;             {MIDIPascal Filters}



  PROCEDURE InitMPFilters;
    VAR
       count: integer;
  BEGIN
    {MIDIPascal Filters }
    FOR count := resetFilters TO filter8 DO
       MPFilters[count] := 0;
    MPFilters[filter1] := 1;              {set filter1 (Active Sensing) on}
  END; {InitMPFilters}
```

```
PROCEDURE DoActiveSenseFilter;
  BEGIN
    IF MPFilters[filter1] = 1 THEN
      MidiFilter(Filter1, ActiveSense, ActiveSense, 0)
    ELSE
      MidiFilter(Filter1, 0, 1, 0);
  END; {DoActiveSenseFilter}
```

MIDIPascal has eight built-in data filters that you can set up with the *MIDIFilter* procedure. MIDIFilter takes a filter number, low-data limit, high-data limit, and a skip count. The filter numbers are 0-8 (0 is used to reset all eight filters). MIDIFilter can remove a range of data values that you specify with low- and high- data limits. Setting both the low- and high-limits to the same value filters out one value. Setting the low-limit value to 0 turns the filter off. The skip count allows you to specify the number of additional bytes to be filtered out following a byte that is within the data range.

The MIDIPascal *interface file* declares nine constants you can use in place of the numbers (filter0 through filter8). Later, we will build a routine for our MPFilters menu item that allows the user to turn the eight filters on and off. We'll use some of the same variables used by that routine in DoActiveSense, so we show the initialization procedure, *InitMPFilters*, here. InitMPFilters initializes a nine-element array (*MPFilters*) with the value of element 1 set to 1, and all of the other elements set to 0. We use this array to hold the state of each filter. A value of 1 indicates that the filter is on; 0 indicates that the filter is off. In its initial state then, the array represents Filter1 set to on and Filter2—Filter8 set to off. Filter1 will be used set to remove Active Sensing messages from the MIDI data stream. (We'll preset the data values for the other filters, too.)

The DoActiveFilter procedure checks the current value of the first element of the MPFilterArray (Filter1). If it is 1, It calls MIDIFilter with the low- and high-data limits set for *ActiveSense*. This has previously been declared as a constant equal to $FE (the value of MIDI's Active Sense status byte). Since this is a 1-byte message, the skip count parameter passed to MIDIFilter is 0. When the program is intialized, Filter1 will always be set to 1. Later on, however, the user may want to turn this filter off. If so, the value of Filter1 will be 0. In that case, DoActiveSense calls MIDIFilter with the low-data limit set to 0 to disable the filter.

After turning on the Active Sensing filter, MIDIInit sets up the port configuration as follows:

MIDI Configuration

```
CONST
{From MIDIPascal interface file}
     halfMeg = 0;                     {MIDI Port constants}
     oneMeg = 1;
     twoMeg = 2;
     commPort = 3;
     printerPort = 4;

     resetMidi = 0;                   {Midi constants}
     inputEnable = 1;
     inputDisable = 2;
     outputEnable = 3;
     outputDisable = 4;
     clearInput = 5;
     clearOutput = 6;



  VAR
{From RTL Init file}
     theSCSI, ClockMhz: integer;      {MIDI Configuration variables}



  PROCEDURE InitConfiguration;
  BEGIN
     {MIDI Configuration }
     theSCSI := commPort;
     ClockMhz := oneMeg;
  END;



  PROCEDURE SetMIDIPort;
  BEGIN
     MidiPort(ClockMhz);
     MidiPort(theSCSI);
     MIDI(resetMIDI);
  END;
```

The procedure consists of three MIDIPascal calls.

MidiPort (ClockMhz) sets the interface clock rate to the current value of our global variable *ClockMhz*.

MidiPort(theSCSI) sets the interface to the current value of our global variable *theSCSI*.

These two variables are initialized in the *InitConfiguration* procedure. theSCSI is set to *commPort*, MIDIPascal's global constant for the modem port. ClockMhz is set to *oneMeg*—MIDIPascal's global constant for 1 MHz.

The third MIDIPascal call, *MIDI(resetMIDI)*, clears and enables the input and output buffers.

Set Up the Menu Bar

```
set up and display  RTL's menus:

        Set up the Apple menu
        Set up the File menu
        Set up the MIDI menu
        Set up the Thru menu
        Set up the Map menu

        Display the menu bar
```

Each menu is set up with a separate procedure. After all of the menus have been built, we use the Toolbox routine *DrawMenuBar* to display our menu.

```
PROCEDURE SetUpMenus;
BEGIN
  SetUpAppleMenu;
  SetUpFileMenu;
  SetUpMIDIMenu;
  SetUpOutMenu;
  SetUpThruMenu;
  SetUpMapMenu;
  DrawMenuBar;
END; {SetUpMenus}
```

Respond to Any Event

identify and resond to any events:
    find out if an event has occured

    If so, find out what type of event it was

    depending on the type of event,

        process mouse down events

        process key down events

        ignore any other events

    If the user has selected Quit from the file menu
        Shut down the desk accessory if one is open
    or else
        Tell the program the user is finished

This is where RTL will respond to the user's mouse selections of menu choices. The Toolbox routine *GetNextEvent* is used to retrieve an event from the Mac. Data about the event is returned in an event record variable called *theEvent*. The event record holds five types of data related to the event:

- *theEvent.what* holds the event *type* —key down, mouse down, etc.

- *theEvent.message* holds event-dependent data—key or character codes of key down events.

- *theEvent.when* holds the time the event occurred (on the Mac's system clock).

- *theEvent.where* holds the mouse location (in global screen coordinates) when the event happens.

- *theEvent.modifiers* holds the state of the modifier keys and mouse button.

Once the event record is returned by GetNextEvent, a case stucture is used to process the event depending on the value of the *theEvent.what* field. To keep our RTL code down to a reasonable size, we are only interested in mouse down events. However, we left a "hook" in our *DoEvent* routine that you can use to process KeyDown and AutoKey events in your own variations of this shell.

RTL will let the user stop the program with the standard File menu item Quit. However, RTL will allow the user to open desk accessories (DA) from the Mac's Apple menu, and if Quit is selected while a DA is opened, the action should close the DA, not RTL. Our design covers this possibility by using another flag to tell *DoEvent* whether or not a DA has been opened. If the *DAOpened* flag is true, DoEvent closes the DA. If it is false, DoEvent sets the *finished* flag to true. This causes the Level 1 REPEAT ... UNTIL loop to stop and the program calls DoShutDown and quits.

```
VAR
    Quitting, Finished: boolean;
    theEvent: EventRecord;
    DAOpened :boolean;

  PROCEDURE DoEvent;
  BEGIN
    IF GetNextEvent(EveryEvent, theEvent) THEN

      CASE theEvent.what OF

         MouseDown:
           IF NOT Quitting THEN
             DoMouseDown;

         KeyDown, AutoKey:
           IF NOT Quitting THEN
             DoKeysDown;

         OTHERWISE
           {don't do anything}
         END {Case theEvent}

      ELSE IF quitting THEN

      IF DAOpened = True THEN
         ShutDownDskAcc

      ELSE
         Finished := True

  END; {do event}
```

Level 4 Procedures

At this point the procedures that initialize the variables used by the fifteen MIDI program operations would be designed and coded. There are so many variables to declare that we decided to show them later on when we look at the MIDI-related code for each example. That way you can see the variables in context with the code that will use them.

Set Up Apple Menu

```
set up Apple Menu:
        create a new menu titled "apple symbol"
        add an item called "About Real Time MIDI Lab"
        add a line to the menu
        add all available desk accessories to the menu
        place the menu  in the menu bar
```

This procedure is entirely made up of a series of Toolbox calls that build a new menu. (Be sure to read about these in *Inside Macintosh*.) Menus and the items they contain are referred to by number. Rather than referencing a menu by number, such as menu 1, item 1, it's much more convenient to declare a set of global constants. This allows you to refer to menus and item by name. Here are the global constants we declared for RTL's Apple menu.

Some Toolbox routines require a "handle" that points to the menu's location in memory. The handle is created by *NewMenu*. The global variable *AppleMenu* is assigned the handle value by *NewMenu*.

```
CONST
        AppleMenuID = 1;              {resource ID of Apple menu }
        AboutItem = 1;               {ID of "About... " item

VAR
        AppleMenu: MenuHandle;
```

NewMenu creates a new menu with *AppleMenuID* (1) as its reference number, and uses the Apple symbol as a title string (ASCI character 20).

AppendMenu adds new items to a menu. You tell it which menu by passing it a menu handle, in this case *AppleMenu* , and you tell it how to display the items by passing it a series of strings such as About Real-Time MIDI Lab. You can call *AppendMenu* once for each item, as we do here, or once for each menu, as we'll show you in our other menu-building procedures.

AddResMenu is used here to add the names of all desk accessories (resource type "DRVR") to the menu.

InsertMenu places the menu into the current menu bar.

```
PROCEDURE SetUpAppleMenu;
  BEGIN
    AppleMenu := NewMenu(AppleMenuID, Chr(20));
    AppendMenu(AppleMenu, 'About Real Time MIDI Lab... ');
    AppendMenu(AppleMenu, '————————————————');
    AddResMenu(AppleMenu, 'DRVR');                        {add DA names to menu}
    InsertMenu(AppleMenu, 0);

  END;{ SetUpAppleMenu }
```

Here are the menu globals and procedure that set up our File, MIDI, Out, Thru, and Mapping menus. These routines are the bottom level of our menu initialization tasks. We list the menu globals for each menu with the appropriate procedure. In the actual program code, all of these are declared together in a single Pascal *unit* callled *RTLabMenuGlobals*.

Set Up File Menu

```
CONST
    FileMenuID = 101;
    QuitItem = 1;

VAR
  FileMenu: MenuHandle;

PROCEDURE SetUpFileMenu;
  BEGIN
    FileMenu := NewMenu(FileMenuID, 'File');
    AppendMenu(FileMenu, 'Quit');
    InsertMenu(FileMenu, 0);
  END;{SetUpFileMenu}
```

Set Up MIDI Menu

```
CONST
    MIDIMenuID = 102;
    ConfigureItem = 1;
    MIDIFiltersItem = 2;

VAR
    MIDIMenu: MenuHandle;

PROCEDURE SetUpMIDIMenu;
BEGIN
    MIDIMenu := NewMenu(MIDIMenuID, 'MIDI');
    AppendMenu(MIDIMenu, 'Configuration; MIDIFilters');
    InsertMenu(MIDIMenu, 0);
END;{SetUpMIDIMenu }
```

Set Up Out Menu

```
CONST
    OutMenuID = 103;
    NoteTestItem = 1;
    KeyTestItem = 2;
    SendItem = 4;
    PanicItem = 6;

VAR
    OutMenu: MenuHandle;

PROCEDURE SetUpOutMenu;
BEGIN
    OutMenu := NewMenu(OutMenuID, 'Out');
    AppendMenu(OutMenu, 'Note Test;Keyboard Test;(-;Send Message;(-;Panic');
    InsertMenu(OutMenu, 0);
END;{SetUpOutMenu }
```

Note the use of the open parenthesis character to *disable* a menu item and the use of a single "-" to set up a line in the menu. (See *Inside Macintosh* for details.)

```
CONST
    ThruMenuID = 104;
    ThruTestItem = 1;
    ThruItem = 3;
    DataDisplayItem = 4;
    RSFilterItem = 5;
    ChanFilterItem = 6;

VAR
   ThruMenu: MenuHandle;

PROCEDURE SetUpThruMenu;
BEGIN
   ThruMenu := NewMenu(ThruMenuID, 'Thru');
   AppendMenu(ThruMenu, 'Thru Test;(-;MIDI Thru')
   AppendMenu(ThruMenu,'Display Data;Running Status Filters');
   InsertMenu(ThruMenu, 0);
END;{SetUpThruMenu }
```

Set Up Mapping Menu

```
CONST
    MapMenuID = 105;
    ChannelMapItem = 1;
    ControlMapItem = 3;
    ProgramMapItem = 4;
    VelocityMapItem = 5;
    TransposeMapItem = 7;
    HarmonyMapItem = 8;

VAR
    MapMenu: MenuHandle;

PROCEDURE SetUpMapMenu;
BEGIN
   MapMenu := NewMenu(MapMenuID, 'Mapping');
   AppendMenu(MapMenu, 'Channel;(-;Controller')
   AppendMenu(MapMenu,'Program Change;Velocity;(-;Note Map;Harmony Map ');
   InsertMenu(MapMenu, 0);
END;{SetUpMapMenu }
```

Respond to Mouse Down Events

---

process mouse down events:
   find out where the mouse was when pressed

   depending on where the mouse is

        respond to mouse click in "desktop"

        respond to mouse click in menu bar

        respond to mouse click in DA

   ignore mouse clicks anywhere else

The Toolbox routine *FindWindow* looks at the *theEvent.where* field and assigns a part code to *thePart*. A case structure is used to handle the mouse down event based on the value of *thePart*. The values we use for each case are predefined Macintosh constants.

InDesk: the mouse was clicked in the Mac's empty desktop.

InMenuBar: the mouse was clicked in the menu bar.

InSysWindow: the mouse was clicked in a system window (desk accessory).

In our program we don't do anything if the mouse is pressed in the Mac desktop, but we've left a hook here in case you want to add a routine of your own.

If the mouse was clicked in the menu bar, we call *DoMenuHit* to process it.

If the mouse was clicked in a system window, we call the Toolbox routine *SystemClick* to process the mouse event for us. For example, if the user has opened a desk accessory and clicks on its close box, SystemClick will take care of shutting down the DA.

```
PROCEDURE DoMouseDown;
  VAR
    whichWindow: WindowPtr;
    thePart: integer;

BEGIN
  thePart := FindWindow(theEvent.where, whichWindow);
  CASE thePart OF
    InDesk:
      ; {Don't do anything}

    InMenuBar:
      DoMenuHit;

    InSysWindow: {takes care of click in DA window}
      SystemClick(theEvent, whichWindow);

    OTHERWISE
      {don't do anything}
  END {case thePart}
END;
```

Level 5 Procedures

Respond to Clicks in the Menu Bar

respond to mouse click in the menu bar:
       get the location of the mouse click in the menu
       do whatever is required by the selected item

The Toolbox routine *MenuSelect* is passed *theEvent.where*. It assigns a value to the variable *MenuPick*. This variable is then passed to our *DoMenuChoice* procedure which uses it to determine which item in which menu was selected.

```
PROCEDURE DoMenuHit;
  VAR
    MenuPick: longint;

BEGIN
  MenuPick := MenuSelect(theEvent.where);
  DoMenuChoice(MenuPick);
END; {DoMenuHit}
```

Level 6 Procedures

Get the Menu Choice

```
do whatever is required by the selected item:
        find out which menu was selected

        find out which item in the menu was selected

        depending on the menu selected,

                if no menu is selected
                        do nothing

                for the apple menu
                        perform the selected operation

                for the File menu
                        perform the selected operation

                for the MIDI menu
                        perform the selected operation

                for the Out menu
                        perform the selected operation

                for the Thru menu
                        perform the selected operation

                for the Mapping menu
                        perform the selected operation

        unhighlight the menu title
```

Finding out which menu and item is simply a matter of decoding the *MenuPick* variable. Its high-order word contains the code of the Menu ID and its low-order word contains the code of the menu item. The codes are zero if no menu or item is selected. We use the Toolbox routines *HiWord* and *LoWord* to decode the variable and assign the values to *MenuID* and *ItemID*. A case structure is used to handle the menu selection based on the value of *MenuID*. We use the global menu ID constants we defined previously as the value for each case. If no selection was made (for example, the mouse may have been clicked in the menu bar, but not on any menu title), we don't do anything. If a selection was made, a procedure that handles all the items for a given menu is called. It is passed the *ItemID* so that it can, in turn, call the appropriate procedure for the selected program operation.

After the program operation is executed, the Toolbox call *HiLiteMenu(0)* unhighlights the menu title. (The Mac automatically highlights the menu for you when the selection is made, but it's your responsibility to unhighlight it.)

```
PROCEDURE DoMenuChoice;{(MenuPick:longint)}
  CONST
    noSelection = 0;

  VAR
    MenuID, ItemID: integer;

BEGIN
  MenuID := HiWord(MenuPick);
  ItemID := LoWord(MenuPick);

  CASE MenuID OF
    noSelection:
      ;{no action taken}

    AppleMenuID:
      AppleCmd(ItemID);

    FileMenuID:
      FileCmd(ItemID);

    MIDIMenuID:
      MIDICmd(ItemID);

    OutMenuID:
      OutCmd(ItemID);

    ThruMenuID:
      ThruCmd(ItemID);

    MapMenuID:
      MapCmd(ItemID)
  END; {Case MenuID}

  HiliteMenu(0)

END; {DoMenuChoice}
```

Level 7 Procedures

Get the Menu Command

---

perform the selected menu operation:

    depending on the item number

        do first item

        do second item
        :
        :
        do last item

We use the same structure for all of our *MenuCmd* procedures. A case structure is used to handle the item selection based on the value of *ItemID*. We use the global itemID menu constants previously defined for the value of each case. Depending on the value of the Item ID, the appropriate *DoItem* procedure is called.

The one exception is the *AppleCmd* procedure. Since we want RTL to allow the user to open and close DAs, and DAs are opened from the Apple menu, we must include the routine to open the DAs in this procedure.

If *AppleCmd* is passed an item ID value that is greater than our previously declared *AboutItem*, a DA has been selected from the menu. The Toolbox routine *GetItem* returns the name of the selected DA. Then the *OpenDeskAcc* Toolbox routine is used to open the DA. Then we set our *DAOpened* flag to true so *DoEvent* can identify a user request to quit the DA from the file menu and close the DA instead of RTL.

Get Apple Commands

```
PROCEDURE AppleCmd (ItemID: integer);
   VAR
      DskAccID: integer;
      DskAccName: str255;
BEGIN
   CASE ItemID OF
      AboutItem:
         DoAbout;

      OTHERWISE
         BEGIN
            GetItem(AppleMenu, itemID, DskAccName);
            DskAccID := OpenDeskAcc(DskAccName);
            DAOpened := True;
         END;
   END {case}
END;
```

Here are the *MenuCmd* procedures for the remaining menus.

Get File Commands

```
PROCEDURE FileCmd (ItemID: integer);
BEGIN
   CASE ItemID OF
      QuitItem:
         DoQuit
   END {case}
END;
```

Get MIDI Commands

```
PROCEDURE MIDICmd (ItemID: integer);
BEGIN
   CASE ItemID OF
      ConfigureItem:
         DoConfigure;

      MIDIFiltersItem:
         DoMIDIFilters

   END {case}
END;
```

Get Out Commands

```
PROCEDURE OutCmd (ItemID: integer);
BEGIN
  CASE ItemID OF
    NoteTestItem:
      DoNoteTest;

    KeyTestItem:
      DoKeyTest;

    SendItem:
      DoSend;

    PanicItem:
      DoPanic

  END {case}
END;
```

Get Thru Commands

```
PROCEDURE ThruCmd (ItemID: integer);
BEGIN
  CASE ItemID OF
    ThruTestItem:
      DoThrutest;

    ThruItem:
      DoThru;

    DataDisplayItem:
      DoDataDisplay;

    RSFilterItem:
      DoRSFilter;

  END {case}
END;
```

Get Mapping Commands

```
PROCEDURE MapCmd (ItemID: integer);
BEGIN
   CASE ItemID OF
      ChannelMapItem:
         DoChannelMap;

      ControlMapItem:
         DoControlMap;

      ProgramMapItem:
         DoProgramMap;

      VelocityMapItem:
         DoVelocityMap;

      TransposeMapItem:
         DoTransposeMap;

      HarmonyMapItem:
         DoHarmonyMap

   END {case}
END;
```

Level 8 Procedures

Now our program structure is defined down to the point where individual operations are performed. Our first operation is performed when the user selects About Real-Time MIDI Lab. . . from the Apple menu. This is a very simple operation. All we have to do is display an *alert box* that displays a message with the basic information about the program. Here's the design:

Do About

```
Do About :
         set the message to
         MIDI Real Time Lab by Steve De Furia:

         Display the alert
```

We have designed several general purpose "utility" procedures and functions that can be used by any routine for simple tasks. The *DoAbout* procedure uses one of these–*TellUser*–to display an alert with our message.

```
PROCEDURE DoAbout;
BEGIN
   TellUser(AboutAlertID, 'Real Time MIDI Lab by Steve De Furia');
END; {DoAbout}
```

Here is the code for *TellUser*. It takes an *alertID* and message string. The alert has already been created in a resource file. Its *reference constant* is declared as a global constant in our program. The alert is a small window with an "empty" static text box and a continue button. The Toolbox routine *ParamText* is used to substitute the message string into the alert's empty text field. The *Alert* Toolbox routine displays the alert (with our message) and waits for the user to dismiss it by hitting enter, return, or clicking on the button with the mouse.

```
CONST
   AboutAlertID = 1313;

PROCEDURE TellUser; {(AlertID: integer; message: str255)}
VAR
     dontCare: integer;

BEGIN
   ParamText(message, '', '', '');
   dontCare := Alert(AlertID, NIL);
END; {TellUser}
```

Do Quit

```
DoQuit:
          tell RTL that the user selected quit from the file menu
```

The *DoQuit* procedure is very simple. All it has to do is set the *quitting* flag to true. This signals the *DoEvent* procedure that the user selected quit.

```
PROCEDURE DoQuit;
BEGIN
   Quitting := True;
END; {DoQuit }
```

At this point we can run and test the complete RTL shell. To do this, we create a "dummy" procedure for each *DoItem*. Here's the design for our dummy routines:

Dummy Procedure

---

dummy do item procedure:

   draw a window that displays

   "this procedure is not implemented"

Now we can compile and run the program. All of the menus will be displayed and we can select any item from any menu. If we select a DA from the Apple Menu, it will open. We can close it by clicking in its close box or by selecting quit. If we select About RTL... we see our message. If we select any other item, we see an alert that displays the name of the procedure that called it. This is a good technique to exercise the complete user interface of any program you build. If there's something wrong, or you want to make some changes, now is the time to do it—before you've installed the routines that perform the operations selected from the menus. Here are the dummy versions of our *DoItem* routines. In the next section, we'll look at the complete code for each MIDI routine.

Do Configure

```
PROCEDURE DoConfigure;
BEGIN
   TellUser(AboutAlertID, 'Configure is not implemented.');
END; {Configure}
```

Do MIDI Filters

```
PROCEDURE DoMIDIFilters;
BEGIN
   TellUser(AboutAlertID, 'MIDI Filters are not implemented.');
END; {MIDIFilters }
```

Do Note Test

```
PROCEDURE DoNoteTest;
BEGIN
   TellUser(AboutAlertID, 'Note Test is not implemented.');
END; {NoteTest}
```

Do Key Test

```
PROCEDURE DoKeyTest;
  BEGIN
    TellUser(AboutAlertID, 'Keyboard Test is not implemented.');
  END;
```

Do Send

```
PROCEDURE DoSend;
BEGIN
   TellUser(AboutAlertID, 'Send Message is not implemented.');
END; {Send}
```

Do Panic

```
PROCEDURE DoPanic;
BEGIN
   TellUser(AboutAlertID, 'Panic is not implemented.');
END; {Panic}
```

Do Thru Test

```
PROCEDURE DoThruTest;
BEGIN
   TellUser(AboutAlertID, 'Thru Test is not implemented.');
END; {ThruTest}
```

Do MIDI Thru

```
PROCEDURE DoThru;
  BEGIN
    TellUser(AboutAlertID, 'MIDI Thru is not implemented.');
  END; {Thru}
```

Do Display Data

```
PROCEDURE DoDataDisplay;
BEGIN
   TellUser(AboutAlertID, 'Data Display is not implemented.');
END; {DataDisplay}
```

Do Running Status Filters

```
PROCEDURE DoRSFilter;
BEGIN
   TellUser(AboutAlertID, 'Running Status Filters are not implemented.');
END; {RSFilter}
```

Do Channel

```
PROCEDURE DoChannelMap;
   BEGIN
      TellUser(AboutAlertID, 'Channel Mapping is not implemented.');
   END; {Channel}
```

Do Controller

```
PROCEDURE DoControlMap;
BEGIN
   TellUser(AboutAlertID, 'Controller Mapping is not implemented.');
END; {ControlMap}
```

Do Program Change

```
PROCEDURE DoProgramMap;
BEGIN
   TellUser(AboutAlertID, 'Program Change Mapping is not implemented.');
END; {ProgramMap}
```

Do Velocity

```
PROCEDURE DoVelocityMap;
BEGIN
   TellUser(AboutAlertID, 'Velocity Mapping is not implemented.');
END; {VelocityMap}
```

Do Note Map

```
PROCEDURE DoTransposeMap;
BEGIN
   TellUser(AboutAlertID, 'Note mapping is not implemented.');
END; {TransposeMap}
```

Do Harmony Map

```
PROCEDURE DoHarmonyMap;
  BEGIN
    TellUser(AboutAlertID, 'Harmony Mapping is not implemented.');
  END; {Harmony Map}
```

Building the Program Operation Routines

Now that we've built the shell, we can develop each of RTL's program operations. In the specification for each operation, we listed the variables (and their valid ranges) that we would need for each operation. We also specified that the RTL program would use *dialog windows* to get variable values from the user.

Rather than building our dialogs from scratch within the program code, we made a new *resource file*, RTLAB0.rsrc, with ResEdit, and created the dialogs using ResEdit's DLOG and DITL editors. The resource file is linked to the program by selecting Lightspeed Pascal's *Use Resource File* Run option.

Each dialog has a unique ID number which allows us to call it from within our program. Each item within the dialog also has an ID number which we use to access it from our code. Our program uses the following types of dialog items:

- *Static text*: a text string of up to 241 characters that is displayed, but can't be selected or altered by the user

- *Editable text box*: a box which the user can select with the mouse or tab key, and type in up to 241 characters

- *Radio buttons*: a small round "button" that is selected by clicking on it with the mouse. When selected, the radio button will be lit if previously unlit, and unlit if previously lit. When there is more than one radio button grouped together, only one button at a time should be lit. The value of a lit button is 1, the value of an unlit button is 0. Note that these are *integer*, not *boolean*, values

- *Check boxes*: a small square box that can be selected by clicking on it with the mouse. When selected, the box will be checked with an X if previously unchecked, and unchecked if previously checked. The value of a checked box is 1, the value of an unchecked box is 0. Note that these are *integer*, not *boolean*, values

- *Push buttons*: a rounded rectangle that surrounds a label like done, cancel, or continue. Push buttons are selected by clicking on them with the mouse

The Mac expects dialog item #1 to be the *default button*. This button, like the continue button of an alert, can be pushed by hitting the enter or return key. If you don't want to use a default button, don't use 1 as an ID number for any items. If you do, you should show the user which button is the default button by drawing a bold border around it. This is done by defining the default button as a *user item* and drawing it with the *DrawUserCtrl* Toolbox call. We take a shortcut here by using our *BoldOKButton* procedure. It draws a bold border around the *display rectangle* of item number 1. Be aware that, as used in RTL, this procedure doesn't automatically redraw the border if the dialog is covered by another window and then redrawn.

We have created several small utility procedures to help us display dialogs and update their controls. These are general purpose tools used by all of our *DoDlog* procedures. Before we look at these procedures, let's look at the utilities.

Displaying Resource Dialogs

```
PROCEDURE ShowResDialog;{DLOGID,defaultState}
BEGIN
   TheDialog := GetNewDialog(DLOGID, NIL, WindowPtr(-1));
   SetPort(TheDialog);
   IF defaultState = On THEN
     BoldOKButton;
   DrawDialog(TheDialog);
END; {ShowResDialog}
```

ShowResDialog is used to display a previously defined resource dialog window and the items it contains. It calls the Toolbox routine *GetNewDialog* with an ID for the dialog we want and gets the dialog from the resource file. Next, *SetPort* is used to set the Mac's current drawing port to the dialog window.

Most of RTL's dialogs contain *default buttons*. These should always have a boldface border. Along with the *DLOGID* parameter, ShowResDlog takes a *defaultState* parameter. If defaultState is "true," then ShowResDlog calls our *BoldOKButton* to draw the border. Finally, the Toolbox routine *DrawDialog* is called to display the dialog on the screen.

Bold the OK Button

```
PROCEDURE BoldOKButton;
    VAR
        DlogType: integer;
        dispRect: rect;
        DlogHandle: handle;
        cntrlHandle: controlHandle;
        curState: PenState;

    BEGIN
        GetPenState(curState);
        GetDItem(theDialog, OK, Dlogtype, DlogHandle, dispRect);
        PenSize(3, 3);
        InsetRect(dispRect, -4, -4);
        FrameRoundRect(dispRect, 16, 16);
        SetPenState(curState);
    END;{Bold OKButton}
```

BoldOKButton is based on the Mac convention of always using item #1 as the default button. A Mac global constant *OK* is used to represent item #1. All of the procedures used in BoldOKButton are Toolbox routines.

Before it does any drawing, BoldOKButton uses the *GetPenState* routine to store the current state of QuickDraw's pen. Then *GetDItem* is used to get the *display rectangle* of the OK item (item # 1). Next, *PenSize* sets the pen to 3x3 pixels. (This will draw a bold line.) *InsetRect* expands the display rectangle of the OK button by 4 pixels, and *FrameRoundRect* draws the expanded rectangle with the bold pen. Finally, *SetPenState* is called to reset the pen to its original state.

Reset Dialog Controls

```
PROCEDURE ResetDlogCntrl (theDlogItem, theParameter, theValue: integer);
    VAR
        DlogType: integer;
        DlogRect: rect;
        DlogHandle: handle;
        cntrlHandle: controlHandle;

BEGIN
    GetDItem(theDialog, theDlogItem, Dlogtype, DlogHandle, DlogRect);
    cntrlHandle := ControlHandle(DlogHandle);
    IF theParameter = theValue THEN
        SetCtlValue(cntrlHandle, 1)
    ELSE
        SetCtlValue(cntrlHandle, 0);
END; {ResetDlogCntrl}
```

ResetDlogCntrl is used to set radio buttons or check boxes to show the current values of a variable. *theDlogItem* is the item ID of the control being reset. *theParameter* is the value of the variable being checked; *theValue* is the value it is checked against. If theParameter and theValue are equal, the control is turned on. If they are unequal, the control is turned off. We use ResetDlogCntrl at the beginning of any dialog routine that has radio buttons and/or check boxes. All of the procedures called by ResetDlogCntrl are Toolbox routines.

GetDItem is used to get the handle (memory location) of the item being checked. Pascal's *type-casting* feature is used in the statement "cntrlHandle := ControlHandle(DlogHandle)" to convert the dialog handle to a control handle. *SetCtlValue* uses the controlhandle to update the control with the new value.

Reset Check Boxes

```
PROCEDURE ResetCheckBox (selectedBox: integer);
  VAR
    DlogType, boxFlag: integer;
    DlogRect: rect;
    DlogHandle: handle;
    cntrlHandle: controlHandle;
BEGIN
  GetDItem(theDialog, selectedBox, Dlogtype, DlogHandle, DlogRect);
  cntrlHandle := ControlHandle(DlogHandle);
  boxFlag := GetCtlValue(cntrlHandle);
  boxFlag := ToggleFlag(boxFlag);
  SetCtlValue(cntrlHandle, boxFlag);
END; {ResetCheckBox}



FUNCTION ToggleFlag (flag: integer): integer;
BEGIN
  flag := ABS(Flag - 1);          {reverse 1 to 0 or 0 to1}
  ToggleFlag := flag;
END;{ToggleFlag}
```

ResetCheckBox is used to reverse the value of a check box when it is selected by the user. If the box is checked, selecting it removes the check. If it is unchecked, selecting it puts an X in the box. The control value of a checked box is 1, the value of an unchecked box is 0. We use ResetCheckBox in all dialog routines that have check boxes. Whenever the routine detects that the user has clicked on a check box, ResetCheckBox is called to toggle it from 1 to 0 or from 0 to 1.

Like ResetDlogCntrol, ResetCheckBox makes extensive use of Toolbox routines. *GetDItem* gets the handle to the dialog item and the handle is converted to a control handle by type-casting. *GetCrtlValue* assigns the box's current value to our variable *boxFlag.* Next we use our own utility function *ToggleFlag* to toggle the value of boxFlag from 1 to 0 or from 0 to 1. Finally, *SetCntrlValue* is used to reset the control to the value of boxFlag.

Reset Radio Buttons

```
PROCEDURE ResetRadioList (lowButton, hiButton, selectedButton: integer);
  VAR
    DlogSelection, DlogType, theButton: integer;
    DlogRect: rect;
    DlogHandle: handle;
    cntrlHandle: controlHandle;
BEGIN
  DlogSelection := selectedButton;
  FOR theButton := lowButton TO hiButton DO
    BEGIN
      GetDItem(theDialog, theButton, Dlogtype, DlogHandle, DlogRect);
      cntrlHandle := ControlHandle(DlogHandle);
      IF theButton = selectedButton THEN
        SetCtlValue(cntrlHandle, 1)
      ELSE
        SetCtlValue(cntrlHandle, 0);
    END;{for count}
END; {ResetRadioList}
```

ResetRadioList is used to reset all of the radio buttons in a group so that the last button selected is lit, and all of the others are turned off. Radio buttons are generally used when the user is given more than one choice for a parameter. For example, we use a group of three radio buttons to allow the user to select an interface clock rate. The user may select any of the three rates, but only one can be active at a time. It is our responsibility to see to it that the buttons are lit and unlit properly when any button in a group is selected. This is done by keeping the item numbers for each group of radio buttons in a series. (The clock-rate radio buttons are numbered 5 to 7.) ResetRadioList checks all of the buttons in the series and unlights all but the currently selected button. Here again, we make good use of the Toolbox.

ResetRadioList is given the values of the lowest and highest ID numbers of the radio buttons in the group, and the ID number of the selected button. A FOR loop is used to check each button in the group. The loop's counter, *theButton,* is set to the ID number of the lowest button in the group.

GetDItem gets the handle to theButton and the handle is converted to a control handle by type-casting. If theButton is equal to the ID of the selected button, *SetCtlValue* is used to set the button's value to 1. If theButton is not equal to the ID of the selected button, *SetCtlValue* is used to set the button's value to 0. The value of theButton is incremented and the process repeats until all of the buttons in the group have been reset.

Display Numbers in Text Boxes

```
PROCEDURE NumberToItem (theDialog: DialogPtr; DlogItem, theNumber: Integer);
  VAR
    DlogType: integer;
    DlogRect: rect;
    DlogHandle: handle;
    thetext: str255;

BEGIN
  GetDItem(theDialog, DlogItem, Dlogtype, DlogHandle, DlogRect);
  NumToString(theNumber, theText);
  SetIText(DlogHandle, thetext);
END;{NumberToItem}
```

NumberToItem is used whenever we want to display a number in a dialog's *editable text box*. Text boxes can only display strings of characters. Many of our program's variables are integer values. In order to display them in a text box, we must convert the number to its string equivalent, then display the string in the text box. NumberToItem handles the conversion and resets the text box as well. All of the procedures used are from the ToolBox. *GetDItem* gets the handle to the item. *NumToString* converts the integer value to a Pascal string. *SetIText* puts the string into the edit box.

Checking for Range Errors

It is always a good idea to check input values to see if they are within the legal range of the procedures that will be using them. If they are not, an error message should be displayed. Many of RTL's dialogs allow the user to type in number values that are used by the program's MIDI routines. In every case, we check the value to see if it is within the range limits we've defined. If not, the value displayed in the dialog window is reset to a default value and an alert tells the user what the range limits for that particular value are.

Numbers are typed into editable text boxes, so before we can check their value, we must first convert them from character strings to integers. We use the *NumberFromItem* function to handle getting the string from the dialog and converting it to an integer. It uses only Toolbox routines.

Get Number from Text Box

```
FUNCTION NumberFromItem (theDialog: DialogPtr; DlogItem: Integer): integer;
   VAR
      DlogType: integer;
      DlogRect: rect;
      DlogHandle: handle;
      thetext: str255;
      theNumber: Longint;

BEGIN
   GetDItem(theDialog, DlogItem, Dlogtype, DlogHandle, DlogRect);
   GetIText(DlogHandle, thetext);
   StringToNum(theText, theNumber);
   NumberFromItem := theNumber;
END;{NumberFromItem}
```

GetDItem gets the handle to the text box. *GetIText* gets the text string. *StringToNum* converts the string to an integer.

Check Data for Out of Range Error

```
FUNCTION InDataRange (dataValue, lowLimit, hiLimit: integer): boolean;
BEGIN
   IF (dataValue < lowLimit) OR (dataValue > hiLimit) THEN
      InDataRange := FALSE
   ELSE
      InDataRange := TRUE;
END;{InDataRange}
```

The *InDataRange* function checks a value against an upper and lower limit. If the value is within the two limits, the function returns a true. If the value is outside the range limits, the function returns a false.

From the specifications we can see that we need to handle twelve different data ranges:

MIDI data, 0-127; arpeggio length 1-8; arpeggio speed 1-15; 8-bit byte values 0-255; polyphony 1-4; MIDI channel values 1-16; controller values, mod wheel(1) – data decrement (97); scale factor values ±10; status values 128-255; harmony values ± two octaves; duration values 0-100; and delay values 0-60.

The twelve different types of values are assigned code numbers and declared as constants.

Create an Error Message List

```
CONST
    {errorList array codes}
    dataValueCode = 1;
    lengthValueCode = 2;
    speedValueCode = 3;
    byteValueCode = 4;
    polyphonyValueCode = 5;
    channelValueCode = 6;
    controlValueCode = 7;
    scaleValueCode = 8;
    statusValueCode = 9;
    harmonyValueCode = 10;
    durationValueCode = 11;
    delayValueCode = 12;

VAR
    ErrorList: ARRAY[dataValueCode..delayValueCode] OF str255;
```

A 12-element, global string array variable is declared. When RTL is initialized, the procedure *InitErrorList* loads the error messages into the string array. The appropriate value code is used as the subscript for each message.

```
PROCEDURE InitErrorList;
  BEGIN
    {error messages for CheckValue function calls}
    ErrorList[dataValueCode] := 'MIDI data values must be between 0 - 127';
    ErrorList[lengthValueCode] := 'Length values must be between 1 - 8';
    ErrorList[speedValueCode] := 'Speed values must be between 1- 15';
    ErrorList[byteValueCode] := 'MIDI byte values must be between 0 - 255';
    ErrorList[polyphonyValueCode] := 'Polyphony values must be between 1-4';
    ErrorList[channelValueCode] := 'Channel values must be between 1-16';
    ErrorList[controlValueCode] := 'Control values must be between 1- 97';
    ErrorList[scaleValueCode] := 'Scale factor values must be ± 10';
    ErrorList[statusValueCode] := 'Status values must between 128 - 255';
    ErrorList[harmonyValueCode] := 'Harmony values must be ± 24';
    ErrorList[durationValueCode] := 'Duration values must be 0 - 100';
    ErrorList[delayValueCode] := 'Delay values must be 0-60';
  END; {InitErrorList}
```

Now that we have the basic tools that we need to get values from the dialog and check them against range limits, as well as a list of error messages, we can build a high-level, range-checking routine that can be used by any of our program operations. This function is called to check the value of any number entered by the user.

Check Value of Dialog Entry

```
FUNCTION CheckValue (theItem, oldValue, valueCode: integer): integer;
  VAR
    newValue, loLimit, hiLimit: integer;
    theMessage: str255;

BEGIN
  CASE valueCode OF
    dataValueCode:
      BEGIN
        theMessage := ErrorList[valueCode];
        loLimit := 0;
        hiLimit := maxDataValue;
      END;

    lengthValueCode:
      BEGIN
        theMessage := ErrorList[valueCode];
        loLimit := 1;
        hiLimit := 8;
      END;

    speedValueCode:
      BEGIN
        theMessage := ErrorList[valueCode];
        loLimit := 1;
        hiLimit := 15;
      END;

    byteValueCode:
      BEGIN
        theMessage := ErrorList[valueCode];
        loLimit := 0;
        hiLimit := SystemReset;
      END;

    polyphonyValueCode:
      BEGIN
        theMessage := ErrorList[valueCode];
        loLimit := 1;
        hiLimit := polyphony;
      END;
```

```
channelValueCode:
  BEGIN
    theMessage := ErrorList[valueCode];
    loLimit := Channel1;
    hiLimit := Channel16;
  END;

controlValueCode:
  BEGIN
    theMessage := ErrorList[valueCode];
    loLimit := ModController;
    hiLimit := DataDecrement;
  END;

  statusValueCode:
  BEGIN
    theMessage := ErrorList[valueCode];
    loLimit := NoteOff;
    hiLimit := SystemReset;
  END;

harmonyValueCode:
  BEGIN
    theMessage := ErrorList[valueCode];
    loLimit := -twoOctaves;
    hiLimit := twoOctaves;
  END;

durationValueCode:
  BEGIN
    theMessage := ErrorList[valueCode];
    loLimit := 0;
    hiLimit := 100;
  END;

delayValueCode:
  BEGIN
    theMessage := ErrorList[valueCode];
    loLimit := 0;
    hiLimit := 60;
  END;
```

```
    OTHERWISE
      BEGIN
        {check Value code with debugger if you have problems here}
        TellUser(AboutAlertID, 'undefined value code passed to CheckData');
        disposDialog(theDialog);
        loLimit := 999;
        hiLimit := -999;
      END;
    END;{case valueCode}

    newValue := NumberFromItem(theDialog, theItem);
    IF NOT InDataRange(newValue, loLimit, hiLimit) THEN
      BEGIN
        TellUser(AboutAlertID, theMessage);
        newValue := oldValue;
        NumberToItem(theDialog, theItem, newValue);
      END;

    CheckValue := newValue;
END; {CheckValue}
```

CheckValue is passed three values. *theItem* is the item ID of the text box being checked. *oldValue* is the default value to which the item is reset if there is an error. *valueCode* is the code number for the data range to be checked.

A CASE structure is used to determine the type of data being checked. Depending on the value of valueCode, *theMesesage* is assigned the correct error message from the ErrorList array, and *loLimit* and *hiLimit* are assigned the appropriate range limit values.

Next, *newValue* is assigned the user-entered value by our NumberFromItem procedure. Then, newValue is checked by InDataRange.

If the value is within the legal range, CheckValue returns the user's value. If the value is out of range, Check value displays an alert with the proper error message, and resets the text box to the default value.

Design of DoDlog Procedures

All RTL *DoDlog* procedures that employ dialogs to get input from the user have the same general design.

DoDlog Procedure

dodialog:

    set the procedure's local variables to the current global values

    display the dialog

    set the dialog's controls to show the current local values

    until the user dismisses the dialog:

        respond to user selection of a control

            update selected radio buttons

            update selected check box

            check values entered for range errors
            reset the local variable to new value

    when the user pushes done, cancel or other button:

        If done button
            reset global values to new local values

        If cancel button
            don't change original global values

        If other button
            execute task specified by other button

    remove the dialog from the screen

MIDI Menu Operations

Configuration Procedures

```
PROCEDURE DoConfigure;
BEGIN
   DoConfigureDLog;
   IF anyChanges THEN
      SetMIDIPort;
END; {Configure}
```

Here is the DoConfigure procedure as it appears in the final version of the program. It calls *DoConfigureDlog* to get configuration settings from the user. If the user dismisses the the dialog by pushing done, DoConfigure sets *anyChanges* to true. If so, DoConfigure calls the *SetMIDIPort* procedure (which we've already seen) and resets the port to the new values. The following screen shows the dialog displayed by DoConfigureDlog.

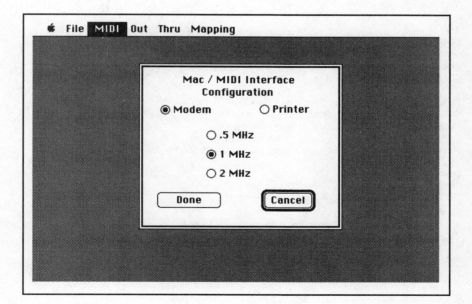

```
CONST
{From MIDIPascal interface file}
      halfMeg = 0;                        {MIDI Port constants}
      oneMeg = 1;
      twoMeg = 2;
      commPort = 3;
      printerPort = 4;

                                          {MIDI Menu Dialogs}
      MIDISetupDlogID = 104;              {Configure  Resource ID's}
      CancelDlogItem = 1;
      DoneDlogItem = 2;
      ModemDlogItem = 3;
      PrinterDlogItem = 4;
      HalfMegDlogItem = 5;
      OneMegDlogItem = 6;
      TwoMegDlogItem = 7;


PROCEDURE DoConfigureDlog;
   VAR
      DlogItem, DlogType, whichSCSI, clockRate, ItemListOffset: integer;
      DlogRect: rect;
      DlogHandle: handle;
BEGIN
   ItemListOffset := 5;
   whichSCSI := theSCSI;
   clockRate := clockMhz;
   ShowResDialog(MIDISetupDlogID, On);

   ResetDlogCntrl(ModemDlogItem, theSCSI, commPort);
   ResetDlogCntrl(PrinterDlogItem, theSCSI, printerPort);
   ResetDlogCntrl(halfMegDlogItem, clockMhz, halfMeg);
   ResetDlogCntrl(oneMegDlogItem, clockMhz, oneMeg);
   ResetDlogCntrl(twoMegDlogItem, clockMhz, twoMeg);

   REPEAT
     BEGIN
       ModalDialog(NIL, DlogItem);
       CASE DlogItem OF
         ModemDlogItem, PrinterDlogItem:
           BEGIN
             ResetRadioList(ModemDlogItem, PrinterDlogItem, DlogItem);
             whichSCSI := DlogItem;
           END;

         HalfMegDlogItem, OneMegDlogItem, TwoMegDlogItem:
           BEGIN
             ResetRadioList(HalfMegDlogItem, TwoMegDlogItem, DlogItem);
             clockRate := DlogItem - ItemListOffset;
           END;
```

```
        OTHERWISE
            {do nothing}
        END {CaseDlogItem}
    END; {repeat}

UNTIL (DlogItem = DoneDlogItem) OR (DlogItem = CancelDlogItem);
IF DlogItem = DoneDlogItem THEN
    BEGIN
        anyChanges := TRUE;              {return done result update global variables}
        theSCSI := whichSCSI;
        ClockMhz := clockRate;
    END

ELSE
    anyChanges := False;               {return cancel result, don't change global variables}
    DisposDialog(TheDialog);
END;{DoConfigureDlog}
```

DoConfigureDlog allows the user to set new values for the global port and clock-rate variables, *theSCSI* and *ClockRate*. The first step in the procedure is to declare a local version of these variables to hold the updated values entered when the user clicks the mouse on the dialog's controls. The local variables used to hold the results of the user's interaction with the dialog window are *whichSCSI* and *clockRate*. Here are the steps in DoConfigure:

The local variables are set to the current values held in the program's globals, theSCSI and ClockMhz. ShowResourceDialog displays the dialog and draws a bold border around the cancel button. The dialog's controls are set to the current settings with calls to ResetDlogCntrl for each control. The Toolbox routine *ModalDialog* reports any user activity in the dialog window. A CASE structure handles user selection of each dialog item. When either the modem or printer buttons are pushed, ResetRadioList resets the radio buttons. whichSCSI is set to dlogItem (the selected port code). When any of the clock rate buttons are pushed, ResetRadioList resets the radio buttons. clockRate is set to dlogItem - ItemlistOffset (the selected clock rate code).

If the user pushes the done button, the global values are set to the local values, and *anyChanges* is set to true. If the user pushes cancel, the global values aren't changed and anyChanges is set to false.

MIDIFilters Procedures

```
PROCEDURE DoMIDIFilters;
BEGIN
  DoMPFilterDlog;
  IF anyChanges THEN
    BEGIN
      SetMPFilters;
      MIDI(resetMIDI);
    END;
END; {MIDIFilters}
```

DoMIDIFilters uses the same general structure as DoConfigure. First, a dialog procedure (*DoMPFilterDlog*) is called to allow the user to change the current settings. After the dialog is dismissed, DoMIDIFIlters calls *SetMP-Filters* to reset the MIDI Pascal filters if the anyChanges flag was set to true by DoMPFilterDlog. The following screen shows the dialog displayed by DoMIDIFiltersDlog.

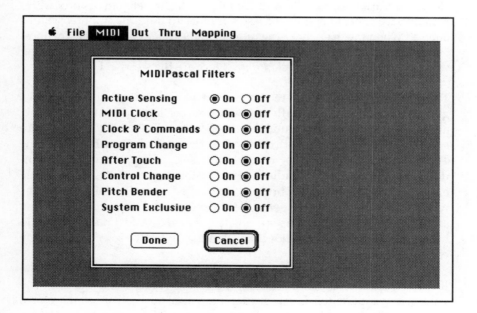

```
CONST
        AllNotesData = $7B;                {MIDI Status Bytes}
        NoteOff = $80;
        NoteOn = $90;
        PolyPressure = $A0;
        ControlChange = $B0;
        ProgramChange = $C0;
        ChannelPressure = $D0;
        PitchBend = $E0;
        SystemMessage = $F0;
        QuarterFrame = $F1;
        SongPointer = $F2;
        SongSelect = $F3;
        TuneRequest = $F6;
        EOX = $F7;
        MIDIClock = $F8;
        MIDIStart = $FA;
        MIDIContinue = $FB;
        MIDIStop = $FC;
        ActiveSense = $FE;
        SystemReset = $FF;

                                           {MIDI Menu Dialogs}
        MPFilterDlogID = 102;              {MIDI Pascal Filter  Resource ID's}
        MPFCancelItem = 1;
        MPFDoneItem = 2;
        MPFActiveOn = 3;
        MPFActiveOff = 4;
        MPFClockOn = 5;
        MPFClockOff = 6;
        MPFClkCmdOn = 7;
        MPFClkCmdOff = 8;
        MPFChangeOn = 9;
        MPFChangeOff = 10;
        MPFAfterTouchOn = 11;
        MPFAfterTouchOff = 12;
        MPFCntrlOn = 13;
        MPFCntrlOff = 14;
        MPFBendOn = 15;
        MPFBendOff = 16;
        MPFSysExOn = 17;
        MPFSysExOff = 18;
```

```
      PROCEDURE DoMPFilterDlog;
        VAR
          DlogItem, DlogType: integer;
          DlogRect: rect;
          DlogHandle: handle;
          theMPFilter: MPFilterArray;
          count, theDlogItem: integer;
      BEGIN
        ShowResDialog(MPFilterDlogID, On);

        theDlogItem := MPFActiveOn;
{the first item in the filter radio list}
        FOR count := 1 TO 8 DO
{for each of the filters...}
          BEGIN
            theMPFilter[count] := MPFilters[count];
{set local array to current global values}
            ResetDlogCntrl(theDlogItem, MPFilters[count], 1);        {update filter's ON display}
            ResetDlogCntrl(theDlogItem + 1, MPFilters[count], 0);    {update  OFF display}
            theDlogItem := theDlogItem + 2;
{increment to next filter}
          END;

        REPEAT
          BEGIN
            ModalDialog(NIL, DlogItem);
            CASE DlogItem OF

              MPFActiveOn, MPFActiveOff:
                BEGIN
                  ResetRadioList(MPFActiveOn, MPFActiveOff, DlogItem);
                  IF DlogItem = MPFActiveOn THEN
                    theMPFilter[1] := 1
                  ELSE
                    theMPFilter[1] := 0;
                END;
```

```
        MPFClockOn, MPFClockOff:
            ;
        MPFClkCmdOn, MPFClkCmdOff:
            ;
        MPFChangeOn, MPFChangeOff:
            ;
        MPFAfterTouchOn, MPFAfterTouchOff:
            ;
        MPFCntrlOn, MPFCntrlOff:
            ;
        MPFBendOn, MPFBendOff:
            ;
        MPFSysExOn, MPFSysExOff:
            BEGIN
                ResetRadioList(MPFSysExOn, MPFSysExOff, DlogItem);
                IF DlogItem = MPFSysExOn THEN
                    theMPFilter[8] := 1
                ELSE
                    theMPFilter[8] := 0;
            END;

        OTHERWISE
            {do nothing}
        END {CaseDlogItem}
    END; {repeat}

    UNTIL (DlogItem = MPFDoneItem) OR (DlogItem = MPFCancelItem);
    IF DlogItem = MPFDoneItem THEN
        BEGIN
            anyChanges := True;
            FOR count := 1 TO 8 DO              {relplace the global values with the local array values}
                MPFilters[count] := theMPFilter[count];
        END

    ELSE
        anyChanges := False;                          {cancel: don't change anything}
    DisposDialog(TheDialog);
END;{DoMPFilterDisplay}
```

DoMPFilterDlog follows the same design as all of our other DoDlog procedures. To save space we show only the CASE structures for Filter1 and Filter8. The structure for the other filters is exactly the same, except in each instance the subscript for *theMPFilter* is set to the appropriate filter number. The complete listing is given in Appendix A.

If the anyChanges flag is true, then DoMPFilters will call SetMPFilters when the dialog is dismissed. It, in turn, calls eight routines, one for each MIDIPascal filter.

Set the MPFilters

```
PROCEDURE SetMPFilters;
BEGIN
    DoActiveSenseFilter;
    DoMClockFilter;
    DoMClockCmdsFilter;
    DoSystemFilter;
    DoAfterTouchFilter;
    DoControllerFilter;
    DoPChangeFilter;
    DoBenderFilter;
END;{SetMPFilters}
```

The DoActiveSense procedure that was previously presented is shown again here with the seven other MIDI filter procedures. They are all exactly the same, except each one is set to filter out a different type of MIDI message. Note that Program Change, Channel Pressure, Control Change, and Pitch Bend messages are more than one byte long and require the skip count variable to be set accordingly.

You can use the procedures as is in any of your MIDI programs when you want to set up data filters. Be aware, however, that the MIDIPascal filters don't handle Running Status transmission—when status bytes for Channel Voice messages are not sent unless the status changes. We'll show you how to filter out Running Status data with our RSFilter routines.

MPFilter Procedures

```
PROCEDURE DoActiveSenseFilter;
BEGIN
   IF MPFilters[filter1] = 1 THEN
      MidiFilter(Filter1, ActiveSense, ActiveSense, 0)
   ELSE
      MidiFilter(Filter1, 0, 1, 0);
END; {DoActiveSenseFilter}




PROCEDURE DoMClockFilter;
BEGIN
   IF MPFilters[filter2] = 1 THEN
      MidiFilter(Filter2, MIDIClock, MIDIClock, 0)
   ELSE
      MidiFilter(Filter2, 0, 1, 0);
END;




PROCEDURE DoMClockCmdsFilter;
BEGIN
   IF MPFilters[filter3] = 1 THEN
      MidiFilter(Filter3, MIDIClock, MIDIStop, 0)
   ELSE
      MidiFilter(Filter3, 0, 1, 0);
END;




PROCEDURE DoPChangeFilter;
BEGIN
   IF MPFilters[filter4] = 1 THEN
      MidiFilter(Filter4, ProgramChange, ProgramChange, 1)
   ELSE
      MidiFilter(Filter4, 0, 1, 0);
END;




PROCEDURE DoAfterTouchFilter;
BEGIN
   IF MPFilters[filter5] = 1 THEN
      MidiFilter(Filter5, ChannelPressure, ChannelPressure, 2)
   ELSE
      MidiFilter(Filter5, 0, 1, 0);
END;
```

```
PROCEDURE DoControllerFilter;
BEGIN
   IF MPFilters[filter6] = 1 THEN
      MidiFilter(Filter6, ControlChange, ControlChange, 2)
   ELSE
      MidiFilter(Filter6, 0, 1, 0);
END;




PROCEDURE DoBenderFilter;
BEGIN
   IF MPFilters[filter7] = 1 THEN
      MidiFilter(Filter7, PitchBend, PitchBend, 2)
   ELSE
      MidiFilter(Filter7, 0, 1, 0);
END;




PROCEDURE DoSystemFilter;
BEGIN
   IF MPFilters[filter8] = 1 THEN
      MidiFilter(Filter8, SystemMessage, SystemMessage, 0)
   ELSE
      MidiFilter(Filter8, 0, 1, 0);
END;
```

Out Menu Operations

The program operations selected from the Out menu call routines that transmit MIDI Voice Messages from the Mac. Three of the operations—*Note Test*, *Keyboard Test*, and *Send Message*—employ DoDlog procedures to get input from the user before transmitting MIDI data. We won't go over the complete dialog procedure for each routine since the code for displaying the dialog, for updating dialog controls, and for text boxes are all quite similar. Instead, we'll focus on the special features of each DoDlog procedure such as how it updates RTL's global variables, and the MIDI routines it uses. The fourth operation, *Panic*, uses a different kind of display routine that we'll look at along with its MIDI routines.

MIDI Globals

At this point, we should declare global constants and types that can be used by our MIDI routines. Here is the complete listing of global constant and type declarations that are used by the various MIDI routines in RTL. You'll find that many of these globals can be useful in any MIDI program; we've put them in a separate file, *RTLab Globals,* that you can include with a USES statement into any of your own Pascal programs.

Real-Time MIDI Lab Global Declarations

```
CONST

Constants for MIDI filters and general MIDI processing}
      StatusMask = $F0;
      ChannelMask = $0F;
      Channel16 = 16;
      Channel1 = 1;

{MIDI Status Bytes}
      AllNotesData = $7B;
      NoteOff = $80;
      NoteOn = $90;
      PolyPressure = $A0;
      ControlChange = $B0;
      ProgramChange = $C0;
      ChannelPressure = $D0;
      PitchBend = $E0;
      SystemMessage = $F0;
      QuarterFrame = $F1;
      SongPointer = $F2;
      SongSelect = $F3;
      TuneRequest = $F6;
      EOX = $F7;
      MIDIClock = $F8;
```

```
      MIDIStart = $FA;
      MIDIContinue = $FB;
      MIDIStop = $FC;
      ActiveSense = $FE;
      SystemReset = $FF;


{MIDI Controller ID's}
      ModController = 1;
      BreathController = 2;
      FootController = 4;
      PTimeController = 5;
      DataEntryMSB = 6;
      VolumeController = 7;
      BalanceController = 8;
      PanController = 10;
      SustainSwitch = 64;
      PortamentoSwitch = 65;
      SostentutoSwitch = 66;
      SoftPedalSwitch = 67;
      DataIncrement = 96;
      DataDecrement = 97;
      LocalControl = 122;
      AllNotesOff = 123;

      MaxStatusValue = 255;
      MaxDataValue = 127;
      minDataValue = 0;
      MinOnVelocity = 1;
      OffVelocity = 0;
      MiddleC = 60;
      twoOctaves = 24;
      Forte = 127;
      minorThird = 3;
      majorThird = 4;
      Triad = 2;
      seventhChord = 7;

      Polyphony = 4;
      ScaleSize = 12;

      Column1 = 25;{display values for positioning pen}
      Row1 = 40;
      VerticalLimit = 190;
      HorizontalLimit = 375;
      vertOffset = 10;
      horzOffset = 35;
```

```
VAR
    dataDrawRect: Rect;
    tabCount: integer;


TYPE
    MPFilterArray = ARRAY[0..8] OF integer;
    RSFilterArray = ARRAY[1..5] OF integer;
    ChannelArray = ARRAY[Channel1..Channel16] OF integer;
    MIDIData = 0..MaxDataValue;
    MIDIStatus = 128..MaxStatusValue;
    MIDIByte = 0..255;
    ChordLimit = 1..Polyphony;
    MIDIDataArray = ARRAY[0..MaxDataValue] OF MIDIData;
    ChordArray = ARRAY[1..Polyphony] OF MIDIData;
    ScaleArray = ARRAY[1..ScaleSize] OF integer;

    MIDIMessage = RECORD
        size, status, data1, data2: integer
      END;
    MIDIMessageList = ARRAY[1..9] OF MIDIMessage;
```

NoteTest Procedures

```
PROCEDURE DoNoteTest;
BEGIN
  DoNoteTestDlog;
  MIDI(ResetMIDI);
END; {NoteTest}
```

When Note Test is selected from the menu, the *DoNoteTest* procedure is called. The note testing routines are run from within a DoDlog procedure, *DoNoteTestDlog*. After the dialog is dismissed, DoNoteTest resets MIDI (clears and enables both MIDI buffers).

Here is the dialog displayed by DoNoteTestDlog, and the globals used to reference its dialog item list.

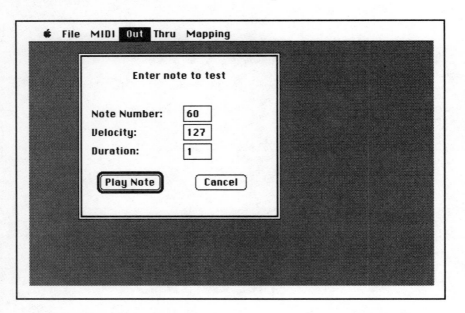

```
{OUT Menu Dialogs}
{    Note Test  Resource IDs}
     NoteTestDlogID = 200;
     NTestNoteItem = 1;
     NTestVelocityItem = 2;
     NTestDurationItem = 3;
     NTestPlayItem = 4;
     NTestCancelItem = 5;
```

Here are the global variables used by the routines and the initialization procedure that is called from InitParameters when RTL is first started.

```
VAR
    theNote, theVelocity: MIDIData;
    theDuration: integer;


{  initialize   Note Test  variables}

    PROCEDURE InitNoteTest;
    BEGIN
{    Note Test }
        theNote := MiddleC;
        theVelocity := Forte;
        theDuration := 1;
    END;
```

Here is an abbreviated listing of the code for DoNoteTestDlog. We've replaced the code for updating variables and handling dialog controls and text boxes with comments. DoNoteTestDlog performs these tasks using the same routines as all of our other DoDlog procedures.

```
PROCEDURE DoNoteTestDlog;
    VAR
        DlogItem, DlogType, thisNote, thisVelocity, thisDuration: integer;
        DlogRect: rect;
        DlogHandle: handle;
BEGIN
    {set local variables to current global values}

    {display dialog}
    {set controls and text boxes to current values}

REPEAT
    BEGIN
        ModalDialog(NIL, DlogItem);
        CASE DlogItem OF

        {for each control and text box:}
            {update local  variables to new values set by the user}
```

```
        NTestPlayItem:
            BEGIN
                theNote := thisNote;{pass local to global}
                theVelocity := thisVelocity;
                theDuration := thisDuration;
                PlayTestNote;     {play global}
            END;
          OTHERWISE
              ;{       do nothing}
        END {CaseDlogItem}
      END; {repeat}
    UNTIL DlogItem = NTestCancelItem;
    DisposDialog(TheDialog);
    ;
  END;{DoNoteTestDlog}
```

When the user pushes the Play Note button in the dialog window, Do
NoteTestDlog assigns the global variables *theNote, theVelocity*, and *duration*
to the values currently displayed, then calls *PlayTestNote*.

Play a Note

```
PROCEDURE PlayTestNote;
  VAR
      level1count, level2count: integer;
BEGIN
  MIDIOut(NoteOn);
  MIDIOut(theNote);
  MIDIOut(theVelocity);

  IF theDuration > 0 THEN
    BEGIN
      FOR level1count := 1 TO 10 * theduration DO
        FOR level2count := 1 TO 500 DO
            ;                   {wait for a while...}

      MIDIOut(NoteOff);      {then send note off}
      MIDIOut(theNote);
      MIDIOut(OffVelocity);
    END;
END;{PlayTestNote}
```

When called, this routine transmits a complete 3-byte Note On message using MIDIPascal's *MIDIOut* command. MIDIOut simply sends a byte to the MIDI OUT port. PlayTestNote sends out our global constant *NoteOn* (Note On channel 1), then transmits the note number and velocity value currently displayed in the note test dialog.

If the duration value in the dialog is 0, the procedure stops. The note will continue to sustain since no Note Off message was sent. You can turn it off by entering a velocity value of 0 in the dialog and pushing play note again. (You can also stop ringing notes by selecting Panic—more on that later.)

If the duration value is from 1 to 100, PlayTestNote uses it to set a loop count that delays the program. When the count is complete, PlayTestNote transmits a complete Note Off message for the same note number and velocity.

The user can play any note at any velocity level directly from the dialog window.

Keyboard Test Procedures

```
PROCEDURE DoKeyTest;
  BEGIN
    DoKeyTestDlog;
    MIDI(resetMIDI);
  END; {KeyTest}
```

When the Keyboard Test is selected from the menu, the *DoKeyTest* procedure is called. The keyboard testing routines are run from within a DoDlog procedure, *DoKeyTestDlog*. After the dialog is dismissed, DoKeyTest resets MIDI (clears and enables both MIDI buffers).

Here is the dialog displayed by DoKeyTestDlog, and the globals used to reference its dialog item list.

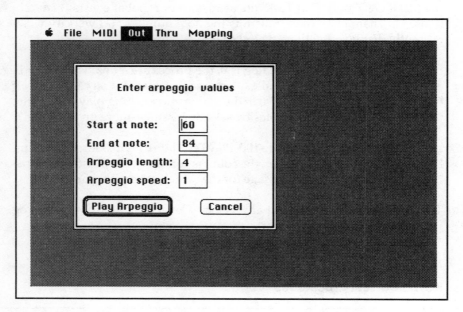

```
{OUT Menu Dialogs}
{    Keyboard Test Resource IDs}
     KTestDlogID = 201;
     KTestPlayItem = 1;
     KTestCancelItem = 2;
     KTestStartItem = 3;
     KTestEndItem = 4;
     KTestLengthItem = 5;
     KTestSpeedItem = 6;
```

Here are the global variables used by the routines and the initialization procedure that is called from InitParameters when RTL is first started.

```
VAR
    StartNote, EndNote: MIDIData;
    ArpLength, ArpSpeed: integer;


{initialize Keyboard Test variables}

    PROCEDURE InitKeyboardTest;
    BEGIN
{     Keyboard test}
    StartNote := MiddleC;
    EndNote := MiddleC + 24;
    ArpLength := 4;
    ArpSpeed := 1;
    END; {InitKeyboardTest}
```

Here is an abbreviated listing of the code for DoKeyTestDlog. We've replaced the code for updating variables and handling dialog controls and text boxes with comments.

```
PROCEDURE DoKeyTestDlog;
    VAR
    DlogItem, DlogType: integer;
    DlogRect: rect;
    DlogHandle: handle;

    thisStart, thisEnd, thisLength, thisSpeed: integer;

BEGIN
    {set local variables to current global values}

    {display dialog}
    {set controls and text boxes to current values}

    REPEAT
    BEGIN
        ModalDialog(NIL, DlogItem);
        CASE DlogItem OF

        {for each control and text box:}
            {update local  variables to new values set by the user}
```

```
            KTestPlayItem:
              BEGIN
                StartNote := thisStart;       {local to global}
                EndNote := thisEnd;
                ArpLength := thisLength;
                ArpSpeed := thisSpeed;
                PlayKeyTest;
              END;
            OTHERWISE
              ;{         do nothing}
        END {Case DlogItem}
      END; {repeat}
    UNTIL DlogItem = KTestCancelItem;
    StartNote := thisStart;
    EndNote := thisEnd;
    ArpLength := thisLength;
    ArpSpeed := thisSpeed;

    DisposDialog(TheDialog);
  END;{DoKeyTestDlog}
```

When the user pushes the Play Arpeggio button in the dialog window, DoKeyTestDlog assigns the global variables *StartNote, EndNote, ArpLength,* and *ArpSpeed* to the values currently displayed, then calls *PlayKeyTest.*

Our keyboard test consists of transmitting a sequence of Note On and Note Off messages over any range of MIDI note numbers. Rather than just transmitting the notes in serial order (play note 1, play note 2, play note 3, etc.), we designed a routine that would play an arpeggio pattern. The arpeggio is created by playing a note, adding an interval value to the note number and then playing the next note. The resulting pattern has "skips" between each note (play note 1, play note 5, play note 9, and so on).

To make the pattern more musical, we add a few twists to the routine that performs it. We actually use two different intervals in our pattern. (The arpeggio alternates between minor and major third intervals.) We play the pattern once in ascending order and then play a variation of the pattern in descending order.

To play all the notes in a given range with our key test, we play the entire pattern starting on the lowest note in the range, then play it again starting on the next highest note, and so on, until it has been played starting once on each note in the range.

The user can set the starting (lowest) note, the ending (highest) note, the length (number of notes), and speed of the arpeggio.

Depending on the length setting, a single arpeggio may span more than two octaves on the keyboard. We include an range checking routine so we don't play illegal notes (less than 0 or greater than 127). Here is the design and code for PlayKeyTest:

Play Key Test

```
PlayKeyTest:
        For each note in the range do the following:
                play the ascending arpeggio

                play the descending arpeggio
```

Play Arpeggio Up

```
play the ascending arpeggio:
        For  the number of notes specified by the length value

                play the note

                move note's value up a minor third

                if the note is higher than MIDI's note range
                        reset note to lowest note in the user's range

                play the note

                move note's value up a minor third

                if the note is higher than MIDI's note range
                        reset note to top note in the user's range
                        stop playing the arpeggio
```

Play Arpeggio Down

play the descending arpeggio:
     For 1 less than the number of notes specified by length

          play the note

          move note's value up a major third

          if the note is lower than MIDI's note range
               reset to lowest note in the user's range
               stop playing the arpeggio

          play the note

          move note's value down a minor sixth

          if the note is lower than MIDI's note range
               reset to lowest note in the user's range
               stop playing the arpeggio

```
PROCEDURE PlayKeyTest;
   VAR
      firstNote, lastNote, count1, count2, loopSize: integer;
      ticks, time: longint;
      hiLimit, lolimit, swing: integer;
      interval1, interval2: integer;
BEGIN
   hiLimit := maxDataValue;
   loLimit := minDataValue;
   ticks := ArpSpeed;
   swing := (ticks * 1);
   interval1 := minorThird;
   interval2 := majorThird;
   lastNote := startNote;
   loopSize := EndNote - StartNote;

{Start of loop for  each note in the range }

   FOR count2 := 1 TO loopSize DO
      BEGIN
         firstNote := lastNote;
```

```
{play ascending arpeggio}
        BEGIN
            FOR count1 := 1 TO ArpLength DO
                BEGIN
                    DoOneNote(firstNote, Forte, swing);
                    firstNote := FirstNote + interval1;
                    IF FirstNote > hiLimit THEN
                        BEGIN
                            firstNote := StartNote;
                            leave;
                        END; {leave check}
                    DoOneNote(firstNote, Forte, ticks);
                    firstNote := FirstNote + interval2;
                    IF FirstNote > hiLimit THEN
                        BEGIN
                            firstNote := endNote; {don'tgo over end note}
                            leave;
                        END; {leave check}
                END;

{play descending arpeggio}
            FOR count1 := 1 TO ArpLength - 1 DO
                BEGIN
                    DoOneNote(firstNote, Forte, ticks);
                    firstNote := FirstNote + interval2;
                    IF FirstNote < loLimit THEN
                        BEGIN
                            firstNote := StartNote;
                            leave;
                        END; {leave check}
                    DoOneNote(firstNote, Forte, swing);
                    firstNote := FirstNote - (interval1 + interval2);
                    ;
                    IF FirstNote < loLimit THEN
                        BEGIN
                            firstNote := StartNote; {don't go under start note}
                            leave;
                        END; {leave check}
                END;
            lastNote := lastNote + 1;
{End of Loop}
        END;
      END;
  END;
```

PlayKeyTest calls on *DoOneNote* to actually play the notes of the arpeggio. DoOneNote calls *PlayNote* to transmit a Note On message for the current arpeggio note, then it uses the Toolbox routine *delay* to pause for a short time. Finally, PlayNote is called again to transmit a Note Off message for the current arpeggio note.

```
PROCEDURE DoOneNote (keyNumber, velocityData: MIDIData; ticks: longint);
  VAR
    time: longint;
BEGIN
  PlayNote(keyNumber, theVelocity);
  delay(ticks, time);
  PlayNote(keyNumber, OffVelocity);
END;{doOneNote}
```

```
PROCEDURE PlayNote (keyNumber, velocityData: MIDIData);
BEGIN
  MIDIOut(NoteOn);
  MIDIOut(keyNumber);
  MIDIOut(velocityData);
END;{ PlayNote (keyNumber, velocityData)}
```

We set the length of the delay by passing DoOneNote the *swing* or *ticks* value in PlayKeyTest. In our code, swing and ticks are each equal to the *ArpSpeed* value set by the user. We alternate between swing and ticks so you can experiment with rhythm variations of the arpeggio. Alter the "swing := (ticks * 1); " statement to "swing := (ticks * 2);" and you will hear the arpeggio played with a swing rhythm.

Send Message Procedures

```
PROCEDURE DoSend;
BEGIN
{ TellUser(AboutAlertID, 'Send Message is not implemented.');}
  DoSendDlog;
  MIDI(resetMIDI);
END; {Send }
```

When Send Message is selected from the menu, the *DoSend* procedure is called. The message sending routine is run from within a DoDlog procedure, *DoSendDlog*. After the dialog is dismissed, DoSend resets MIDI (clears and enables both MIDI buffers).

Here is the dialog displayed by DoSendDlog, and the globals used to reference its dialog item list.

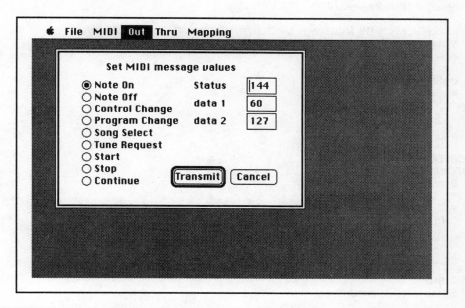

```
{OUT Menu Dialogs}
{    Send ResourceIDs}
     SendTransmitItem = 1;
     SendCancelItem = 2;
     SendDlogID = 202;
     SendNoteOnItem = 3;
     SendNoteOffItem = 4;
     SendCChangeItem = 5;
     SendPChangeItem = 6;
     SendSSelectItem = 7;
     SendTuneRqstItem = 8;
     SendStartItem = 9;
     SendStopItem = 10;
     SendContinueItem = 11;
     SendStatusItem = 12;
     SendData1Item = 13;
     SendData2Item = 14;
```

Here are the global variables used by the routines and a partial listing of the initialization procedure that is called from InitParameters when RTL is first started. We show only the code that initializes the first and last message records here. See the complete RTL listing in Appendix A for the entire procedure.

```
VAR
  SendList: MIDIMessageList;

  MNoteOn, MNoteOff, MCChange, MPChange, MSSelect, MTRqst: MIDIMessage;
  MStart, MStop, MContinue: MIDIMessage;


  theStatus: MIDIStatus;
  theData1: MIDIData;
  theData2: MIDIData;



PROCEDURE InitSendMessage;
  BEGIN
{    Send Message}

    WITH MNoteOn DO
      BEGIN
        size := 3;
        status := NoteOn;
        data1 := MiddleC;
        data2 := Forte;
      END;
    SendList[1] := MNoteOn;

{    initialize other messages here!}

    WITH MContinue DO
      BEGIN
        size := 1;
        status := MIDIContinue;
        data1 := -1;
        data2 := -1;
      END;
    SendList[9] := MContinue;

  END; {InitSendMessage}
```

Here is an abbreviated listing of the code for DoSendDlog. We've replaced the code for updating variables, and handling dialog controls and text boxes, with comments. DoSendDlog differs slightly from our other DoDlog procedures in that the number of text boxes it displays is dependent on the message type selected with the radio buttons. For example, a Note On message (3 bytes) requires three boxes, while a Program Change message (2 bytes) only requires two. Whenever the user selects a new message, we check the *size* field of the *Send* record and hide or show the appropriate text boxes with the Toolbox routines, *HideDItem* and *ShowDItem*. (These routines will function with Mac Plus and later versions of the Macintosh.)

```
PROCEDURE DoSendDlog;
  VAR
    DlogItem, DlogType, ItemListOffset: integer;
    DlogRect: rect;
    DlogHandle: handle;
    count: integer;
    thisMessage: MIDIMessageList;
    Send: MIDIMessage;
    thisSize, thisStatus, thisData1, thisData2: integer;

BEGIN
  {set local variables to current global values}

  {display dialog}
  {set controls and text boxes to current values}

  REPEAT
    BEGIN
      ModalDialog(NIL, DlogItem);
      IF (DlogItem >= SendNoteOnItem) AND (DlogItem <= SendContinueItem) THEN
        BEGIN
          ResetRadioList(SendNoteOnItem, SendContinueItem, DlogItem);
          Send := thisMessage[DlogItem - ItemListOffset];

          IF Send.size = 1 THEN
            BEGIN
              HideDItem(theDialog, SendData1Item);              ...............
          HideDItem(theDialog, SendData2Item)
            END

          ELSE IF send.size = 2 THEN
            BEGIN
              ShowDItem(theDialog, SendData1Item);
              HideDItem(theDialog, SendData2Item)
            END

          ELSE
            BEGIN
```

```
            ShowDItem(theDialog, SendData2Item);
          END;

          NumberToItem(theDialog, SendStatusItem, Send.status);
          NumberToItem(theDialog, SendData1Item, Send.data1);
          NumberToItem(theDialog, SendData2Item, Send.Data2);
        END
      ELSE
        CASE DlogItem OF

        {for each control and text box:}
        { update local  variables to new values set by the user}

          SendTransmitItem:
            BEGIN
              PlayMessage(Send);
            END;
          OTHERWISE
{       do nothing}
          END {CaseDlogItem}
      END; {repeat}
    UNTIL DlogItem = SendCancelItem;
    DisposDialog(TheDialog);
  END;{DoSendDlog}
```

When the user pushes the Transmit button in the dialog window, DoSendDlog calls *PlayMessage*. PlayMessage transmits a MIDI message with the values currently displayed in the dialog window.

```
PROCEDURE PlayMessage (theMessage: MIDIMessage);
BEGIN
  CASE theMessage.size OF
    1:   {1 byte message format}
      MIDIOut(theMessage.status);

    2:   {2 byte message format}
      BEGIN
        MIDIOut(theMessage.status);
        MIDIOut(theMessage.data1);
      END;

    3:   {3 byte message format}
      BEGIN
        MIDIOut(theMessage.status);
        MIDIOut(theMessage.data1);
        MIDIOut(theMessage.data2);
      END;
  END; {case theMessage.size}

END;{ PlayMessage}
```

PlayMessage checks the size field of the message record passed to it by DoSendDlog and uses a CASE structure to determine how many bytes to transmit.

Panic Procedures

```
PROCEDURE DoPanic;
BEGIN
  DoPanicDlog;
END; {Panic}
```

When Panic is selected from the menu, the *DoPanic* procedure is called. DoPanic displays a dialog window that contains no controls, only static text. Then it calls *KillAllNotes* to repeatedly transmit Note Off messages for all notes on all channels. KillAllNotes continues transmitting Note Off messages until the user clicks the mouse.

Here is the dialog displayed by DoPanic and the global used to reference it.

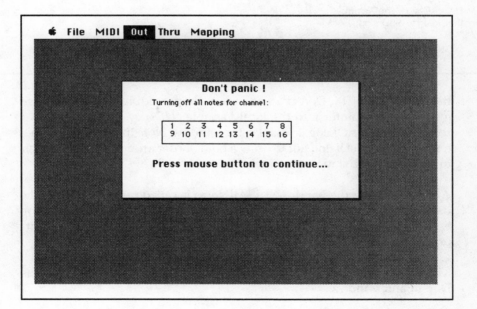

```
{OUT Menu Dialogs}
{     Panic Resource IDs}
      PanicDlogID = 101;
```

Here is the complete code for DoPanicDlog.

```
PROCEDURE DoPanicDlog;

VAR
      oldDialog: DialogPtr;
      DlogItem: integer;

BEGIN
   oldDialog := theDialog;
   ShowResDialog(PanicDlogID, OFF);

   REPEAT

      KillAllNotes;

   UNTIL button;

   DisposDialog(TheDialog);
   theDialog := oldDialog;

   END;{ DoPanicDlog}
```

Before displaying the Don't Panic window, the procedure stores the current global dialog pointer into the local variable *oldDialog*. Then it calls our routine, ShowResDialog, to display the window. Note that the off parameter tells ShowResDialog not to draw a bold border around item #1 (which in this case is the static text string, "Don't panic!")

After displaying the window, KillAllNotes is called repeatedly until the user clicks the mouse button. Once the mouse has been clicked, the dialog is removed from the screen and the global dialog pointer is restored to its original value.

KillAllNotes uses QuickDraw routines to display what it's doing in the Don't Panic window.

```
PROCEDURE KillAllNotes;
   VAR
      tabCount, channel, keyNumber: integer;
      row, column: integer;
      displayRect: rect;
BEGIN
   WITH displayRect DO
      BEGIN
         top := 50;
         left := 50;
         bottom := 80;
         right := 215;
      END;
   frameRect(displayRect);
   row := 30;
   column := 35;
   tabCount := 1;
   moveTo(column, row);

   textFont(Geneva);
   textSize(9);
   WriteDraw(' Turning off all notes for channel: ');

   row := row + 30;
   moveTo(column, row);

   FOR channel := 0 TO 15 DO
      BEGIN
         MIDIOut(ControlChange + channel);
         MIDIOut(AllNotesData);
         MIDIOut(0);
         MIDIOut(NoteOff + channel);
         IF tabCount = 9 THEN
            BEGIN
               tabCount := 1;
               row := row + 10;
            END; {if tabCount}
         tabCount := tabCount + 1;
         moveTo((column - 15) * tabCount, row);
         WriteDraw(channel + 1);
         FOR keyNumber := 0 TO 127 DO {running status transmission}
            BEGIN
               MIDIOut(KeyNumber);
               MIDIOut(0);
            END; {for KeyNumber}
      END; {for channel}
   EraseRect(displayRect);
END;{KillAllNotes}
```

First, it sets up a display rectangle and draws a border around it. Then it changes the text font to Geneva, text size 9, and prints the string *Turning off all notes for channel:*.

Next it transmits a MIDI All Notes Off message for channel 1 and uses QuickDraw's *writeDraw* routine to display the channel number on the screen. After drawing the channel number, it transmits an individual Note Off message for all notes (0-127). We use Running Status transmission here. The Note Off status byte is sent only once, followed by 128 pairs of note number/velocity bytes.

After all 128 Note Off messages are sent, the channel number is incremented. (The channel number is the control variable, *channel*, of the FOR loop.) The entire process repeats until all notes for all sixteen MIDI channels have been sent.

Every time the channel is incremented, QuickDraw's pen is moved to the right by the value of *column* (35 pixels) before the next channel number is displayed. For the ninth channel, the pen is moved to its original horizontal position, and lowered by the value of *row* (30 pixels). The QuickDraw procedure *MoveTo* is used to manipulate the location of the pen. After Note Offs have been sent out over each channel, the display rectangle is erased.

Thru Menu Operations

The program operations selected from the Thru menu call routines that demonstrate ways to read incoming MIDI data, process it in real-time, and transmit it to the OUT port in its original form, or altered by the program.

Thru Test is a simple MIDI continuity tester based on the design example we examined in Part 3.

The major program operation of RTL is *MIDI Thru,* which processes many types of MIDI data simultaneously. The variables for this operation are set from other RTL menus.

Display Data allows you to view MIDI data as it travels through the Mac. You can, for example, see the effect of different settings of the MIDI Filters window on the data stream.

Running Status Filters sets the values for the filter routines used by MIDI Thru.

Thru Test Procedures

```
PROCEDURE DoThruTest;
BEGIN
  DoThruTestDlog;
END; {ThruTest}
```

When Thru Test is selected from the menu, the *DoThruTest* procedure is called. The test routine is run from within a DoDlog procedure, *Do-ThruTestDlog*.

Here is the dialog displayed by DoThruTestDlog, and the globals used to reference its dialog item list.

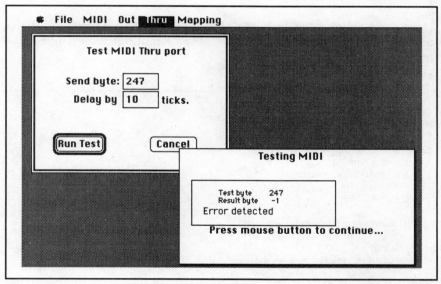

```
        DataWindowID = 217; {resource ID of data display window}

{THRU Menu Dialogs
{     ThruTest Resource IDs}
        ThruTestDlogID = 204;
        ThruTestRunItem = 1;
        ThruTestCancelItem = 2;
        ThruTestSendItem = 3;
        ThruTestRepeatItem = 4;
```

Here are the global variables used by the routines and the initialization procedure that is called from InitParameters when RTL is first started.

```
VAR
    ThruTestFlag: boolean;
    testByte: MIDIByte;
    repeatCount: integer;



{initialize Thru Test variables}
PROCEDURE InitThruTest;
  BEGIN
{    Thru Test }
    testByte := EOX;
    repeatCount := 10;
  END; { InitThruTest}
```

Here is an abbreviated listing of the code for DoThruTestDlog. We've replaced the code for updating variables and handling dialog controls and text boxes with comments.

```
PROCEDURE DoThruTestDlog;
  VAR
    DlogItem, DlogType: integer;
    DlogRect: rect;
    DlogHandle: handle;
    thisByte, thisRepeat: integer;

    dontCare: longint;
BEGIN
  {set local variables to current global values}

  {display dialog}
  {set controls and text boxes to current values}


  REPEAT
    BEGIN
      ModalDialog(NIL, DlogItem);
      CASE DlogItem OF

      {for each control and text box:}
        { update local  variables to new values set by the user}
```

```
              ThruTestRunItem:
                 BEGIN
                    repeatCount := thisRepeat;
                    testByte := thisByte;
                    ThruTestFlag := TRUE;
                    DoTest;
                 END;
              OTHERWISE
                 ;{       do nothing}
           END {CaseDlogItem}
        END; {repeat}
     UNTIL (DlogItem = ThruTestCancelItem);
     DisposDialog(TheDialog);
END;{ThruTestDlog}
```

When the user pushes the RunTest button in the dialog window, Do-ThruTest assigns the global variables *repeatCount* and *testByte* to the currently displayed values, then calls *DoTest*.

```
PROCEDURE DoTest;
   VAR
      oldDialog: DialogPtr;
      DlogItem, DlogType: integer;
      dlogRect: rect;
      displayRect: rect;
      DlogHandle: handle;
      thetext: str255;
BEGIN
   oldDialog := theDialog;
   DlogItem := 1;
   theText := 'Testing MIDI Thru';

   TheDialog := GetNewDialog(PanicDlogID, NIL, WindowPtr(-1));
   SetPort(TheDialog);
   GetDItem(theDialog, DlogItem, Dlogtype, DlogHandle, DlogRect);
   SetIText(DlogHandle, thetext);
   DrawDialog(TheDialog);

   WITH displayRect DO
      BEGIN
         top := 40;
         left := 15;
         bottom := 100;
         right := 200;
      END;
   frameRect(displayRect);
   insetRect(displayRect, 5, 5);
   REPEAT
```

```
    BEGIN
       RunTheTest;
       eraseRect(displayRect);
    END;
  UNTIL button;
  DisposDialog(TheDialog);
  theDialog := oldDialog;
  setPort(theDialog);
END;{DoTest}
```

DoTest stores a pointer to the Thru Test dialog window, then gets a new dialog window from the resource file. It is the same one we used for the Don't Panic window. The static text in item #1 is reset to the string, "Testing MIDI Thru."

Next, a display rectangle is set up and framed and the display rectangle is shrunk by 5 pixels. We do this so that subsequent calls to eraseRect won't erase the border we just drew.

Finally, *RunTheTest* procedure is called. After the test is performed, the display rectangle is erased. This removes the data drawn there by Run-TheTest. This continues until the user clicks the mouse.

```
PROCEDURE RunTheTest;
  VAR
     count, InByte: integer;
     delayFactor, dontCare: longint;
BEGIN
  textFont(geneva);
  textSize(9);

  delayFactor := repeatCount;

  MIDIOut(testByte);
  delay(delayFactor, dontCare);
  MIDIIn(InByte);

  moveTo(50, 60);
  writeDraw('Test byte ');
  moveTo(100, 60);
  WriteDraw(testByte);

  moveTo(50, 70);
  writeDraw('Result byte');
  moveTo(100, 70);
  WriteDraw(inByte);
```

```
    IF testByte <> InByte THEN
      BEGIN
        textSize(12);
        moveTo(30, 85);
        WriteDraw('Error detected');
        textSize(9);
        delay(60, dontCare);
      END;
END;{RunTheTest}
```

The test consists of transmitting the *testByte* value with MIDIOut, waiting the number of ticks specfified by the user, and then reading the IN port with MIDIIn.

The value of the test byte and the result byte are drawn in the display rectangle in 9-point Geneva text.

If the two values don't match, "Error detected" is printed in 12-point Geneva text.

When an error occurs, RunTheTest resets the delay value to 60 for subsequent tests in the current run. This is more than enough delay to compensate for Mac IIs or Macs with accelerator cards.

Display Data Procedures

```
PROCEDURE DoDataDisplay;
BEGIN
  DoThruDlog;
END; {DataDisplay}
```

When Display Data is selected from the menu, the *DoDataDisplay* procedure is called. DoDataDisplay calls *DoThruDlog,* which displays a window with no controls, only static text.

Here is the dialog displayed by DoThruDlog and the global used to reference it.

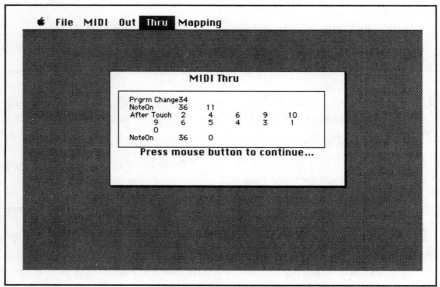

DataWindowID = 217; {resource ID of data display window}

Here is the complete code for DoThruDlog.

```
PROCEDURE    DoThruDlog;

    VAR
        oldDialog: DialogPtr;
        DlogItem, DlogType: integer;
        dlogRect: rect;
        DlogHandle: handle;
        thetext: str255;
BEGIN
    oldDialog := theDialog;
    DlogItem := 1;
    theText := 'MIDI Thru Display';

    TheDialog := GetNewDialog(PanicDlogID, NIL, WindowPtr(-1));
    SetPort(TheDialog);
    GetDItem(theDialog, DlogItem, Dlogtype, DlogHandle, DlogRect);
    SetIText(DlogHandle, thetext);
    DrawDialog(TheDialog);
```

```
    WITH dataDrawRect DO
      BEGIN
        top := 25;        {set dimensions of text display}
        bottom := 100;
        left := 10;
        right := 275;
      END;
    frameRect(dataDrawRect);
    insetRect(dataDrawRect, 5, 5); {don't erase the frame}
    resetPen;
    MIDI(ClearInput);        {clear buffers}
    MIDI(ClearOutput);
    REPEAT
      BEGIN
        MIDIThruDisplay;
      END;
    UNTIL button;
    DisposDialog(TheDialog);
    theDialog := oldDialog;
    setPort(theDialog);
END;{ DoThruDlog}
```

After storing the current dialog pointer in *oldDialog*, DoThruDlog gets a new dialog from the resource file. The static text of item 1 is set to MIDI Thru Display.

Next, a display rectangle is set up and framed, then the display rectangle is shrunk by 5 pixels. (We use the global variable *dataDrawRect* for this.) The pen is moved to the upper left corner of the display rectangle by calling *resetPen*.

The MIDI buffers are cleared and the procedure *MIDIThruDisplay* is called repeatedly until the user clicks the mouse.

```
PROCEDURE MIDIThruDisplay;
  VAR
    inByte: integer;    {this variable holds MIDI data}
BEGIN
  MIDIIn(InByte);        {check In port for data (Inbyte holds result)}
  IF InByte <> -1 THEN {this is only true when Inbyte is valid MIDI data}
    BEGIN
      ProcessMIDI(InByte);
      MIDIOut(InByte); {send the data to the Out port}
    END; {if <>-1}
END; {MIDIThruDisplay}
```

The MIDIThruDisplay procedure shows how simple the design for a MIDI Thru processing routine is. It consists of only three steps:

Get a byte of MIDI data from the IN buffer.
Process the byte (in this case, display its value in the dialog window).
Transmit the byte.

The trick is to perform the processing so quickly that it is invisible to the user. Drawing to the screen, even with QuickDraw, takes considerable processing time. When you run this program operation, you may notice some lag between the time you move a MIDI control and the point at which you hear its effect on the device connected to the Mac interface's OUT port. (When you see just how much data is transmitted by moving that control, you'll understand why there is a delay.)

MIDIPascal's MIDIIn command is used to get a byte from the IN buffer and assign its value to the global variable *inByte*.

If no data is in the buffer, MIDIIn returns a value of -1, and nothing else happens until the routine is called again from the REPEAT . . . LOOP in DoThruDlog.

If inbyte is any other value, it is processed by the routine *ProcessMIDI* and then transmitted to the OUT port with MIDIOut.

```
PROCEDURE ProcessMIDI (InByte: integer); {parse MIDI  status and data}
BEGIN
   textFont(geneva);
   textSize(9);

   IF InByte > maxDataValue THEN
      DoStatusByte(InByte)
   ELSE
      DoDataByte(InByte);
END;{ProcessMIDI}
```

ProcessMIDI first sets the text font and size that we'll use in the display. Then it calls one of two routines, *DoStatusByte* or *DoDataByte*, depending on the value of inByte. If inByte's value is greater than 127, it is a MIDI status byte.

```
PROCEDURE DoStatusByte (InByte: integer); {process status byte}
BEGIN
   SetUpStatusDraw;
   DrawStatusByte(InByte);
END;{DoStatusByte}
```

DoStatusByte moves the pen to the first column of a new row by calling *Set-UpStatusDraw*. Then it finds the type of status and displays its name with *DrawStatusByte*.

```pascal
PROCEDURE SetUpStatusDraw;        {move pen to start of next line}
  VAR
    thePoint: point;
BEGIN
  tabCount := 1;
  GetPen(thePoint);
  thePoint.v := thePoint.v + vertOffset;  {move position down one line}
  IF thePoint.v > 90 THEN {VerticalLimit}
  {check vertical position}
    BEGIN
      thePoint.v := Row1;       {position of  top of display}
      EraseRect(dataDrawRect);    {erase the display rectangle}
    END;
  MoveTo(Column1, thePoint.v);      {move pen}
END;{SetUpStatusDraw}


PROCEDURE DrawStatusByte (InByte: integer); {display MIDI status type}
  VAR
    status: integer;
BEGIN
  status := BitAnd(Inbyte, $f0);
  CASE status OF
    NoteOff:
      WriteDraw('NoteOff');
    NoteOn:
      WriteDraw('NoteOn');
    PolyPressure:
      WriteDraw('Poly Pressure');
    ControlChange:
      WriteDraw('Controller');
    ProgramChange:
      WriteDraw('Prgrm Change');
    ChannelPressure:
      WriteDraw('After Touch');
    PitchBend:
      WriteDraw('Pitch Bend');
    SystemMessage:
      WriteDraw('System Message');
    OTHERWISE
      WriteDraw('UNKNOWN STATUS !!')
  END {case status}
END;{DrawStatus}
```

```
PROCEDURE DoDataByte (InByte: integer); {process data byte}
BEGIN
    SetUpDataDraw;
    DrawDataByte(InByte);
END;{DoDataByte}
```

DoDataByte moves the pen to the next column, or starts a new line if necessary, by calling *SetUpDataDraw*. Then it calls *DrawData* to display the value of inByte.

```
PROCEDURE SetUpDataDraw;        {move pen to next column}
    VAR
        thePoint: point;
BEGIN
    tabCount := tabCount + 1;
    GetPen(thePoint);
    thePoint.h := tabCount * horzOffset;
    IF thePoint.h > 220 THEN {HorizontalLimit}
{check horizontal position}
        BEGIN
            thePoint.h := horzOffset;       {position of left side of display}
            tabCount := 1;
            thePoint.v := thePoint.v + vertOffset;   {move pen down one line}
        END;
    IF thePoint.v > 90 THEN {VerticalLimit}
    {check vertical position}
        BEGIN
            thePoint.v := Row1;        {position of top of display}
            EraseRect(dataDrawRect);        {erase previous display}
        END;
    MoveTo(thePoint.h, thePoint.v);     {move pen to new position}
END;{SetUpDataDraw}


PROCEDURE DrawDataByte (inByte: integer);  {display data value}
BEGIN
    WriteDraw(inByte);
END;{draw data}
```

MIDI Programming Tools

MIDI ThruDisplay demonstrates a basic design for real-time MIDI processing. Of the remaining program operations, all except MIDI Thru and Harmony Map are used to get parameters from the user which will be used by MIDI Thru's processing routines. Before we go on to build MIDI Thru, we should look at some utility procedures and functions that are used to process MIDI data. These routines can be used "as is" in your own MIDI software.

MIDI Data Functions

Get Channel Value

```
FUNCTION GetChannel (byte: integer): integer;
   VAR
      x: integer;
BEGIN
   x := bitAnd(byte, channelMask);
   GetChannel := x;
END;{GetChannel}
```

GetChannel is used to return the channel value of any MIDI Channel Voice Message. It uses the Toolbox routine *bitAnd* to AND the value of the byte with the constant *channelMask*. The mask sets the upper four bits of the byte value to 0, leaving the channel value in the lower four bits. The value of the function is the channel ID of the byte.

Get Status Value

```
FUNCTION GetStatus (byte: integer): integer;
   VAR
      X: integer;
BEGIN
   x := bitAnd(byte, statusMask);
   GetStatus := x;
END; {GetStatus}
```

GetStatus is used to return the status value of any MIDI Status byte. It uses the Toolbox routine *bitAnd* to AND the value of the byte with the constant *statusMask*. The mask sets the lower four bits of the byte value to 0, leaving the status value in the upper four bits. The value of the function is the status ID of the byte.

Get Pitch Value

```
FUNCTION GetSemitone (key: integer): integer;
   VAR
     x: integer;

BEGIN
  x := (key MOD 12) + 1;
  GetSemitone := x;
END;{GetSemitone}
```

GetSemiTone is used to return the pitch value of any MIDI note number. The value returned by the function is a code for each pitch of a chromatic scale (C= 1, C# = 2, D = 3 ... B = 12).

Invert MIDI Data

```
FUNCTION InvertData (byte: integer): integer;
   VAR
     x: integer;
BEGIN
  x := maxDataValue - byte;
  InvertData := x;
END;
```

InvertData is used to invert the data value of any MIDI data byte. The value returned by the function is equal to the value of the data byte subtracted from 127 (the maximum MIDI data value).

Wait for MIDI Data

```
FUNCTION WaitForMIDI: integer;
   VAR
     x: integer;
BEGIN
  MIDIIn(x);
  WHILE x = -1 DO
    MIDIIn(x);
  WaitForMIDI := x;
END;{WaitForMIDI}
```

WaitForMIDI is a brute force method of returning a MIDI byte without having to process "no data in buffer" result codes. Once called, it will call MIDIIn indefinitely until a valid MIDI byte is received, then it will return its value.

Wait for MIDI or Mouse

```
FUNCTION MIDIorMouse: integer;
   VAR
      x: integer;
BEGIN
   MIDIIn(x);
   WHILE (x = -1) AND (button = false) DO
      BEGIN
         MIDIIn(x);
      END;
   MIDIorMouse := x;
END; {MIDIorMouse}
```

MIDIorMouse is similar to WaitForMIDI except that it checks for mouse clicks between calls to MIDIIn. This allows the user to interrupt a routine, and it still cuts down on the overhead required to process result code errors.

MIDI Mapping

Several of our routines make use of *mapping* to alter the value of MIDI bytes. Mapping is used here to mean reassigning a source value to a target value. For example, reassign channel 1 to channel 3, or reassign program number 24 to program number 6. We use a simple array for our maps. The array is dimensioned with one element for each possible data value, and initialized so that the value of each element is set to the value of that element's subscript. Here's how we set up an array for program mapping:

```
CONST
   MaxDataValue = 127;
   minDataValue = 0;


TYPE
   MIDIDataArray = ARRAY[minDataValue..MaxDataValue] OF MIDIData;

VAR
   ProgramMaps: MIDIDataArray;


PROCEDURE InitPrgrmChangeMaps;
   VAR
      count: integer;
BEGIN
{    Program Change Mapping}
   FOR count := minDataValue TO MaxDataValue DO
      ProgramMaps[count] := count;
END; {InitPrgrmChangeMaps}
```

In the initialized state, source program numbers (the array subscripts) and target program numbers (the element values) are the same. The Program Change menu selection of RTL allows the user to alter the value of any element in the ProgramMaps array. Now we can map any source program number to any target program number with a single statement:

```
theMIDIByte := ProgramMaps[theMIDIByte];
```

The statement uses the value of the incoming MIDI byte to point to an element in the array. If that element has been changed by the user, theMIDIByte is assigned the new value. Otherwise, it is assigned its original value.

To execute program mapping from within our MIDI Thru design, we have to check the incoming data and watch for a Program Change status byte. Once the status byte is received, the next data byte will be a program number, so we reassign its value with the mapping statement. Using this scheme, we actually reassign *all* program numbers, whether they have been changed from their initial values or not.

We use the same technique to map note numbers, controller numbers, and channel numbers in addition to program numbers in RTL's MIDI Thru program operation.

Parsing Running Status MIDI Data

In order to process any incoming MIDI data, the program must know to what kind of message the data belongs. Normally, data bytes are preceded by a status byte that identifies the message. The MIDI spec allows devices to transmit the seven *Channel Voice* messages: Note On, Note Off, Control Change, Program Change, Channel Pressure, Polyphonic Key Pressure, and Pitch Bend Change using Running Status.

Under Running Status, it is not necessary to resend the status byte for messages of the same status. A series of 10 Note On messages can be sent by first sending the Note On status byte, then following it with ten pairs of note number and velocity data bytes. Notes can be turned on and off by without changing status by sending velocity values of 0 with the note numbers you wish to turn off.

The receiver must assume that all data bytes are of the same type (in this case, Note On) until a new status byte is received. When the next status byte is received, the receiver must adopt the new status. The only exception is that MIDI System Real-Time messages may interrupt a Running Status transmission. These are single-byte messages used to send timing data that can occur anywhere in the MIDI data stream.

A real-time MIDI program must keep track of the current status so it can process untagged data bytes properly. Here is a basic design for parsing Running Status:

Process Running Status MIDI Data

```
parsing running status transmissions:
      get a byte from MIDI In

      if the byte is a status byte (more than 127) :
            update runningStatus

      if the byte is a data byte (127 or less)
            process byte based on the value of runningStatus:

                        process Note On
                        process Note Off
                        :
                        :
                        process SysEx

      send the byte to MIDI Out
```

Here is a basic design for the "update the Running Status" portion of the example.

Update Running Status

```
update runningStatus:
        get the status of the byte

        assign runningStatus based on the status of the byte:

                If status is any Channel Voice status
                        runningStatus = status

                If status is System Real Time
                        runningStatus doesn't change
```

We execute this design in the code for MIDI Thru and we also include in the design the ability to filter out data that is transmitted under Running Status. Before we look at MIDI Thru, let's examine the routines that set values for the variables they use.

Running Status Filters Procedures

```
PROCEDURE DoRSFilter;
BEGIN
   DoRSFilterDlog;
END; { RSFilter}
```

When Running Status Filters is selected from the menu, the *DoRSFilterDlog* procedure is called. The procedure displays a dialog that lets the user set running status filter variables that are used by MIDI Thru.

Here is the dialog displayed by DoRSFilterDlog, and the globals used to reference its dialog item list.

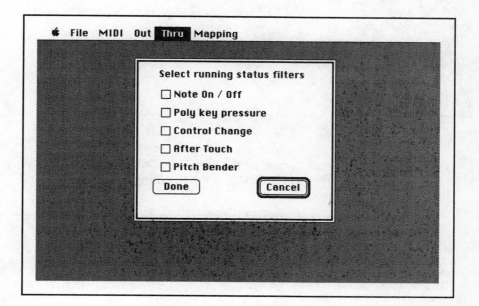

```
{THRU Menu Dialogs}
RSFilterDlogID = 207;          {Running Status Filter Resource IDs}
RSFilterCancelItem = 1;
RSFilterDoneItem = 2;
RSFilterNoteItem = 3;
RSFilterPPressItem = 4;
RSFilterCChangeItem = 5;
RSFilterATouchItem = 6;
RSFilterPBendItem = 7;
```

Here are the global variables used by the routines and the initialization procedure that is called from InitParameters when RTL is first started.

```
VAR
   {Running Status Filters}
   RSFilters: RSFilterArray;

PROCEDURE InitRSFilters;
   VAR
      count: integer;
BEGIN
   FOR count := 1 TO 5 DO
      RSFilters[count] := 0;
END; {InitRSFilters}
```

Here is an abbreviated listing of the code for DoRSFilterDlog. We've replaced the code for updating variables and handling dialog controls and text boxes with comments.

```
PROCEDURE DoRSFilterDlog;
   VAR
      DlogItem, DlogType, ItemListOffset: integer;
      DlogRect: rect;
      DlogHandle: handle;
      thisRSFilter: RSFilterArray;
      FilterID: integer;
      count: integer;

BEGIN
   {set local variables to current global values}

   {display dialog}
   {set controls and text boxes to current values}
```

```
REPEAT
  BEGIN
    ModalDialog(NIL, DlogItem);
    CASE DlogItem OF

    {for each control and text box:}
        {update local  variables to new values set by the user}

    END {Case DlogItem}
  END; {repeat}

UNTIL (DlogItem = RSFilterDoneItem) OR (DlogItem = RSFilterCancelItem);
IF DlogItem = RSFilterDoneItem THEN
  BEGIN
    FOR count := 1 TO 5 DO     {set global array to new values}
        RSFilters[count] := thisRSFilter[count];
  END

ELSE
    ;{Cancel: don't change anything}
  DisposDialog(TheDialog);
END;{DoRSFilterDlog}
```

When the user pushes the done button, the current settings of the five Running Status filters are loaded into the *RSFilters* array.

Channel Procedures

```
PROCEDURE DoChannelMap;
BEGIN
  DoChannelMapDlog;
END; {Channel}
```

When Channel is selected from the menu, the *DoChannelMap* procedure is called. The procedure displays a dialog that lets the user set channel mapping variables that are used by MIDI Thru. The user can reassign any source channel number to any target channel number.

Here is the dialog displayed by DoChannelMapDlog, and the globals used to reference its dialog item list.

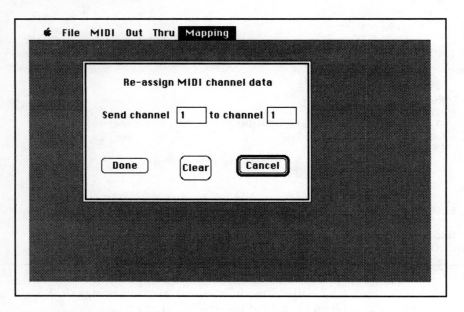

```
{MAPPING Menu Dialogs}
ChanMapDlogID = 209;                    {Channel Map ResourceIDs}
ChanMapCancelItem = 1;
ChanMapDoneItem = 2;
ChanMapClearItem = 3;
ChanMapSourceItem = 4;
ChanMapDestItem = 5;



VAR
    {Channel Mapping}
    ChanMaps: ChannelArray;
    ChanMapOffsetFlag, ChanMapReassignFlag: integer;
```

Here are the global variables used by the routines, and the initialization procedure that is called from InitParameters when RTL is first started.

```
PROCEDURE InitChannelMaps;
  VAR
     count: integer;
BEGIN
  FOR count := Channel1 TO Channel16 DO
     ChanMaps[count] := count;

  ChanMapOffsetFlag := 1;
END; {InitChannelMaps}
```

Here is an abbreviated listing of the code for DoChannelMapDlog. We've replaced the code for updating variables and handling dialog controls and text boxes with comments.

```
PROCEDURE DoChannelMapDlog;
  VAR
     DlogItem, DlogType: integer;
     DlogRect: rect;
     DlogHandle: handle;

     thisChannel: ChannelArray;
     count, thisSourceChannel, thisTargetChannel: integer;
     thisOffsetFlag, thisReassignFlag: integer;

BEGIN
  {set local variables to current global values}

  {display dialog}
  {set controls and text boxes to current values}

  REPEAT
    BEGIN
      ModalDialog(NIL, DlogItem);
      CASE DlogItem OF
        ChanMapSourceItem:
          BEGIN
            thisSourceChannel := CheckValue(DlogItem, Channel1, channelValueCode);
            NumberToItem(theDialog, ChanMapDestItem, thisChannel[thisSourceChannel]);
          END;

        ChanMapDestItem:
          BEGIN
            thisTargetChannel := CheckValue(DlogItem, Channel1, channelValueCode);
            thisChannel[thisSourceChannel] := thisTargetChannel;
          END;
```

```
    ChanMapClearItem:
      BEGIN
        FOR count := Channel1 TO Channel16 DO
          thisChannel[count] := count;
        NumberToItem(theDialog, ChanMapSourceItem, Channel1);
        NumberToItem(theDialog, ChanMapDestItem, thisChannel[Channel1]);
      END;

      OTHERWISE
        {do nothing}
    END {CaseDlogItem}
  END; {repeat}

UNTIL (DlogItem = ChanMapDoneItem) OR (DlogItem = ChanMapCancelItem);
IF DlogItem = ChanMapDoneItem THEN
  FOR count := Channel1 TO Channel16 DO
    ChanMaps[count] := thisChannel[count]

ELSE
  ;{Cancel: don't change anything}
  DisposDialog(TheDialog);
END;{DoChannelMapDlog}
```

We've listed the code that handles the entries into both text boxes here. Note that when the user enters a new value for *thisSourceChannnel*, we use NumberToItem to display the current value of *thisTargetChannel*. When the user pushes the clear button, the local array variable for the channel maps, *thisChannel*, is reset to the initialized state (no reassignments). The same techniques are used for the Controller and Program Change DoDialog procedures as well. When the done button is pushed, the current values of the channel mapping array are loaded into the global variable *ChanMaps*.

Controller Procedures

```
PROCEDURE DoControlMap;
BEGIN
  DoControlMapDlog;
END; {ControlMap}
```

When Controller is selected from the menu, the *DoContolMapDlog* procedure is called. The procedure displays a dialog that allows the user to reassign any MIDI source controller to any MIDI target controller.

Here is the dialog displayed by DoControlMap, and the globals used to reference its dialog item list.

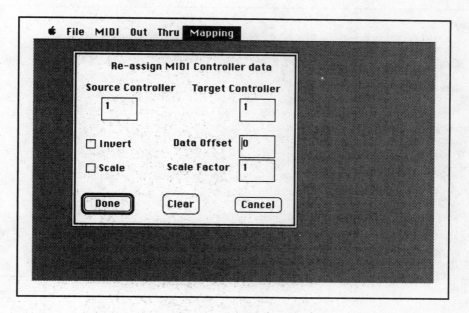

```
{MAPPING Menu Dialogs}
ControlMapDlogID = 215;          {Control Mapping Resource IDs}
ControlDoneItem = 1;
ControlClearItem = 2;
ControlCancelItem = 3;
ControlOffsetItem = 4;
ControlSFactorItem = 5;
ControlInvertItem = 6;
ControlScaleItem = 7;
ControlSourceItem = 8;
ControlTargetItem = 9;
```

Here are the global variables used by the routines and the initialization procedure that is called from InitParameters when RTL is first started.

```
VAR
  {Controller Mapping}
  ControlMaps: MIDIDataArray;
  CntrlInvertFlag, CntrlScaleFlag: integer;
  CntrlOffset: MIDIData;
  CntrlSFactor: integer;



PROCEDURE InitControllerMaps;
  VAR
    count: integer;
BEGIN
  FOR count := ModController TO DataDecrement DO
    ControlMaps[count] := count;

  CntrlInvertFlag := 0;
  CntrlScaleFlag := 0;
  CntrlOffset := 0;
  CntrlSFactor := 1;
END;
```

Here is an abbreviated listing of the code for DoControlMapDlog. We've replaced the code for updating variables and handling dialog controls and text boxes with comments.

```
PROCEDURE DoControlMapDlog;
  VAR
    DlogItem, DlogType: integer;
    DlogRect: rect;
    DlogHandle: handle;

    thisControl: MIDIDataArray;
    count, thisSourceCntrl, thisTargetCntrl: integer;
    thisInvertFlag, thisScaleFlag: integer;
    thisCntrlOffset, thisCntrlSFactor: integer;

BEGIN
  {set local variables to current global values}

  {display dialog}
  {set controls and text boxes to current values}
```

```
REPEAT
  BEGIN
    ModalDialog(NIL, DlogItem);
    CASE DlogItem OF

    {for each control and text box:}
      {update local  variables to new values set by the user}


    END {CaseDlogItem}
  END; {repeat}

UNTIL (DlogItem = ControlDoneItem) OR (DlogItem = ControlCancelItem);
IF DlogItem = ControlDoneItem THEN
  BEGIN
    CntrlInvertFlag := thisInvertFlag;
    CntrlScaleFlag := thisScaleFlag;
    CntrlOffset := thisCntrlOffset;
    CntrlSFactor := thisCntrlSFactor;
    FOR count := ModController TO DataDecrement DO
      ControlMaps[count] := thisControl[count];
  END

ELSE
  ;{Cancel: don't change anything}
DisposDialog(TheDialog);


    END;{DoControlMapDlog}
```

When the done button is pushed, the current values of the local controller mapping array are loaded into the global variable *ControlMaps*. The offset and scaling factors currently displayed are loaded into *CntrlOffset* and *CntrlSFactor*. The checked or unchecked state of the invert and scale check boxes are loaded into *CntrlScaleFlag* and *CntrlInvertFlag*.

Program Change Procedures

```
PROCEDURE DoProgramMap;
BEGIN
  DoProgramMapDlog;
END; {ProgramMap}
```

When Program Change is selected from the menu, the *DoProgramMap* procedure is called. The procedure displays a dialog that allows the user to reassign any source program number to any target program number.

Here is the dialog displayed by DoProgramMapDlog, and the globals used to reference its dialog item list.

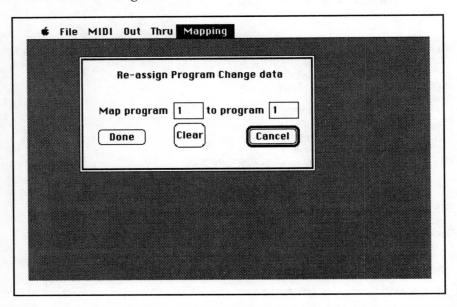

```
     {MAPPING  Menu Dialogs}
     PChangeMapDlogID = 210;        {Program Change Map Resource IDs}
     PChangeCancelItem = 1;
     PChangeDoneItem = 2;
     PChangeClearItem = 3;
     PChangeMapItem = 4;
     PChangeToItem = 5;


 VAR
    {Program Change Mapping}
    ProgramMaps: MIDIDataArray;

PROCEDURE InitPrgrmChangeMaps;
     VAR
        count: integer;
   BEGIN
      FOR count := 0 TO MaxDataValue DO
         ProgramMaps[count] := count;
   END; {InitPrgrmChangeMaps}
```

Here is an abbreviated listing of the code for DoProgramMapDlog. We've replaced the code for updating variables and handling dialog controls and text boxes with comments.

```
PROCEDURE DoProgramMapDlog;
  VAR
    DlogItem, DlogType: integer;
    DlogRect: rect;
    DlogHandle: handle;

    thisMap: MIDIDataArray;
    count, SourceProgram, TargetProgram: integer;

BEGIN
  {set local variables to current global values}

  {display dialog}
  {set controls and text boxes to current values}

  REPEAT
    BEGIN
      ModalDialog(NIL, DlogItem);
      CASE DlogItem OF

      {for each control and text box:}
        {update local  variables to new values set by the user}

      END {CaseDlogItem}
    END; {repeat}

  UNTIL (DlogItem = PChangeDoneItem) OR (DlogItem = PChangeCancelItem);
  IF DlogItem = PChangeDoneItem THEN
    BEGIN
      FOR count := 0 TO MaxDataValue DO
        ProgramMaps[count] := thisMap[count];
    END

  ELSE
    ;{Cancel: don't change anything}
  DisposDialog(TheDialog);
END;{ DoProgramMapDlog}
```

When the done button is pushed, the current values of the local program mapping array are loaded into the global variable *ProgramMaps*.

Velocity Procedures

```
PROCEDURE DoVelocityMap;
BEGIN
  DoVelocityMapDlog;
END; {VelocityMap}
```

When Velocity is selected from the menu, the *DoVelocityMapDlog* procedure is called. The procedure displays a dialog that allows the user to enter settings for MIDI Thru's velocity processing routines.

Here is the dialog displayed by DoVelocityMapDlog, and the globals used to reference its dialog item list.

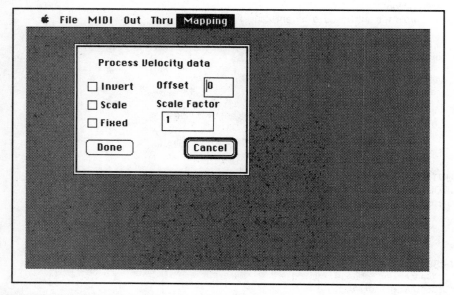

```
{MAPPING  Menu Dialogs}
VelocityMapDlogID = 211;          {Velocity Map Resource IDs}

VCancelItem = 1;
VDoneItem = 2;
VInvertItem = 3;
VScaleItem = 4;
VFixedItem = 5;
VOffsetItem = 6;
VSFactorItem = 7;
```

```
VAR
  {Velocity Mapping}
  VInvertFlag, VScaleFlag, VFixedFlag: integer;
  VOffset: MIDIData;
  VSFactor: integer;



PROCEDURE InitVelocity;
BEGIN
  VInvertFlag := 0;
  VScaleFlag := 0;
  VFixedFlag := 0;
  VOffset := 0;
  VSFactor := 1;
END; {InitVelocity}
```

Here are the global variables used by the routines and the initialization procedure that is called from InitParameters when RTL is first started.

```
PROCEDURE DoVelocityMapDlog;
    VAR
        DlogItem, DlogType, VelocityOffset: integer;
        DlogRect: rect;
        DlogHandle: handle;

        thisInvertFlag, thisScaleFlag, thisFixedFlag: integer;
        thisVOffset, thisVSFactor: integer;

    BEGIN
        {set local variables to current global values}
        {display dialog}
        {set controls and text boxes to current values}

        REPEAT
          BEGIN
            ModalDialog(NIL, DlogItem);
            CASE DlogItem OF

            {for each control and text box:}
                {update local  variables to new values set by the user}

            END {CaseDlogItem}
          END; {repeat}
```

```
UNTIL (DlogItem = VDoneItem) OR (DlogItem = VCancelItem);
IF DlogItem = VDoneItem THEN
  BEGIN
    VInvertFlag := thisInvertFlag;
    VScaleFlag := thisScaleFlag;
    VFixedFlag := thisFixedFlag;
    VOffset := thisVOffset;
    VSFactor := thisVSFactor;
  END
ELSE
  ;{Cancel: don't change anything}
DisposDialog(TheDialog);
END;{DoVelocityMap}
```

When the done button is pushed, the current values of the local variables for
the invert, scale, and fixed check boxes are loaded into the global variables,
V*InvertFlag*, *VScaleFlag*, and*VFixedFlag*. The currently displayed offset and
scale factor are loaded into *VOffset* and *VSFactor*.

Note Map Procedures

```
PROCEDURE DoTransposeMap;
BEGIN
  DoTransposeDlog;
END; {TransposeMap}
```

When Note Map is selected from the menu, the *DoTranposeDlog* procedure
is called. The procedure displays a dialog that allows the user to enter values
that MIDIThru will use to transpose note numbers within a given range by
as much as two octaves up or down.

Here is the dialog displayed by DoTransposeDlog, and the globals used to reference its dialog item list.

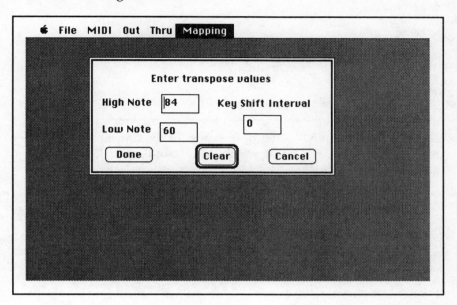

```
{MAPPING Menu Dialogs}
TransposeDlogID = 212;              {Key Transpose Resource IDs}
TransposeClearItem = 1;
TransposeCancelItem = 2;
TransposeDoneItem = 3;
TransposeHiNoteItem = 4;
TransposeLoNoteItem = 5;
TransposeKeyShiftItem = 6;


VAR
  {Transpose}
  HiTransposeNote, LoTransposeNote: MIDIData;
  NoteMap: MIDIDataArray;
  KeyTranspose: integer;
```

```
PROCEDURE InitTranspose;
  VAR
    count: integer;
BEGIN
  {Transpose}
  FOR count := 0 TO MaxDataValue DO
    NoteMap[count] := count;
  HiTransposeNote := MiddleC + twoOctaves;
  LoTransposeNote := MiddleC;
  KeyTranspose := 0;
END; {InitTranspose}
```

Here is an abbreviated listing of the code for DoTransposeDlog. We've replaced the code for updating variables and handling dialog controls and text boxes with comments.

```
PROCEDURE DoTransposeDlog;
  VAR
    DlogItem, DlogType: integer;
    DlogRect: rect;
    DlogHandle: handle;
    thisHiNote, thisLoNote, thisShift, count: integer;
BEGIN
  {set local variables to current global values}
  {display dialog}
  {set controls and text boxes to current values}

  REPEAT
  BEGIN
    ModalDialog(NIL, DlogItem);
    CASE DlogItem OF

      TransposeHiNoteItem:
        BEGIN
          thisHiNote := CheckValue(DlogItem, MiddleC + 24, dataValueCode);
          IF thisHiNote + thisShift > maxDataValue THEN
            BEGIN     {reset KeyTranspose so it works with this hi note value}
              thisShift := maxDataValue - thisHiNote;
              NumberToItem(theDialog, TransposeKeyShiftItem, thisShift);
            END;
        END;

      TransposeLoNoteItem:
        BEGIN     {reset KeyTranspose so it works with this lo note value}
          thisLoNote := CheckValue(DlogItem, MiddleC, dataValueCode);
          IF thisLoNote + thisShift < 0 THEN
            BEGIN
              thisShift := -thisLoNote;
              NumberToItem(theDialog, TransposeKeyShiftItem, thisShift);
            END
        END;
```

```
                TransposeKeyShiftItem:
                  BEGIN
                    thisShift := CheckValue(DlogItem, 0, harmonyValueCode);
                    IF thisLoNote + thisShift < 0 THEN
                      BEGIN        {reset lo note to work with this key shift value}
                        thisLoNote := -thisShift;
                        NumberToItem(theDialog, TransposeLoNoteItem, thisLoNote);
                      END
                    ELSE IF thisHiNote + thisShift > maxDataValue THEN
                      BEGIN        {reset hi note to work with this key shift value}
                        thisHiNote := maxDataValue - thisShift;
                        NumberToItem(theDialog, TransposeHiNoteItem, thisHiNote);
                      END;
                  END;

                TransposeClearItem:
                  BEGIN
                    InitTranspose;
                    thisHiNote := HiTransposeNote;
                    thisLoNote := LoTransposeNote;
                    thisShift := KeyTranspose;
                    NumberToItem(theDialog, TransposeHiNoteItem, thisHiNote);
                    NumberToItem(theDialog, TransposeLoNoteItem, thisLoNote);
                    NumberToItem(theDialog, TransposeKeyShiftItem, thisShift);
                  END;

                OTHERWISE
                    ;{       do nothing}
              END {CaseDlogItem}
          END; {repeat}

      UNTIL (DlogItem = TransposeDoneItem) OR (DlogItem = TransposeCancelItem);
      IF DlogItem = TransposeDoneItem THEN
        BEGIN
          FOR count := thisLoNote TO thisHiNote DO
            {add KeyTranspose value to note numbers}
            NoteMap[count] := NoteMap[count] + thisShift;

          HiTransposeNote := thisHiNote;
          LoTransposeNote := thisLoNote;
          KeyTranspose := thisShift;
        END

      ELSE
        ;{Cancel: don't change anything}
      DisposDialog(TheDialog);
    END;{DoTransposeDlog}
```

If the user enters new values for *thisHighNote*, *thisLoNote*, or *thisShift*, that are out of the range of the current displayed values, the routine will reset the other values to work with the newly entered one. When the done button is pushed, *thisShift* is added the elements of *NoteMap* within the transpose range.

MIDI Thru Procedures

```
PROCEDURE DoThru;
BEGIN
   DoMIDIThru;
END; {Thru}
```

When MIDI Thru is selected from the menu, the *DoMIDIThru* procedure is called. This is our main MIDI processing routine. It uses the variables set with the Running Status Filters, Channel, Controller, Program Change, and Velocity menus to modify MIDI data in real-time. The design for DoMIDI Thru looks like this:

DoMIDIThru

```
DoMIDIThru:
        get a byte from MIDI In

        if the byte is a status byte (more than 127) :
                update  runningStatus and set filter flag
        if the byte is a Channel Voice status byte:
                re-assign the channel number

        if the byte is a data byte (127 or less):
                process byte based on the value of  runningStatus:

                        Note On and Note Off data
                                process note number and velocity data

                        Control Change data
                                process controller data

                        Program Change data
                                re-assign program number

        if filter flag is off for this type message:
                send the byte to MIDI OUT
```

DoMIDIThru keeps track of Running Status and also checks to see if the user has turned on a Running Status filter for the current status. If a filter is on, messages of that type are not transmitted by MIDIThru. This is the design of the Update*Status* procedure, which is called every time DoMIDIThru receives a status byte.

Update Running Status

```
update runningStatus:
        set SkipByte flag to false
        set byteCount to 1

        get the status of the byte

        assign runningStatus based on the status of the byte:

                Note On or Note Off
                        If Note On/Off filter is on
                                SkipByte is true
                        If Note On/Off filter is off
                                runningStatus = status

                Polyphonic Key Pressure
                        If Poly Key Pressure filter is on
                                SkipByte is true
                        If Poly  Key Pressure  filter is off
                                runningStatus = status

                Control Change
                        If Control Change filter is on
                                SkipByte is true
                        If Control Change  filter is off
                                runningStatus = status
                Program Change
                        runningStatus = status

                Channel Pressure
                        If After Touch filter is on
                                SkipByte is true
                        If After Touch  filter is off
                                runningStatus = status
```

```
Pitch Bend
        If Pitch Bend filter is on
                SkipByte is true
        If Pitch Bend  filter is off
                runningStatus = status

System Common
                runningStatus = status

System Exclusive
                runningStatus = status

If status is System Real Time
        runningStatus doesn't change
```

Here is the complete code for MIDIThru and UpdateStatus.

```
PROCEDURE DoMIDIThru;
    VAR
       inChannel: integer;

BEGIN
   REPEAT
      MIDIIn(theMIDIByte);
      IF theMIDIByte <> -1 THEN
         BEGIN
            IF theMIDIByte >= NoteOff THEN
               DoUpdateStatus;

            IF (theMIDIByte >= NoteOff) AND (theMIDIByte < SysEx) THEN
               ChannelizeStatus;

            IF theMIDIByte <= maxDataValue THEN
               CASE RunningStatus OF
                  NoteOn, NoteOff:
                     ProcessNoteData;

                  PolyPressure:
                     ;

                  ControlChange:
                     ProcessControlData;

                  ProgramChange: {re-assign program number to mapped value}
                     theMIDIByte := ProgramMaps[theMIDIByte];
```

```
              ChannelPressure:
                 ;
              PitchBend:
                 ;
              OTHERWISE
                 ;

              END; {Case RunningStatus}

         IF SkipByte = False THEN
              MIDIOut(theMIDIByte);
         END; {if byte ,.-1}

    UNTIL Button;
    END;{DoMIDIThru}


PROCEDURE DoUpdateStatus;
    VAR
        status: integer;
    BEGIN
      SkipByte := False;                    {when this is false bytes are Xmitted by MIDIThru}
      byteCount := 1;                        {new status, so reset byte counter to 1}

      status := GetStatus(theMIDIByte);
      CASE Status OF
        NoteOn, NoteOff:
          BEGIN
            IF RSFilters[1] = 1 THEN         {if the RSFilter box is checked}
              BEGIN
                SkipByte := True;            {bytes with this status won't be sent out}
              END
            ELSE
              RunningStatus := Status;       {updated to new running status}
          END;

        PolyPressure:
          BEGIN
            IF RSFilters[2] = 1 THEN
              BEGIN
                SkipByte := True;
              END
            ELSE
              RunningStatus := Status;
          END;
```

```
      ControlChange:
         BEGIN
           IF RSFilters[3] = 1 THEN
             BEGIN
                SkipByte := True;
             END
           ELSE
             RunningStatus := Status;
         END;

      ProgramChange:
         RunningStatus := Status;

      ChannelPressure:
         BEGIN
           IF RSFilters[4] = 1 THEN
             BEGIN
                SkipByte := True;
             END
           ELSE
             RunningStatus := Status;
         END;

      PitchBend:
         BEGIN
           IF RSFilters[5] = 1 THEN
             BEGIN
                SkipByte := True;
             END
           ELSE
             RunningStatus := Status;
         END;

      OTHERWISE                                {take care of System Common and SysEx status bytes}
         IF Status < MIDIClock THEN            {ignore System  Real Time bytes      }
             RunningStatus := Status;
    END; {Case Status}
END;{DoUpdateStatus}
```

After updating the *RunnngStatus* variable, MIDIThru channelizes all MIDI Voice Channel messages by calling *ChannelizeStatus*.

Channel Mapping

```
PROCEDURE ChannelizeStatus;
  VAR
     inputChannel: integer;
BEGIN
  inputChannel := GetChannel(theMIDIByte) + 1;
  theMIDIByte := RunningStatus + ChanMaps[inputChannel] - 1;
END;{ChannelizeStatus}
```

ChannelizeStatus reassigns the channel number by using the current value as a subcript to the *ChanMaps* array.

ProcessNoteData is called when data bytes pass through MIDIThru and RunningStatus = NoteOn or NoteOff.

Note Mapping and Velocity Processing

```
PROCEDURE ProcessNoteData;
BEGIN
  CASE ByteCount OF
    1: {process note number}
      BEGIN
        byteCount := 2;
        theMIDIByte := NoteMap[theMIDIByte];
      END;

    2: {process velocity data}
      BEGIN
        byteCount := 1;
        IF theMIDIByte > minOnVelocity THEN
          BEGIN
            IF VFixedFlag = 1 THEN
              theMIDIByte := VOffset
            ELSE IF VScaleFlag = 1 THEN
              BEGIN
                theMIDIByte := (theMIDIByte + VOffset) * VSFactor;
                IF theMIDIByte > maxDataValue THEN
                  theMIDIByte := maxDataValue
                ELSE IF theMIDIByte < MinOnVelocity THEN
                  theMIDIByte := minOnVelocity;
              END;
            IF VInvertFlag = 1 THEN
              theMIDIByte := InvertData(theMIDIByte);
          END;
      END;

    OTHERWISE
      ;{do nothing}
  END;
END;{ ProcessNoteData}
```

In order to process the data properly, the routine uses the variable *byteCount* to keep track of which byte of the note on message is currently held in the global variable *theMIDIByte*. If byteCount=1, data bytes are key numbers; if byteCount=2, data bytes are velocity data. A CASE structure uses byte-Count as its control variable to switch to the correct processing routine.

If the byte is a note number, its value is used as a subscript to the *NoteMap* array. If the byte is velocity data, its processing is determined by the settings of the *VFixed*, *VOffset*, and *VInvert* flags. If the VFixedFlag=1, the byte is assigned the value of *VOffset*. If the VScaleFlag=1, the value of the byte is multiplied by the value of VS*Factor*. If the new value is outside the range of MIDI data values (0-127), it is reset to the highest (or lowest) legal value. If the VInvertFlag=1, then *InvertData* is called to invert the value of the byte.

ProcessControlData is called when data bytes pass through MIDIThru and RunningStatus = Note On or Note Off.

Controller ID Mapping and Controller Data Processing

```
PROCEDURE ProcessControlData;
BEGIN
   CASE byteCount OF
     1: {first data byte (controller ID}
        BEGIN
           byteCount := 2;                              {increment byte counter}
           theMIDIByte := ControlMaps[theMIDIByte];     {re-assign to mapped value}
        END;

     2: {second data byte (controller value}
        BEGIN
           byteCount := 1;                              {reset Byte counter}
           IF CntrlScaleFlag = 1 THEN
             BEGIN
                theMIDIByte := theMIDIByte + CntrlOffset;
                IF theMIDIByte > maxDataValue THEN
                   theMIDIByte := maxDatavalue;
             END;
           IF CntrlInvertFlag = 1 THEN
             theMIDIByte := InvertData(theMIDIByte);
        END;

     OTHERWISE
        ;{do nothing}
   END;
END;{ProcessControlData}
```

Like ProcessNoteData, this procedure uses byteCount to switch processing to the appropriate routine for either controller ID or controller value. If the byte is a controller ID, its value is used as a subscript to the *ControlMaps* array. If the byte is a controller value, it is processed in accordance with the setting of *CntrlScaleFlag* and *CntrlInvertFlag*. These routines are similar to the ones used to process velocity data in ProcessNoteData.

Mapping Menu Operations

Harmony Procedures

```
PROCEDURE DoHarmonyMap;
BEGIN
  DoHarmonyMapDlog;
END; {Harmony Map }
```

When Harmony Map is selected from the menu, the *DoHarmonyMapDlog*
procedure is called. The procedure displays a dialog that allows the user to
enter range and polyphony and scale values for real-time, auto-harmoniza-
tion routines.

Here is the dialog displayed by DoHarmonyDlog, and the globals used to
reference its dialog item list.

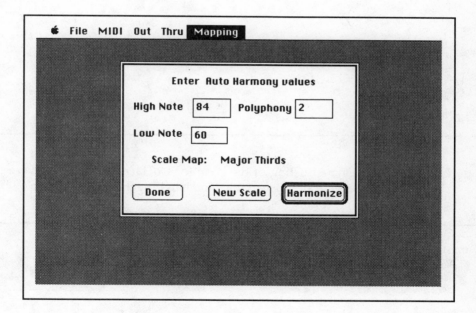

```
{MAPPING menu}
HarmonyDlogID = 213;              {Auto Harmony Resource IDs}
HarmonizeItem = 1;
HarmonyDoneItem = 2;
HarmonyNewScaleItem = 3;
HarmonyHiNoteItem = 4;
HarmonyLoNoteItem = 5;
HarmonyPolyItem = 6;
HarmonyScaleMapItem = 7;



VAR
  {Auto Harmony}
  HiHarmonyNote, LoHarmonyNote: MIDIData;
  HarmonyMap: ChordArray;
  HarmonySize: ChordLimit;



PROCEDURE InitAutoHarmony;
  VAR
    count: integer;
BEGIN
  {Auto Harmony}
  FOR count := 1 TO ScaleSize DO
    HarmonyMap[count] := majorThird;
  HiHarmonyNote := MiddleC + twoOctaves;
  LoHarmonyNote := MiddleC;
  HarmonySize := Triad;
END; {InitAutoHarmony}
```

Here is an abbreviated listing of the code for DoHarmonyDlog. We've replaced the code for updating variables and handling the dialogs controls and text boxes with comments.

```
PROCEDURE DoHarmonyMapDlog;
  VAR
    DlogItem, DlogType: integer;
    DlogRect: rect;
    DlogHandle: handle;
    HarmonyDialog: DialogPtr;
    thisHiNote, thisLoNote, thisSize: integer;
    thisScaleName: str255;
```

```
BEGIN
   {set local variables to current global values}

   {display dialog}
   {set controls and text boxes to current values}

   REPEAT
      BEGIN
         ModalDialog(NIL, DlogItem);
         CASE DlogItem OF

         {for each control and text box:}
            {update local  variables to new values set by the user}

            HarmonyNewScaleItem:
               BEGIN
                  DoScaleMapDlog;
                  theDialog := HarmonyDialog;
                  GetDItem(theDialog, HarmonyScaleMapItem, Dlogtype, DlogHandle, DlogRect);
                  SetIText(DlogHandle, ScaleName);
               END;

            HarmonizeItem:
               BEGIN
                  HarmonySize := thisSize;
                  HiHarmonyNote := thisHiNote;
                  LoHarmonyNote := thisLoNote;
                  PlayHarmony;
               END;

            OTHERWISE
               ;{do nothing}
         END {CaseDlogItem}
      END; {repeat}

   UNTIL DlogItem = HarmonyDoneItem;
   DisposDialog(TheDialog);
END;{DoHarmonyMapDlog}
```

If the New Scale button is pushed, then *DoScaleMapDlog* is called and a new dialog window is displayed. The user can use that dialog window to enter new harmony values for the twelve pitches of the chromatic scale.

If the Harmonize button is pushed, the *PlayHarmony* procedure is called.

Harmonize MIDI Notes

```
PROCEDURE PlayHarmony;
  VAR
    byte1, keyData, velocityData, status: integer;
BEGIN {PlayHarmony}
  MIDI(ClearInput);
  MIDI(ClearOutput);

  REPEAT
    BEGIN
      MIDIIn(byte1);
      IF byte1 <> -1 THEN
        BEGIN

          IF byte1 >= NoteOff THEN
            status := GetStatus(byte1);

          CASE status OF
            NoteOff, NoteOn:
              BEGIN

                CASE GetStatus(byte1) OF
                  NoteOn:
                    BEGIN
                      MIDIOut(byte1);
                      keyData := WaitForMIDI;
                      velocityData := WaitForMIDI;
                      MIDIOut(keyData);
                      MIDIOut(velocityData);
                      IF (keyData > LoHarmonyNote) AND (Keydata < HiHarmonyNote) THEN
                        SendHarmony(keyData, velocityData);
                    END;{byte1=NoteOff,NoteOn}

                  OTHERWISE
                    BEGIN
                      keyData := byte1;
                      velocityData := WaitForMIDI;
                      MIDIOut(keyData);
                      MIDIOut(velocityData);
                      IF (keyData > LoHarmonyNote) AND (Keydata < HiHarmonyNote) THEN
                        SendHarmony(keyData, velocityData);
                    END;{otherwise byte1 = runningstatus data}

                END;{case GetStatus(byte1)}
              END;{ status = NoteOff,NoteOn}
            OTHERWISE
              MIDIout(byte1);
          END;{Case Status}
        END;{byte1<> -1}
    END; {repeat loop}
  UNTIL button;
END;{PlayHarmony}
```

PlayHarmony uses a CASE structure to select the processing routines for all incoming bytes. The control variable of the CASE structure is *status*. Its value is the value of the last received status byte. When a Note On message is detected, the routine waits for the next two data bytes (which will be the key and velocity data for the note). Next it checks to see if the key number is within the range set by *LoHarmonyNote* and *HiHarmonyNote*. If it is, *SendHarmony* is called.

Sending Harmony Data

```
PROCEDURE SendHarmony (key, velocity: integer);
  VAR
    i, scaleNumber: integer;

BEGIN{SendChord}
  FOR i := 1 TO HarmonySize DO
    BEGIN
      scaleNumber := GetSemitone(key);
      key := key + ScaleMap[scaleNumber];
      MIDIOut(key);
      MIDIOut(velocity);
    END; {for i}
END;
```

SendHarmony transmits a chord for every note played. The number of notes in the chord is set by the value of *HarmonySize*. For each note in the chord, SendHarmony adds a separate harmony interval by using the pitch value of the note (C #= 1, C# = 2, etc.) as the subscript to the *ScaleMap* array. The harmony interval is set by adding the value of the *ScaleMap* element to the key number.

Scale Map Procedures

Here is the dialog and globals used by *DoScaleMapDlog*:

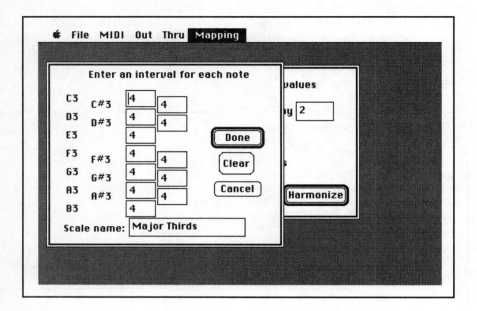

```
ScaleMapDlogId = 214;          {Scale Map ResourceIDs}
ScaleMapDoneItem = 1;
ScaleMapCancelItem = 2;
ScaleMapClearItem = 3;
ScaleMapCItem = 4;
ScaleMapCsItem = 5;
ScaleMapDItem = 6;
ScaleMapDsitem = 7;
ScaleMapEItem = 8;
ScaleMapFItem = 9;
ScaleMapFsItem = 10;
ScaleMapGItem = 11;
ScaleMapGsItem = 12;
ScaleMapAItem = 13;
ScaleMapAsItem = 14;
ScaleMapBItem = 15;
ScaleMapNameItem = 16;
```

```
VAR
  {ScaleMap}
  ScaleMap: ScaleArray;
  ScaleName: str255;


PROCEDURE InitScaleMap;
  VAR
    count: integer;
BEGIN
  {ScaleMap}
  FOR count := 1 TO ScaleSize DO
    ScaleMap[count] := 4;
  ScaleName := 'Major Thirds';
END; { }
```

Here is an abbreviated listing of the code for DoScaleMapDlog. We've
replaced the code for updating variables and handling dialog controls and
text boxes with comments.

```
PROCEDURE DoScaleMapDlog;
  VAR
    DlogItem, DlogType, ItemListOffset: integer;
    DlogRect: rect;
    DlogHandle: handle;
    thisScale: ScaleArray;
    count, theScaleItem, ScaleID: integer;
    thisScaleName: str255;

BEGIN
  {set local variables to current global values}
  {display dialog}
  {set controls and text boxes to current values}

  REPEAT
    BEGIN
      ModalDialog(NIL, DlogItem);
      CASE DlogItem OF

      {for each control and text box:}
        {update local  variables to new values set by the user}
```

```
            ScaleMapClearItem:
              BEGIN
                InitScaleMap;
                theScaleItem := ScaleMapCItem;
                FOR count := 1 TO ScaleSize DO
                  BEGIN
                    thisScale[count] := ScaleMap[count];
                    NumberToItem(theDialog, theScaleItem, thisScale[count]);
                    theScaleItem := theScaleItem + 1;
                  END;
                thisScaleName := ScaleName;
                GetDItem(theDialog, ScaleMapNameItem, Dlogtype, DlogHandle, DlogRect);
                SetIText(DlogHandle, thisScaleName);
              END;

            OTHERWISE
              ;{        do nothing}
        END {CaseDlogItem}
      END; {repeat}

  UNTIL (DlogItem = ScaleMapDoneItem) OR (DlogItem = ScaleMapCancelItem);
  IF DlogItem = ScaleMapDoneItem THEN
      BEGIN
        FOR count := 1 TO ScaleSize DO
          ScaleMap[count] := thisScale[count];
        GetDItem(theDialog, ScaleMapNameItem, Dlogtype, DlogHandle, DlogRect);
        getIText(DlogHandle, thisScaleName);
        ScaleName := thisScaleName;
      END

  ELSE
    ;{Cancel: don't change anything}
  DisposDialog(TheDialog);
END;{DoScaleMapDlog}
```

Part Five

Building a BASIC MIDI Application

Part 5

Building a BASIC MIDI Application

Application 2: SysEx MIDI Lab

SysEx Lab is a "laboratory" for exploring non-real-time (System Exclusive) MIDI programming techniques: It demonstrates MIDI concepts on two levels. It will show the programmer how to write MIDI code in BASIC with MIDIBASIC, and will also show examples of practical non-real-time MIDI applications. Here are the major elements of MIDI programming demonstrated by SysEx Lab:

- How to configure the Mac to work with any MIDI interface

- How to decode and encode "nibblized" data using MIDIBASIC's *GetMIDI* command

- How to transmit and receive System Exclusive *dump request* and *bulk data* messages for any MIDI device that uses "one way" protocols. SysEx Lab gives specific examples of the format used for these MIDI devices: Yamaha DX7 II, TX802; Southworth Music, JamBox 4, J.L. Cooper, MSB+; and Lexicon LXP-1

- How to transmit and receive System Exclusive *dump request* and *bulk data* messages for any MIDI device that uses "handshaking" protocols. SysEx Lab gives specific examples of the format used by Casio's CZ synthesizers: CZ1, CZ1000, CZ5000, and CZ230s

- How to store, access and display data bytes within a bulk dump

The SysEx lab also provides examples of several Macintosh programming techniques:

- How to use QuickBASIC's built-in, high-level Macintosh routines in place of Mac Toolbox routines.

- How to *Save* and *Open* files using the *mini finder* dialog window

- How to tag files with a *type* when saving them

- How to view files by *type* when opening them

215

- How to set up an event-driven application that uses the mouse or *command key equivalents* to choose program operations from pull-down menus

- How to build an *empty shell* to test program design

Specification of SysEx MIDI Lab

Here is the basic specification we used to design SysEx MIDI Lab.

Specification of the User Interface

- All program operations will be accessed via menu choices selected with the mouse or command key equivalents

- The program will use PRINT statements to display information to the user

- The program will use the Mac's *mini finder* dialog window to save and open files

Specifications of the Program Operations

Each program operation is linked to a separate menu item. The specifications for SysEx Lab's operations are listed in the order that they appear on the application's menus. For each program operation there is a *description* of what the operation should do. Where appropriate, the description is followed by a list of *variables* that will be used by the operation, and the *initialized* value of each variable.

This specification served as the "bible" for the design and coding phases of the program development. The variables identified in the specifications were written into the code using the same name (shown here in italics).

File Menu

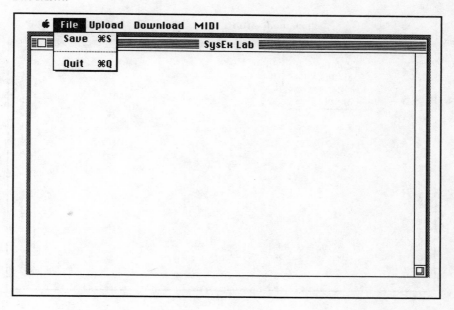

Save

Description
When selected, display the standard Mac *mini finder* dialog window. If there is a bulk dump file in the buffer, allow the user to name and save the file. Files saved with SysExLab will be "typed" to indicate whether one-way or handshaking routines will be required to transmit the file when it is opened.

Variables
FileName$ holds the name of the current file. File names are tagged with sXl1 for one-way transfers and sXl2 for handshaking transfers.

Quit

When selected, shut down the program and return to the Macintosh finder.

Upload Menu

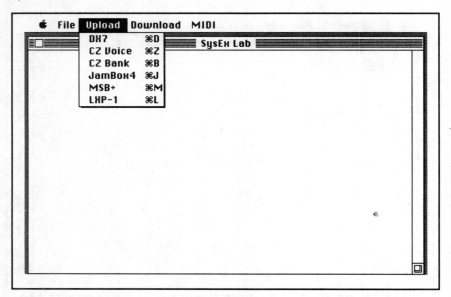

DX7

Description

When selected, transmit a *voice edit buffer request* message through the MIDI OUT port, and wait for the DX7 to transmit edit buffer data. Retrieve the data by putting it into a string buffer. Print messages that show the user the data in the request message sent by the Mac and the number of bytes sent back by the DX7. If there is no response to the request, print a "time out" error message.

Variables

DX7DumpRequest is an array that holds the request message. *DX7$* is a string buffer that holds the bulk data.

Initialized Values

The size of the request message is 5 bytes. The size of the data dump is 163 bytes.

CZ Voice

Description

When selected, prompt the user for a voice number and then transmit a *Send1 request* for that voice through the MIDI OUT port. Wait for the CZ synthesizer to transmit *Ready1* message. Transmit a *Continue* message to the CZ synthesizer and wait for it to send back a *timbre data* dump.

Casio data is transmitted as a series of 4-bit "nibbles" (an 8-bit byte with no data in the upper four bits). Retrieve and decode the data and put it into a string buffer. Print messages that show the user the data in the request message sent by the Mac, the voice number being received, the number of raw bytes sent back by the CZ230s, and the number of decoded bytes put into the buffer. If there is no response to the request, print a "time out" error message. Transfer the decoded data into a bank buffer that can hold up to 100 individual sets of timbre data.

Variables

CZRequest1 is an array that holds the request message. *CZReady* is an array that holds the ready message. *CZTimbre1$* is a string buffer that holds the bulk data for a single timbre (parameters for one voice). *CZBank$* is a buffer that can hold 100 sets of CZ timbre data.

Initialized Values

The size of the request message is 7 bytes. The size of the receive message is 6 bytes. The raw size of the data dump is 257 bytes. The size of the decoded data dump is 129 bytes. The size of the 100 sets of data dumps is 12,900 bytes.

CZ Bank

Description

The complete CZ Voice operation is performed repeatedly (up to 100 times) until all of the voice numbers from the starting voice number through the ending voice number have been received. The timbre data is decoded and transferred into the bank buffer.

Variables

CZBank1 holds the starting voice and *CZBank32* holds the ending voice. All other variables are the same ones described previously for CZ Voice.

Initialized Values

The starting voice number is set to 0. The ending voice number is set to 3.

MSB+

Description

When selected, transmit a *full dump request* message through the MIDI OUT port, wait for the MSB+ to transmit its full dump data, and retrieve the data by putting it into a string buffer. Print messages that show the user the data in the request message sent by the Mac and the number of bytes sent back by the MSB+. If there is no response to the request, print a "time out" error message.

Variables

MSBRequest is an array that holds the request message. *MSB$* is a string buffer that holds the bulk data.

Initialized Values

The size of the request message is 5 bytes. The size of the data dump is 1,029 bytes.

LXP-1

Description

When selected, transmit an *all parameters dump request* message through the MIDI OUT port, wait for the LXP-1 to transmit its parameter dump data, and retrieve the data by putting it into a string buffer. Print messages that show the user the data in the request message sent by the Mac and the number of bytes sent back by the LXP-1. If there is no response to the request, print a "time out" error message.

Variables

LXPRequest is an array that holds the request message. *LXP$* is a string buffer that holds the bulk data.

Initialized Values

The size of the request message is 7 bytes. The size of the data dump is 7,176 bytes.

Download Menu

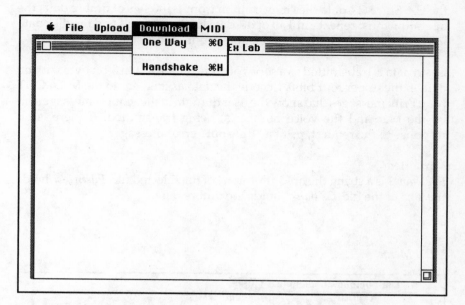

One Way

Description
When selected, show the standard Mac mini finder dialog window used to open files. Display only files that have been previously saved and typed as one-way transfers (type "sXl1"). Once the user selects a file, open it and transmit the data through the MIDI OUT port. Print messages telling the user the name of the file being sent, how many bytes long it is, and display the data for each byte as it is sent.

Variables
FileName$ is a string the holds the name of the selected file. *FileSize%* hold the size of the file. *ByteCount%* holds the number of the byte currently being transmitted, and *X%* holds the value of the byte.

Handshake

Description
When selected, show the standard Mac mini finder dialog window used to open files. Display only files that have been previously saved and typed as handshake transfers (type "sXl2"). Once the user selects a file, transmit a *Receive1 request* for that voice through the MIDI OUT port. Wait for the CZ

synthesizer to transmit a *Ready1* message. Transmit the *timbre data* dump to the CZ. Since CZ data files may contain from 1-100 sets of timbre data, the operation must repeat until all of the data has been sent. Load the disk data into a string buffer and count the number of timbre sets in the file.

Casio data is transmitted as a series of 4-bit "nibbles" (an 8-bit byte with no data in the upper four bits). Encode the data as it is sent to the MIDI OUT port. Print messages that show the user the data in the request message sent by the Mac and the voice number(s) being transmitted. If there is no response to the request, print a "time out" error message.

Variables
FileName$ is a string the holds the name of the selected file. *FileSize%* holds the size of the file. *CZBank$* holds the timbre data.

MIDI Menu

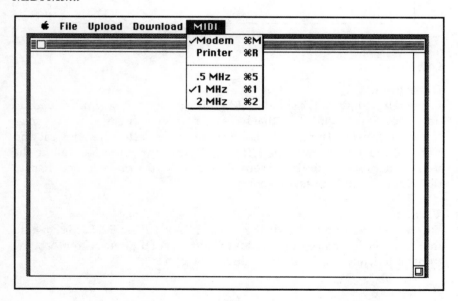

Modem

Description
When selected, reset the MIDI port to the modem port. Confirm the selection by putting a check mark next to the modem menu item.

Variables
Port% holds the setting of the MIDI port

Printer

Description
When selected, reset the MIDI port to the printer port. Confirm the selection by putting a check mark next to the printer menu item.

Variables
Port% holds the setting of the MIDI port.

.5 MHz

Description
When selected, reset the MIDI port to .5 MHz. Confirm the selection by putting a check mark next to the .5 MHz menu item.

Variables
clockRate% holds the setting of the MIDI clock rate.

1 MHz

Description
When selected, reset the MIDI port to 1 MHz. Confirm the selection by putting a check mark next to the 1 MHz menu item.

Variables
clockRate% holds the setting of the MIDI clock rate.

2 MHz

Description
When selected, reset the MIDI port to 2 MHz. Confirm the selection by putting a check mark next to the 2 MHz menu item.

Variables
clockRate% holds the setting of the MIDI clock rate.

Building the Shell for SysEx MIDI Lab

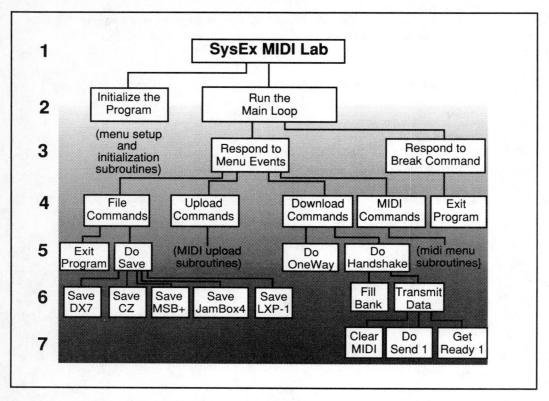

The illustration shows the level structure of the SysEx MIDI Lab program. Like Real-Time MIDI Lab, this program is designed in levels. In this section we'll examine the overall design of the program and build the complete shell.

SysEx Lab is written in QuickBASIC and takes advantage of many of the language's built-in Macintosh commands—like MENU, SYSTEM, and MOUSE—instead of calling Toolbox routines directly from QuickBASIC. You'll see that it's quite simple to create a Mac-like program with menus, mouse, and other powerful Macintosh features without having to use the Toolbox. However, since the Macintosh commands are specific only to QuickBASIC, we won't cover them with the same detail we used for the more universal Toolbox routines. Be sure to refer to your QuickBASIC manuals for the complete details of these commands.

Level 1

Main Program

```
Main Program:
        initialize the program
        main loop:
```

Level 2 Subroutines

Initialize the Program

```
initialize the program:
        initialize BASIC
        initialize SysEx variables
        set compiler flag
        initialize main window
        set up and display SysEx menus
        initialize MIDIBASIC
```

Initialize BASIC

```
CLEAR ,90000!,5000

compiled% = 0                                  'Toggle for compiled/interpreted versions (1 = compiler)
    FOR i%=1 TO PEEK(&H910)
      libname$=libname$+CHR$(PEEK(&H910+i%))
      NEXT
    IF compiled% THEN LIBRARY libname$ ELSE LIBRARY "MIDIBASIC"

    'Use ResEdit to install MIDIBASIC Code resources,
    'otherwise, the program will compile but not run.

DEFLNG a-Z
OPTION BASE 1
```

The first statement sets the memory size for the program. The *compiled%* variable is used to set the *code library* name for the program. When the program is compiled, this is set to 1 and the program uses its own name to reference the MIDIBASIC code. (These must be installed with ResEdit.) If compiled% is set to 0, the programs use MIDIBASIC as the library name. The

DFLNG statement makes the default variable a long integer; OPTION BASE 1 makes 1 the default starting subscript for arrays.

Initialize SysEx Variables

```
                                          'MIDIBASIC Variables
halfMeg% = 0
oneMeg% = 1
twoMeg%= 2
modem% = 3
printer% = 4
ClearIn% = 5
ClearOut% = 6
mode% = 0
count%= 0
result% = 0
loHiMode% = 1
maxBufferSize% = 5000
TempBufferSize = 8500
CheckOn = 2
CheckOff = 1
port% = modem%
clockRate% = oneMeg%


MSBFlag = 1                               'flags for file type
JamFlag = 2
DX7Flag = 3
LXPFlag = 4
CZ1Flag = 5
CZ32Flag =6
noDataFlag = 0
DumpFlag=noDataFlag


' SyxEx  Format Variables
' string buffer variable

  temp1$ = SPACE$(1)

'_____

'   MSB Formats

  MSBSize% = 1029                         'size of the MSB edit full dump (in bytes)
  MSB$ = SPACE$(MSBSize%)                 'this string will hold the MSB+ Data
  MSBRequestSize% = 5                     'size of MSB+ Full Dump SysEx request

DIM MSBRequest(MSBRequestSize%)           'Array to hold 5 byte MSB+ request
  MSBRequest(1) = &HF0                    'SysEx
  MSBRequest(2) = &H15                    'JL Cooper ID
  MSBRequest(3) = &HB                     'MSB+ ID Code
  MSBRequest(4) = &H1                     'Full dump request
  MSBRequest(5) = &HF7                    'Last byte: EOX
```

```
'
'   JanBox4 formats

    JamSize% = 304                              'size of the Jam Box edit full dump (in bytes)
    Jam$ = SPACE$(JamSize%)                     this string will hold the Jam Box Data
    JamRequestSize% = 5                         'size of Jam Box Full Dump SysEx request

DIM JamRequest(JamRequestSize%)                 'Array to hold 5 byte MSB+ request
    JamRequest(1) = &HF0                        'SysEx  status
    JamRequest(2) = &H28                        'Southworth ID
    JamRequest(3) = &H17                        'Message Request
    JamRequest(4) = &H18                        'Full dump request
    JamRequest(5) = &HF7                        'Last byte: EOX

'──────────────────── DX7  Formats ────────────────────

    DX7RequestSize% = 5
    DX7Size% = 163                              'size of voice edit buffer dump
    DX7$ = SPACE$(DX7Size%)

DIM DX7DumpRequest(DX7RequestSize%)             'array to hold DX7 II edit request
DX7DumpRequest(1) = &HF0                        'SysEx status
DX7DumpRequest(2) = &H43                        'Yamaha ID
DX7DumpRequest(3) = &H20                        'sub status/ channel 1
DX7DumpRequest(4) = &H0                         'voice edit buffer
DX7DumpRequest(5) = &HF7                        'EOX

'
'   LXP-1 Formats

    LXPRequestSize% = 7
    LXPSize% = 7176                             'size of an LXP's "all parameters" dump
    LXP$ = SPACE$(LXPSize%)

DIM LXPRequest(LXPRequestSize%)                 'array for LXP-1 all registers request
LXPRequest(1) = &HF0                            'SysEx
LXPRequest(2) = &H6                             'Lexicon ID
LXPRequest(3) = &H2                             'LXP-1 ID
LXPRequest(4) = &H30                            'channel 1
LXPRequest(5) = &H64                            'event code = "all registers"
LXPRequest(6) = &H0                             'ignored for "all register" request
LXPRequest(7) = &HF7                            'EOX
```

```
'_____

'  CZ1 Formats

CZTimbre1Size% = 129                       'size in byte of one CZ timbre
TimbresPerVoice% = 100                     'number of voices in a bank.
                                           ' for a CZ-230s
BankSize% = (CZTimbre1Size% * TimbresPerVoice%)
CZBank$ =SPACE$(BankSize%)                 'buffer used to hold CZ voices
CZRequest1Size% = 7                        'size of Request message
CZReadySize% = 6                           'size of Ready message
CZReady$ = SPACE$(CZReadySize%)            'buffer to hold Readt message
RawTimbre1Size% =257                       'size of nibblized data dump
CZTimbre1$ = SPACE$(CZTimbre1Size%)        'buffer to hold de-nibblized data dump

DIM CZRequest1(CZRequest1Size%)            'array for CZ  requests
CZRequest1(1) = &HF0                       'SysEx
CZRequest1(2) = &H44                       'CasioID
CZRequest1(3) = &H0                        'Sub ID1
CZRequest1(4) = &H0                        'Sub ID 2
CZRequest1(5) = &H70                       'channel 1
CZRequest1(6) = &H10                       'op code send rqst H10, receive rqst H20
CZRequest1(7) = &H0                        'internal  voice number 1

CZBank1% = 0                               'start and stop voice numbers
CZBank32% = 3                              'set to four for sends to CZ-230s
```

The values for several sets of global variables are assigned in this block of statements. MIDIBASIC variables are used as parameters for the MIDIBASIC commands. The file type flags are used by SyEx to keep track of the type of data being processed. The SysEx format variables are used to hold bulk dump data and request messages. There are five different sets of SysEx format variables. Each set is used to send and receive data to a specific MIDI device. The five devices are: Yamaha DX7 II, Casio CZ-230s, Southworth JamBox4, J.L. Cooper MSB+, and Lexicon LXP-1. The initialization procedure for each device is the same.

First, a *Size%* variable is assigned the size (in bytes) of the device's data dump, then a string variable is dimensioned to that size. Before they can be used by MIDIBASIC, the strings must be dimensioned with a SPACE$ statement. The string will be used by MIDIBASIC's *GetMIDI* and *SendMIDI* commands.

Next, a *RequestSize%* variable is assigned the size (in bytes) of the request message for the device, then a *request* array is dimensioned to the size of the message. After the request array is dimensioned, each of its elements is assigned the appropriate hexadecimal value for the message. (All System Exclusive messages have $F0 as the first element and $F7 as the last.)

The initialization of the CZ format variables is more involved than the others. Casio instruments use handshaking (two-way communication) when data is transferred between CZ instruments and a computer, and several messages are exchanged during the course of a single dump. We'll look into the specifics of CZ initialization when we cover the CZ Voice and CZ Bank program operations.

Every MIDI device capable of sending or receiving System Exclusive messages uses a unique format for its data. The specific details are usually printed in the owner's manual. Our book, **The System Exclusive Book**, lists the complete System Exclusive formats for 150 MIDI devices.

Initialize Main Window

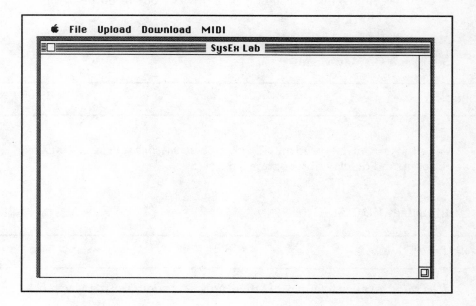

```
screenW%=SYSTEM(5)              'screen height
screenH%=SYSTEM(6)              'screen width
menuBarH%=PEEKW(&HBAA)          'menu bar height
TitleH%=20                      'height of window type 1 title bar
height%=screenH%-(menuBarH%+TitleH%+10)
centerWindow 1,"SysEx Lab",height%,screenW%-10,1,1/2

IF compiled% THEN
   PRINT "Use ResEdit to install MIDIBasic Code resources!"
END IF
```

Initializing the main window for SysEx consists of four steps:

- Get the size of the Macintosh screen.
- Get the height of the menu bar.
- Open a full screen window.
- Print a reminder about installing MIDIBASIC code resources with ResEdit if the program has been compiled.

Setup and Display Menus

```
GOSUB SetUpMenus
```

After the progam has been initialized, the *SetUpMenus* subroutine is called to set up and display the program's menus.

Initialize MIDIBASIC

```
GOSUB INITMIDI
```

INITMIDI is called to initialize MIDIBASIC and configure the Macintosh/ MIDI interface.

Main Loop

```
main loop:
      respond to menu events

      respond to break command
```

```
WHILE 1
   ON MENU   GOSUB DoMenu    :MENU ON
   ON BREAK  GOSUB DoBreak    :BREAK ON
WEND
```

Once started, the main loop of the program responds only to menu activity or the "break" command (apple key-period). If the user makes a menu selection, *doMenu* is called. If the user hits break, *doBreak* is called. After the user's actions are processed, the MENU ON or BREAK ON statements are used to make sure that the loop will continue to receive menu and break events (in case they were disabled by another subroutine).

Level 3 Subroutines

Set Up and Display SysEx Menus

```
set up and display SysEx  menus:
      set up File menu
      set up Upload menu
      set up Download menu
      set up MIDI menu
```

```
SetUpMenus:
   GOSUB SetupFileMenu
   GOSUB SetupUploadMenu
   GOSUB SetupDownloadMenu
   GOSUB SetUpMIDIMenu
RETURN
```

SetUpMenus calls a separate subroutine to build each of SysEx's menus.

Initialize MIDIBASIC

```
initialize MIDIBASIC:
        open MIDIBASIC
        filter out active sensing
        set clock rate
        set port
        clear MIDI buffers
```

```
INITMIDI:
  CALL MIDIopen(maxBufferSize%,maxBufferSize%)
  CALL MIDIFilter(1,254,254,0)                          'Filter out active sensing !!
  CALL MIDIPort(clockRate%)
  CALL MIDIPort(port%)
  GOSUB ClearMIDI
RETURN

ClearMIDI:
  CALL MIDI(ClearIn%)
  CALL MIDI(ClearOut%)
RETURN
```

INITMIDI sets the size of the input and output buffers, creates an Active Sensing filter, and configures the interface clock rate to 1 MHz and the port to the modem port. *ClearMIDI* is called to clear the input and output buffers.

Get the Menu Choice

```
respond to Menu Events:
        find out which menu
        find out which item

        depending on which menu

                for the File menu
                        perform the selected operation

                for the Upload  menu
                        perform the selected operation

                for the Download  menu
                        perform the selected operation

                for the MIDI menu
                        perform the selected operation

                for any other menu
                        Print " unknown menu  id"
```

```
DoMenu:
  MenuID= MENU(0)
  MenuItem= MENU(1)
  CLS
  SELECT CASE MenuID
    CASE 1   :GOSUB FileCmd          'File menu
    CASE 2   :GOSUB UploadCmd        'Upload menu
    CASE 3   :GOSUB DownloadCmd      'Download menu
    CASE 4   :GOSUB MIDICmd          'MIDI menu
    CASE ELSE                        'ignore any other menu
        PRINT "Unknown menuID:" MenuID
  END SELECT
  MENU                               'restore unhighlighted state
RETURN
```

MenuID holds the code for which menu was selected. It is used as the control variable for a SELECT CASE structure which calls the subroutine for the appropriate menu. *MenuItem* holds the value of the selected menu item. It will be used to select the correct subroutine for the user's menu selection.

Respond to Break Command

```
respond to break command:
        print "Leaving SysEx Lab"

        close MIDIBASIC

        stop the program
```

```
DoBreak:
  PRINT "Leaving SysEx Lab"
  LIBRARY CLOSE
  END
```

doBreak shuts down the program. First it prints a sign-off message, then it closes MIDIBASIC and ends the program.

Level 4 Subroutines

Set Up File Menu

```
SetupFileMenu:
  MENU 1,0,1,"File"
  MENU 1,1,1,"Save"        :cmdKey 1,1,"S"
  MENU 1,2,0,"-"
  MENU 1,3,1,"Quit"        :cmdKey 1,3,"Q"
RETURN
```

SetUpFileMenu creates the File menu. The *cmdKey* statements are used to set command key equivalents for each menu item. Refer to the QuickBASIC *Language Reference Manual* for the details of using MENU statements. The three other menus are set up in the same manner.

Set Up Upload Menu

```
SetupUploadMenu:
   MENU 2,0,1,"Upload"
   MENU 2,1,1,"DX7"          :cmdKey 2,1,"D"
   MENU 2,2,1,"CZ Voice"     :cmdKey 2,2,"Z"
   MENU 2,3,1,"CZ Bank"      :cmdKey 2,3,"B"
   MENU 2,4,1,"JamBox4"      :cmdKey 2,4,"J"
   MENU 2,5,1,"MSB+"         :cmdKey 2,5,"M"
   MENU 2,6,1,"LXP-1"        :cmdKey 2,6,"L"
RETURN
```

Set Up Download Menu

```
SetupDownloadMenu:
   MENU 3,0,1, "Download"
   MENU 3,1,1,"One Way "     :cmdKey 3,1,"O"
   MENU 3,2,0,"-"
   MENU 3,3,1,"Handshake"    :cmdKey 3,3,"H"
RETURN
```

Set Up MIDI Menu

```
SetUpMIDIMenu:
   ModemCheck = 2
   PrinterCheck = 1
   halfMegCheck = 1
   oneMegCheck =2
   twoMegCheck = 3
   MENU 4,0,1, "MIDI"
   MENU 4,1,2,"Modem"        :cmdKey 4,1,"M"
   MENU 4,2,1,  "Printer"    :cmdKey 4,2,"R"
   MENU 4,3,0,"-"
   MENU 4,4,1, ".5 MHz"      :cmdKey 4,4,"5"
   MENU 4,5,2,"1 MHz"        :cmdKey 4,5,"1"
   MENU 4,6,1, "2MHz"        :cmdKey 4,6,"2"
RETURN
```

Get the Menu Command

perform the selected menu operation:

      depending on the item number

          do first item

          do second item
          :
          :
          do last item

Get File Commands

```
FileCmd:
  SELECT CASE MenuItem
    CASE 1   :GOSUB DoSave
    CASE 3                            'quit
      LIBRARY CLOSE
      END
    CASE ELSE
      PRINT "Undefined menu item."
  END SELECT
RETURN
```

The *FileCmd* subroutine uses *MenuItem* as the control variable of a SELECT CASE structure that calls the appropriate subroutine for the item selected by the user. If the user has selected save (or command-S), the *DoSave* subroutine is called. If the user has selected quit (or command-Q), FileCmd closes MIDIBASIC and ends the program.

Get Upload Commands

```
UploadCmd:
  MOUSE ON                              'look for mouse clicks during these routines
  SELECT CASE MenuItem
    CASE 1   :GOSUB DoDX7
    CASE 2   :GOSUB DoCZ1
    CASE 3   :GOSUB DoCZ32
    CASE 4   :GOSUB DoJamBox
    CASE 5   :GOSUB DoMSB
    CASE 6   :GOSUB DoLXP
    CASE ELSE
      PRINT "Undefined menu item."
  END SELECT
  MOUSE OFF
RETURN
```

The *UploadCmd* subroutine uses MenuItem to select the appropriate sub-routine to handle the user's menu selection.

Get Download Commands

```
DownloadCmd:
  SELECT CASE MenuItem
    CASE 1   :GOSUB DoOneWay
    CASE 3   :GOSUB DoHandShake
    CASE ELSE
      PRINT "Undefined menu item."
  END SELECT
RETURN
```

The *DownloadCmd* subroutine uses MenuItem to select the appropriate subroutine to handle the user's menu selection.

Get MIDI Commands

```
MIDICmd:
  SELECT CASE MenuItem
    CASE 1   :GOSUB DoModem
    CASE 2   :GOSUB DoPrinter
    CASE 4   :GOSUB DoHalfMeg
    CASE 5   :GOSUB DoOneMeg
    CASE 6   :GOSUB DoTwoMeg
    CASE ELSE
      PRINT "Undefined menu item."
  END SELECT
  PRINT "Reseting Interface"
  CALL MIDIPort(clockRate%)              'reset the MIDI clock rate
  CALL MIDIPort(port%)                   'reset the MIDI port
RETURN
```

The *MIDICmd* subroutine uses MenuItem to select the appropriate subroutine to handle the user's menu selection. In this case, the subroutine called will be used to set new values for the interface configuration. After the subroutine has been executed, MIDICmd uses two MIDIPort statements to reset the interface.

Level 5 Subroutines

At this point, we can complete an empty shell for the program; the routines are designed and coded. Before we get to the specific code for the subroutines that actually handle the SysEx data, we install *dummy* versions of each routine. Each dummy routine prints a message that gives the name of the routine. If we specified that the subroutine will print messages when it is completely executed, then we print a test version of the message here. These routines allow us to run the program and test the user interface along with the major points of our overall design. Here is the general design for a dummy routine:

Dummy Subroutine

```
dummy do item procedure:
        print a message saying the subroutine is not implemented

        print a test version of any messages that will be printed
        by the routine
```

DoSave

```
DoSave:
  IF DumpFlag = noData THEN
     PRINT "There is no data in the buffer to save."
     RETURN
  END IF
  FileName$=FILES$(0,"File to save:")
  IF FileName$="" THEN
     RETURN                             'Cancel was selected
  END IF
  SELECT CASE DumpFlag
     CASE 1      :GOSUB SaveMSBData
     CASE 2      :GOSUB SaveJamData
     CASE 3      :GOSUB SaveDX7Data
     CASE 4      :GOSUB SaveLXPData
     CASE 5,6:GOSUB SaveCZ1Data
     CASE ELSE
        PRINT "Dump type" DumpFlag
  END SELECT
RETURN
```

SaveMSBData

```
SaveMSBData:
    PRINT "Can't save " FileName$
    PRINT "Save routine for dump type" DumpFlag "is not implemented"
RETURN
```

SaveJamData

```
SaveJamData:
    PRINT "Can't save " FileName$
    PRINT "Save routine for dump type" DumpFlag "is not implemented"
RETURN
```

SaveDX7Data

```
SaveDX7Data:
    PRINT "Can't save " FileName$
    PRINT "Save routine for dump type" DumpFlag "is not implemented"
RETURN
```

SaveLXPData

```
SaveLXPData:
    PRINT "Can't save " FileName$
    PRINT "Save routine for dump type" DumpFlag "is not implemented"
RETURN
```

SaveCZ1Data

```
SaveCZ1Data:
    PRINT "Can't save " FileName$
    PRINT "Save routine for dump type" DumpFlag "is not implemented"
RETURN
```

DoDX7

```
DoDX7:
    PRINT "DX7  is not implemented"
    DumpFlag = DX7Flag
    GOSUB DX7Up
RETURN
```

DX7Up

```
DX7Up:   'Upload DX7 Edit Buffer Bulk data
    PRINT ,"Sending DX7 II (TX 802) Edit Buffer Dump Request"
    PRINT "Retrieved"count% "bytes of 'DX7 II Edit Buffer Data."
RETURN   'DX7up
```

DoCZ1

```
DoCZ1:
   PRINT "CZ Voice is not implemented"
   DumpFlag = CZ1Flag
   GOSUB CZ1Up
RETURN
```

CZ1Up

```
CZ1Up:   'Upload CZ1Voice Bulk data
   LOCATE 2,1
   PRINT "Sending CZ1 Send Request 1for voice number :";
   PRINT CZRequest1(7)
RETURN   'CZ1up
```

DoCZ32

```
DoCZ32:
   PRINT "CZ Bank is not implemented"
   DumpFlag = CZ32Flag
RETURN
```

DoJamBox

```
DoJamBox:
   PRINT "JamBox 4 is not implemented"
   DumpFlag = JamFlag
   GOSUB JamUp
RETURN
```

DoJamUp

```
JamUp:   'Upload Jam Box Bulk data
   PRINT ,"Sending JamBox4+ Full Dump Request"
RETURN   'JamUp
```

DoMSB

```
DoMSB:
   PRINT "MSB+  is not implemented"
   DumpFlag = MSBFlag
   GOSUB MSBUp
RETURN
```

MSBUp

```
MSBUp:   'Upload MSB+ bulk dump data
   PRINT, "Sending MSB+ Full Dump Request
RETURN   'MSBUp
```

DoLXP

```
DoLXP:
  PRINT "LXP-1 is not implemented"
  DumpFlag = LXPFlag
  GOSUB LXPUp
RETURN
```

LXPUp

```
LXPUp:   'Upload "all registers" from LXP-1
  DumpFlag = LXPFlag
  PRINT ,"Sending LXP-1 All Register Dump Request"
RETURN   'LXPup
```

DoOneWay

```
DoOneWay:
  PRINT "Trasmit data is not implemented"
RETURN
```

DoHandShake

```
DoHandShake:
  PRINT "This DoHandShake"
  GOSUB TransmitCZData
RETURN
```

TransmitCZData

```
TransmitCZData:
  PRINT"Transmitting voice to CZ here"
RETURN
```

DoModem

```
DoModem:
  PRINT "Modem is not implemented"
RETURN
```

DoPrinter

```
DoPrinter:
  PRINT "Printer is not implemented"
RETURN
```

DoHalfMeg

```
DoHalfMeg:
   PRINT ".5 MHz is not implemented"
RETURN
```

DoOneMeg

```
DoOneMeg:
   PRINT "1 MHz is not implemented"
RETURN
```

DoTwoMeg

```
DoTwoMeg:
   PRINT "2 MHz is not implemented"
RETURN
```

Upload Operations

With the exception of CZ Voice and CZ Bank, all of the Upload program operations use the same design to request and receive bulk data from a MIDI device. You can use this design as a template for your own routines to get System Exclusive data from most MIDI devices.

Upload SysEx Data

```
Get System Exclusive data:
        tell the user what kind of request message is being sent

        clear the input and output buffers

        send the request message

        wait for result from GetMIDI or mouse click

                call GetMIDI to get the expected SysEx data

        If the mouse was clicked, or GetMIDI returns a time out error:
                tell user an error occurred
                set the dump flag to "no data"
                return to the calling subroutine

        If the data was received without error
                tell user how many bytes were retrieved
```

DX7 Subroutines

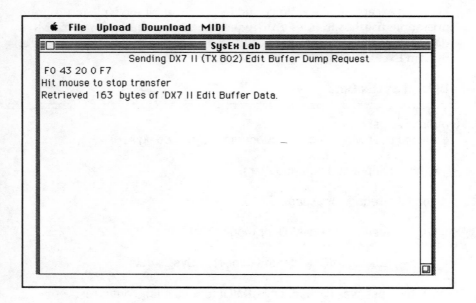

```
DoDX7:
   DumpFlag = DX7Flag
   GOSUB DX7Up
RETURN
```

When DX7 is selected from the menu, *DoDX7* is called. It assigns the *DumpFlag* variable the value of *DX7Flag*. This flag is used by the save routines to determine how many bytes to write to disk. After setting the flag, *DX7Up* is called.

```
DX7Up:
   PRINT ,"Sending DX7 II (TX 802) Edit Buffer Dump Request"
   GOSUB ClearMIDI
   ByteCount = DX7RequestSize%
   FOR J = 1 TO ByteCount
      X% = DX7DumpRequest(J)
      MIDIOut X%
      PRINT " " HEX$(X%);
   NEXT J
   PRINT
   result% =-1
   click% = 0
   PRINT "Hit mouse to stop transfer"
   WHILE result% = -1
      ON MOUSE GOSUB EndIt
      CALL GetMIDI(DX7$,0,count%,result%)
   WEND
   IF result% = 1 THEN
      PRINT "Time out error.  Edit buffer data not received."
      DumpFlag = noData 'reset dump flag on error
      RETURN
   END IF
   PRINT "Retrieved"count% "bytes of 'DX7 II Edit Buffer Data."
RETURN   'DX7up

EndIt:
   result% = 1
RETURN
```

This subroutine follows the basic design we presented at the beginning of this section. First, the routine prints a message informing the user which request is about to be sent. Then, ClearMIDI (which we looked at in the previous section) is called to clear the input and output buffers. We send the request message, one byte at a time, with the MIDIOut command. *ByteCount* is assigned the value of *DX7RequestSize%* which is used as the control variable of a FOR . . . NEXT loop. The loop is used to transmit each element of the *DX7Request* array. When each byte is transmitted, its hex value is printed in the program window.

After the entire message is transmitted, *GetMIDI* is called to retrieve a string of MIDI data from the input buffer. The size of the string must have been previously declared. For the DX7 dump we use the string *D/X/7$*. We set the size of the string with a "SPACE$(DX7Size%)" statement in the initialization block of the program. This is the size of a DX7 II *voice edit buffer dump* (163 bytes). The call to GetMIDI is placed inside a WHILE . . . WEND structure along with an ON MOUSE GOSUB statement (to allow the user to cancel the dump by clicking on the mouse).

The GetMIDI command has its own built-in timing function. When called, it will wait up to 1.5 seconds for the data string to arrive. If no data, or less data than the string size, has arrived within that time, GetMIDI returns an error in its *result%* parameter. If the value of result% is 1, a time out error occurred. If the value is 0, no error occurred. If there is an error, or the user clicks the mouse, the value of the result% variable is set to 1 and the WHILE . . . WEND structure stops. At that point, an error message is printed, the DumpFlag is set to the value of noData, and the program returns to the calling routine.

If the string is received as expected, DX7$ contains 163 bytes of data received from the DX7 and result% is set to 0. The WHILE . . . WEND structure stops and a message telling the user how many bytes were retrieved is printed.

CZ Voice Subroutines

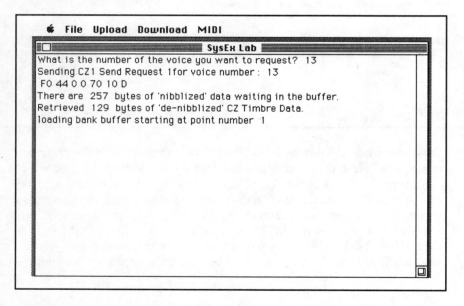

```
DoCZ1:
   DumpFlag = CZ1Flag
   voiceCount% = 1
   PRINT "What is the number of the voice you want to request";
   INPUT voice%
   CZRequest1(7) = voice%
   GOSUB CZ1Up
RETURN
```

When CZ Voice is selected from the menu, *DoCZ1* is called. It assigns the DumpFlag variable the value of *CZ1Flag*. Next, voiceCount% is set to 1 (more on voiceCount% later). After these two variables have been set, the user is prompted to enter a voice number. (This is the one command-line routine in the program.) The *voice%* variable is assigned the value of the voice number entered by the user. The value is inserted into byte 7 of the CZ request message with the "CZRequest1(7) = voice%" statement. The last step of the routine is to call the *CZ1Up* subroutine.

The DX7 dump was an example of a one-way protocol for sending and receiving System Exclusive data. The Mac sends a request message and the DX7 sends a data message. Neither the Mac nor the DX7 checks to see if its messages were received. Casio's CZ instruments use a handshaking protocol. Each device acknowledges that it has received a message before proceeding with the dump. The protocol is a kind of script that both the Mac and the CZ must follow. If the protocol isn't followed exactly, the dump will not be completed. Here is a step-by-step summary of the *Send1 request* protocol to use with CZ instruments:

1. The Mac transmits a *Send1* message for the requested voice number to the CZ and waits for it to send back a *Ready1* message.

2. The CZ acknowledges the *Send1* message by transmitting a *Ready1* message back to the Mac and waits for it to send a *Continue Message*.

3. The Mac acknowledges the *Ready1* message by transmitting a *Continue* message and waits for the CZ to send the *timbre data* for one voice.

4. The CZ acknowledges the *Continue* message by transmitting the *timbre data* for the requested voice to the Mac.

Here is the design we use for the CZ1 upload subroutine:

Upload CZ Timbre Data

```
CZ1 upload:
        tell the user what voice number has been requested

        clear the MIDI buffers

        transmit a Send1 request message

        wait for a Ready1 message


        if no Ready1 message is received:
                tell user an error occurred
                set DumpFlag to "noData"
                return to the calling routine

        if a Ready1 message was received OK:
                transmit a Continue message

        wait for the timbre data

        load the data into the CZBank
```

Here is the code for the subroutine:

```
CZ1Up:   'Upload CZ1 Voice Bulk data
    LOCATE 2,1
    CZRequest1(6) = &H10                      'op code for send1 request
    PRINT "Sending CZ1 Send Request 1 for voice number :" CZRequest1(7)
    GOSUB ClearMIDI
    GOSUB DoSend1
    GOSUB GetReady1
    IF result% = 1 THEN
        PRINT "Request unsuccessful, no response from CZ."
        DumpFlag = noData
        RETURN                                'do not continue with the rest of the routine
    END IF
    GOSUB DoContinue
    GOSUB GetTimbreData
    GOSUB LoadBank
RETURN    'CZ1up
```

CZ1Up calls on several other subroutines to handle the details of the data transfer. To perform each step of the Mac's part of the protocol, we use separate routines: *DoSend1*, *GetReady1*, *DoContinue*, and *GetTimbreData*.

```
DoSend1:
  ByteCount = CZRequest1Size%
  FOR J = 1 TO ByteCount
    X% = CZRequest1(J)
    MIDIOut X%
    PRINT " " HEX$(X%);
  NEXT J
  PRINT
RETURN
```

DoSend1 transmits the Send1 message to the CZ.

```
GetReady1:
Test% = -1
  WHILE Test% = -1                              'wait for CZ to handshake with a ready1 message
  CALL GetMIDI(temp1$, mode%,count%, result%)
  IF temp1$ = CHR$(&HF0) OR result% = 1 THEN
    Test% = 0
  END IF
WEND
IF result% = 1 THEN
    LOCATE 10,1
    PRINT "Time out error.   $F0 never received"
ELSE
WHILE Test% = 0
CALL GetMIDI(temp1$, mode%,count%, result%)
  IF temp1$ = CHR$(&H30) OR result% = 1 THEN
    Test% = -1
  END IF
WEND
IF result% = 1 THEN
    PRINT "Time out error. $30 never received"
END IF
END IF
RETURN
```

GetReady1 waits for the CZ to reply with a Ready1 message. The message is made up of two bytes: $F0 and $30. The GetReady1 subroutine waits for one byte to arrive in the input buffer by calling GetMIDI. (*Temp$* is a 1-byte string.) If the byte doesn't arrive, the value of result% is set to 1 and an error message is generated. If an $F0 arrives, a similar process is used to wait for a $30. When the program returns to CZ1Up, the value of result% is checked. If it is 1, an error message is printed, DumpFlag is set to the value or noData, and the program exits the subroutine. If result% is 0, CZ1Up proceeds with the protocol by calling *DoContinue*.

```
DoContinue:
  X% = &H70
  CALL MIDIOut(X%)
  X% = &H31
  CALL MIDIOut(X%)
RETURN
```

The Continue message also consists of two bytes: $70 and $31. DoContinue transmits them with two MIDIOut statements. After the Continue message is sent, CZ1Up calls GetTimbreData.

```
GetTimbreData:
  WHILE count% < RawTimbre1Size%      'wait for input buffer to fill with 257 bytes (the size of a voice dump)
    CALL InCount(count%)
  WEND
  PRINT "There are" count% "bytes of 'nibblized' data waiting in the buffer."
  DumpFlag = CZ1Flag   'set dump type to Jambox

  CALL GetMIDI(CZTimbre1$,loHiMode%,count%,result%)           'get the voice dump from the buffer
  PRINT "Retrieved"count% "bytes of 'de-nibblized' CZ Timbre Data."
RETURN
```

At this point, we assume that there really is a CZ instrument out there about to send a voice dump, so we don't do any more error checking. (However, it is always a good idea to check for errors *wherever* and *whenever* they may occur.) GetTimbreData waits for the input buffer to fill up with 257 bytes of MIDI data (the number of bytes a CZ transmits for a timbre dump). The *InCount* command is used since it will return the number of bytes in the buffer without removing them. (Successive calls to MIDIIn or GetMIDI can also be used to count the bytes in a buffer, but each call would remove data from the buffer. Calls to MIDIIn remove one byte at a time; calls to GetMIDI remove the number of bytes in its string variable each time.) When all 257 bytes have arrived, a message is printed informing the user, and DumplFlag is set to the value of CZ1Flag.

Casio and other manufacturers transmit their data in nibblized format. Each byte contains data in only the low-order bits of the byte. A single byte of internal Casio data is transmitted as two MIDI bytes. First, a MIDI byte containing the low-order bits of the internal data byte is sent, then a MIDI byte containing the high-order bits is sent. (These values are sent in the low bits of each MIDI byte.) Before your program uses the data, it should de-nibblize it. The GetMIDI command can do that for you. GetMIDI's mode%

parameter can be set for normal or nibblized formats. The *loHiMode%* variable in the statement, "CALL GetMIDI (CZTimbre1$, loHiMode%, count%, result%)," retrieves the data from the buffer *and* de-nibblizes it.

After the timbre data is loaded into *CZTimbre1$*, CZ1Up calls *LoadBank*.

```
LoadBank:
  startPoint% = (voiceCount% * CZTimbre1Size%)-(CZTimbre1Size%-1)
  PRINT "loading bank buffer starting at point number" startPoint%
  MID$(CZBank$,startPoint%) = CZTimbre1$
RETURN
```

We use LoadBank to load CZTimbre1$ into a buffer that can hold up to 100 sets of individual timbre data dumps. In the initialization block, we dimensioned a string variable, *CZBank$*, for this purpose. Its size is 12,900 bytes (100 times the size of a single timbre). Loading or unloading the bank is accomplished with BASIC's string manipulation features. We use MID$ to insert the entire CZTimbre1$ into CZBank$. The variable *startPoint%* is used to point to the starting byte in CZBank$ where CZTimbre1$ is inserted. The starting byte for 1 timbre dump is byte 1. There are 129 bytes in CZTimbre$, so the starting point for the second timbre dump is byte 130, the third is byte 259, and so on. LoadBank calculates the starting point, prints the value, and loads the timbre data into CZBank$.

CZ Bank Subroutines

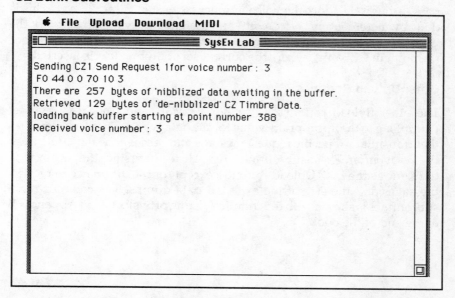

```
DoCZ32:
  DumpFlag = CZ32Flag
  voiceCount% = 1
  FOR voice% = CZBank1% TO CZBank32%
    CZRequest1(7) = voiceCount%  'put the voice number into the request
    GOSUB CZ1Up        ' go get the timbre data fo the voice
    IF result% = 1 THEN
      LOCATE 12,1
      PRINT "Bank dump has stopped after receiving voice number" voice%-1
      RETURN
    END IF
    voiceCount% = voiceCount%+1 'increment the voice being requested
    PRINT "Received voice number :"CZRequest1(7)
  NEXT voice%
RETURN
```

When the user selects CZ Bank, *DoCZ32* is called. This routine uses the values of *CZBank1* and *CZBank32* as the limits to a FOR . . . NEXT loop that calls the CZ1Up routine once for each pass through the loop. This allows us to get a successive series of CZ timbre data dumps from instruments like the CZ101, CZ1000, and CZ230s, which don't have bank dump capabilities. In the initialization block the values for CZBank1 and CZBank 32 are set to 0 and 3 to demonstrate a 4-voice dump. You can use any values from 0 to 99 for these variables. (The most flexible way to set the values would be to allow the user to enter the limits while the program is running.) With each pass through the loop, the voice number requested is raised by 1. This is done by incrementing *voiceCount%* and assigning its value to byte 7 of the CZ request message. LoadBank uses the voiceCount% variable to advance the point in CZBank$, where the current set of timbre data is inserted.

Other Upload Routines

The other upload routines, *DoJamBox*, *DoMSB*, and *DoLXP-1*, each set DumpFlag to the appropriate value for the data type, then call subroutines that transmit the specific request message and retrieve the bulk data from the input buffer. These subroutines are not listed here since they are exactly the same as the DX7 Upload routines, except for the difference in request messages and the size of the expected data dumps. The code for these subroutines is shown with the complete listing of SysEx Lab in Appendix B at the end of the book.

Saving Data to Disk

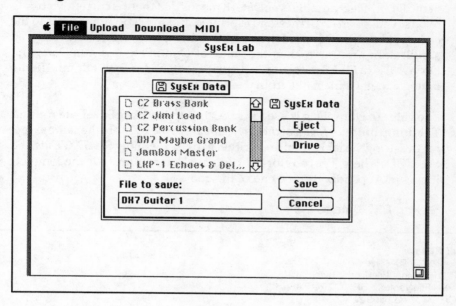

```
DoSave:
  IF DumpFlag = noData THEN
      PRINT "There is no data in the buffer to save."
      RETURN
  END IF
  FileName$=FILES$(0,"File to save:")
  IF FileName$="" THEN
      RETURN 'Cancel was selected
  END IF
  SELECT CASE DumpFlag
      CASE 1      :GOSUB SaveMSBData
      CASE 2      :GOSUB SaveJamData
      CASE 3      :GOSUB SaveDX7Data
      CASE 4      :GOSUB SaveLXPData
      CASE 5,6    :GOSUB SaveCZ1Data
      CASE ELSE
          PRINT "Unknown Dump type" DumpFlag
  END SELECT
RETURN
```

DoSave is called when the user selects save from the File menu. If the value of the DumpFlag variable is noData, it means that there is currently no data to be saved, so an error message is printed and the program returns to the calling subroutine. If one of the Upload routines has successfully retrieved a bulk dump message, then the value of DumpFlag is not noData, and DoSave uses a FILE$ statement to display the standard Save File mini finder dialog and get a file name from the user.

The value of DumpFlag is used to select the appropriate SaveData routine. The dump routines for all of the devices (except the CZs) are the same except for the string variables that are written to disk. We show *SaveDX7Data* and *SaveCZData* here. The code for all of the SaveData routines is in the complete listing in Appendix B at the end of the book.

Saving DX7 Data to Disk

```
SaveDX7Data:
   FileSize% =DX7Size%
   PRINT"Saving" FileSize% "bytes…"
   OPEN FileName$ FOR OUTPUT AS #1
   FOR J = 1  TO FileSize%
      LOCATE 3,1
      WRITE #1,ASC(MID$(DX7$,J,1))
      PRINT "Byte :" J,"Hex Value:"HEX$(ASC(MID$(DX7$,J,1)))
   NEXT J
   CLOSE #1
   PRINT
   NAME FileName$ AS FileName$,"sXl1"                    'types file as one way data
RETURN
```

SaveDX7Data sets the *FileSize%* variable to the value of DX7% and prints the value. Then it opens a file (already named by the user in the DoSave subroutine) for output and uses a FOR...NEXT loop to write the string, one byte at a time, to disk. The ASC command is used to convert the string byte from a character to its ASCII value as it is written to disk. We've included print statements that print the number of the byte being written and its value. The LOCATE command resets the pen to the same position for each print statement, so no time is spent on scrolling text as the dump proceeds. After all of the bytes in the string have been converted and written to disk, the file is closed and renamed. The NAME...AS statement appends "sXl1" to the file name. This will allow us to view only files of this type when we want to download files using the one-way transfer routines.

Saving CZ Data to Disk

```
SaveCZ1Data:
  FileSize% = (startPoint% + CZTimbre1Size%)-1
  PRINT"Saving" FileSize% "bytes…"
  PRINT "length of CZBank$is " LEN(CZBank$)
  OPEN FileName$ FOR OUTPUT AS #1
  FOR J = 1  TO FileSize%
     LOCATE 3,1
     WRITE #1,ASC(MID$(CZBank$,J,1))
     PRINT "Byte :" J,"Hex Value:"HEX$(ASC(MID$(CZBank$,J,1)))
  NEXT J
  CLOSE #1
  PRINT
  NAME FileName$ AS FileName$,"sXl2" 'types file as CZ Timbre data
RETURN
```

SaveCZData is only slightly different from the other SaveData routines. Here, the value of FileSize% is calculated by adding the current value of startPoint% to CZTimbre1Size%, then subtracting 1 from the total. This will give us the number of bytes in CZBank$ that currently hold timbre data. The number will change depending on how many voices were received from the CZ. The names of CZ data files are tagged with "sXL2" to allow us to view only CZ data files when we want to download files using the handshaking transfer routines.

Download Operations

The download operations allow the user to open files previously saved to disk with SaveData routines and transmit them through the MIDI OUT port. Most MIDI devices use a one-way transfer method to receive SysEx data. If the device is enabled to receive SysEx messages, it will load any properly formatted bulk data it receives. We use the subroutine *DoOneWay* to send files to this type of device. Other MIDI devices use a handshaking protocol similar to the CZ protocol presented previously. We use the *DoHandShake* subroutine to handle the required protocol for sending timbre data to CZ instruments.

OneWay Subroutine

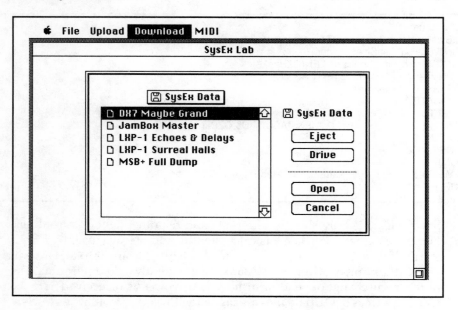

```
DoOneWay:
  FileName$=FILES$(1,"sXl1")
  IF FileName$="" THEN
     RETURN
  END IF
  PRINT FileName$ " is being transmitted."
  ByteCount% = 1
  OPEN FileName$ FOR INPUT AS#1
     WHILE NOT EOF(1)
       INPUT #1, X%
       LOCATE 3,1
       PRINT "Byte :" ByteCount%,"Hex Value:"HEX$(X%)
       ByteCount% = ByteCount% +1
       CALL MIDIOut(X%)
     WEND
  CLOSE #1
RETURN
```

DoOneWay uses a FILE$ statement to display the standard Open File mini finder dialog window. It will only show files that have been previously saved and tagged with "sXl1" when the user selects a file to open.

A message is printed showing the name of the file. The file is opened for input and a WHILE ... WEND structure is used to input the file one byte at a time. Each byte is transmitted with a MIDIOut statement. The number of the byte and its hex value are printed.

Handshake Subroutines

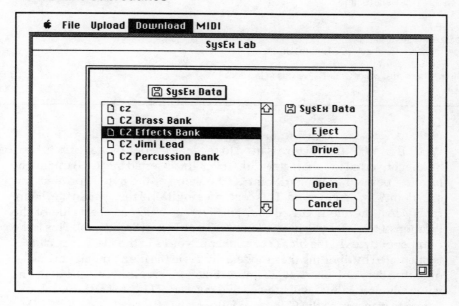

```
DoHandShake:
  voiceCount% = 0
  FileName$=FILES$(1,"sXI2")
  IF FileName$="" THEN
    RETURN
  END IF
  GOSUB FillBank
  PRINT "This file is "FileSize% "bytes long."
  GOSUB TransmitCZData
RETURN
```

DoHandshake sets *voiceCount%* to 0, then uses FILE$ to display the Open File mini finder dialog window. It displays only files that have been previously saved and tagged with "sXl2". When the user selects a file to open, *FillBank* is called.

```
FillBank:
  startPoint% = 1
  OPEN FileName$ FOR INPUT AS #1
  WHILE NOT EOF(1)
    INPUT#1, X%
    MID$(CZBank$,startPoint%,1)=CHR$(X%)
    startPoint% = startPoint%+1
  WEND
  CLOSE #1
  FileSize% = startPoint%-1
  voiceCount% = FileSize%/CZTimbre1Size%
  LOCATE 5,1
  PRINT "There are " voiceCount% "voices in the file."
RETURN
```

FIllBank sets startPoint% to 1 and opens the user-selected file for input. A WHILE . . . WEND structure is used to read the file one byte at a time. Each byte is converted to a character with CHR$ and inserted into CZBank$ at the location pointed at by startPoint%. The value of the byte is printed and startPoint% is incremented. This continues until all of the bytes in the file are read. Then the file is closed and FileSize% is assigned the value of the location of the last byte inserted into CZBank$ (startPoint% - 1). This is the number of bytes in the file. The number of voices in the file, vo*iceCount%*, is calculated by dividing the number of bytes in the file by the size of one set of timbre data (FileSize% / CZTimbre1Size%). This number is printed. The value of voiceCount% will be used by *TransmitCZData* to set the number of voices to transmit to the CZ. After FillBank has finished, *TransmitCZData* is called.

```
TransmitCZData:
  startPoint% = 1
  CZRequest1(6) = &H20           'op code for receive1 request
  CZRequest1(7) = 96             'first programmable voice on CZ-230S
  FOR Z = 1 TO voiceCount%
    CZTimbre1$=MID$(CZBank$,startPoint%,CZTimbre1Size%)
    LOCATE 2,1
    PRINT "Sending CZ1 Receive Request 1 for voice number :" CZRequest1(7)
    GOSUB ClearMIDI
    GOSUB DoSend1
    GOSUB GetReady1
    IF result% = 1 THEN
      PRINT "Request unsuccessful, no response from CZ."
      RETURN                     'dont continue with the rest of the routine
```

```
END IF
CALL SendMIDI(CZTimbre1$,loHiMode%)
X% = &HF7                    'be sure to complete the handshake!
CALL MIDIOut(X%)
startPoint% = startPoint% + CZTimbre1Size%
PRINT "transmitted voice number" CZRequest1(7)
CZRequest1(7) = CZRequest1(7)+1
NEXT Z
RETURN
```

TransmitCZData resets startPoint% to 1 and loads the value $20 into byte 6 of CZRequest1. This is the *op code* byte of the message and the new value changes it from a Send1 message to a Receive1 message. Next, the 96 is loaded into byte 7 of the message. This is the voice number of the first *programmable* voice on a CZ 230s. You can modify this to any number from 0-99, or add a routine that allows the user to enter the value. Next, a FOR . . . NEXT loop is set up using the value of voiceCount% as the upper limit. This allows the routine to transmit the number of voices in the opened file.

For each pass in the loop, a separate set of voice data is transmitted. First, the timbre data for one voice is copied from CZBank$ and inserted into CZTimbre1$. This is done with the MID$ statement. Then a message informs the user which voice number is about to be sent, and the input and output buffers are cleared.

At this point, it is necessary to follow a strict handshaking protocol to send the data for the voice to the CZ. Here is a step-by-step summary of the single-voice *Receive1 request* protocol to use with CZ instruments:

1. The Mac transmits a *Receive1* message for the voice number to be sent to the CZ and waits for it to send back a *Ready1* message.

2. The CZ acknowledges the *Receive1* message by transmitting a *Ready1* message back to the Mac and waits for it to send the *timbre data* for the the voice.

3. The Mac acknowledges the *Ready1* message by transmitting the *timbre data* for the requested voice to the CZ.

4. After sending the *timbre data*, the Mac must send an EOX (End Of Exclusive) byte to signal the CZ that the dump is done.

We use the *DoSend1* routine to send the Ready1 message (since we changed the CZRequest1 array from a Send1 message to a Receive1 message), and GetReady1 to check for a Ready1 message. We've already looked over both of these routines in *CZ Voice Subroutines*, so we won't show the code again here. After the Ready1 message has been received, MIDIOut is called to transmit the data in CZTimbre1$ to the CZ. The mode parameter of MIDIOut is set to the value of loHiMode%. This nibblizes the data into the proper Casio format as it is transmitted to the CZ. Once all of the timbre data has been transmitted, MIDIOut is called to send the 1-byte EOX message required at the end of a dump.

Next, the startPoint% value is increased to point to the start of the next data block in CZBank$, a message is printed confirming that voice was sent, and the value of the voice number byte in the request message is incremented by 1.

This entire transmit process is repeated once for each voice contained in the file opened by the user.

MIDI Operations

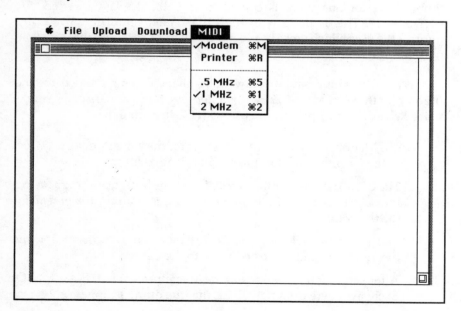

```
MIDICmd:
  SELECT CASE MenuItem
    CASE 1   :GOSUB DoModem
    CASE 2   :GOSUB DoPrinter
    CASE 4   :GOSUB DoHalfMeg
    CASE 5   :GOSUB DoOneMeg
    CASE 6   :GOSUB DoTwoMeg
    CASE ELSE
      PRINT "Undefined menu item."
  END SELECT
  PRINT "Reseting Interface"
  CALL MIDIPort(clockRate%)          'reset the MIDI clock rate
  CALL MIDIPort(port%)               'reset the MIDI port
RETURN
```

When the user selects an item in the MIDI menu, *MIDICmd* selects the subroutine for the appropriate item. Depending on the subroutine selected, the value of either *cloclRate%* or *port%* is updated. After the subroutine has finished updating the variable, the interface configuration is reset with two calls to MIDIPort.

Each of the possible interface configuration parameters for SysEx Lab is displayed as items in the MIDI menu. The parameters currently selected are indicated by placing a check mark to the right of the selected item. The check mark is drawn, or hidden, by using *CheckOn* or *CheckOff* in a QuickBASIC MENU statement.

Modem Subroutine

```
DoModem:
  MENU 4,1,CheckOn                   'reset modem item check mark
  MENU 4,2, CheckOff                 'reset printer item check mark
  port% = modem%
RETURN
```

When Modem is selected from the menu, the Modem item is checked, the Printer item is unchecked, and the port% variable is set to the value of *modem%*.

Printer Subroutine

```
DoPrinter:
  MENU 4,1,CheckOff                  'reset modem item check mark
  MENU 4,2, CheckOn                  'reset printer item check mark
  port% = printer%
RETURN
```

When Printer is selected from the menu, the Printer item is checked, the Modem item is unchecked, and the port% variable is set to the value of *printer%*.

HalfMeg Subroutine

```
DoHalfMeg:
  MENU 4,4,CheckOn          'reset .5 MHz item check mark
  MENU 4,5, CheckOff        'reset 1 MHz item check mark
  MENU 4,6, CheckOff        'reset 2 MHz item check mark
  clockRate% = halfMeg%
RETURN
```

When .5 MHz is selected from the menu, the .5 MHz item is checked, the 1 MHz and 2 MHz items are unchecked, and the port% variable is set to the value of *halfMeg5%*.

OneMeg Subroutine

```
DoOneMeg:
  MENU 4,4,CheckOff         'reset .5 mHz item check mark
  MENU 4,5, CheckOn         'reset 1 mHz item check mark
  MENU 4,6, CheckOff        'reset 2 mHz item check mark
  clockRate% = oneMeg%
RETURN
```

When 1 MHz is selected from the menu, the 1 MHz item is checked, the .5 MHz and 2 MHz items are unchecked, and the port% variable is set to the value of *oneMeg%*.

TwoMeg Subroutine

```
DoTwoMeg:
  MENU 4,4,CheckOff         'reset .5 mHz item check mark
  MENU 4,5, CheckOff        'reset 1 mHz item check mark
  MENU 4,6, CheckOn         'reset 2 mHz item check mark
  clockRate% = twoMeg%
RETURN
```

When 2 MHz is selected from the menu, the 2 MHz item is checked, the .5 MHz and 1 MHz items are unchecked, and the port% variable is set to the value of *twoMeg%*.

Part Six

Appendixes

Appendix A

Procedure and Function Listing for Real-Time MIDI Lab

```
{FIle name:  RTL 00 Globals                                           }
{Description:   Globals for Real Time MIDI Lab program                 }
{Original Date: 9/16/88      By: SDF                                   }


UNIT RTLabGlobals;

INTERFACE

   CONST

      On = TRUE;
      Off = FALSE;
      InSize = 1900;                          {MIDI Input buffer size}
      OutSize = 1900;                         {MIDI Output buffer size

{Constants for MIDI functions and general MIDI processing}
      StatusMask = $F0;
      ChannelMask = $0F;
      Channel16 = 16;
      Channel1 = 1;

{MIDI Status Bytes}
      AllNotesData = $7B;
      NoteOff = $80;
      NoteOn = $90;
      PolyPressure = $A0;
      ControlChange = $B0;
      ProgramChange = $C0;
      ChannelPressure = $D0;
      PitchBend = $E0;
      SystemMessage = $F0;
      QuarterFrame = $F1;
      SongPointer = $F2;
      SongSelect = $F3;
      TuneRequest = $F6;
      EOX = $F7;
      MIDIClock = $F8;
      MIDIStart = $FA;
      MIDIContinue = $FB;
      MIDIStop = $FC;
      ActiveSense = $FE;
      SystemReset = $FF;
```

```
{MIDI Controller ID's}
      ModController = 1;
      BreathController = 2;
      FootController = 4;
      PTimeController = 5;
      DataEntryMSB = 6;
      VolumeController = 7;
      BalanceController = 8;
      PanController = 10;
      SustainSwitch = 64;
      PortamentoSwitch = 65;
      SostentutoSwitch = 66;
      SoftPedalSwitch = 67;
      DataIncrement = 96;
      DataDecrement = 97;
      LocalControl = 122;
      AllNotesOff = 123;

{constants for MIDI  procedures and functions}
      MaxStatusValue = 255;
      MaxDataValue = 127;
      minDataValue = 0;
      MinOnVelocity = 1;
      OffVelocity = 0;
      MiddleC = 60;
      twoOctaves = 24;
      Forte = 127;
      minorThird = 3;
      majorThird = 4;
      Triad = 2;
      seventhChord = 7;
      Polyphony = 4;
      ScaleSize = 12;

{errorList array codes}
      dataValueCode = 1;
      lengthValueCode = 2;
      speedValueCode = 3;
      byteValueCode = 4;
      polyphonyValueCode = 5;
      channelValueCode = 6;
      controlValueCode = 7;
      scaleValueCode = 8;
      statusValueCode = 9;
      harmonyValueCode = 10;
      durationValueCode = 11;
      delayValueCode = 12;
```

```
{constants for QuickDraw routines in Display Data routines}
      Column1 = 25;
      Row1 = 40;
      VerticalLimit = 190;
      HorizontalLimit = 375;
      vertOffset = 10;
      horzOffset = 35;

   TYPE
{useful variable types for MIDI processing routines}

      MPFilterArray = ARRAY[0..8] OF integer;
      RSFilterArray = ARRAY[1..5] OF integer;
      ChannelArray = ARRAY[Channel1..Channel16] OF integer;
      MIDIData = 0..MaxDataValue;
      MIDIStatus = 128..MaxStatusValue;
      MIDIByte = 0..255;
      ChordLimit = 1..Polyphony;
      MIDIDataArray = ARRAY[0..MaxDataValue] OF MIDIData;
      ChordArray = ARRAY[1..Polyphony] OF MIDIData;
      ScaleArray = ARRAY[1..ScaleSize] OF integer;
      MIDIMessage = RECORD
          size, status, data1, data2: integer
        END;
      MIDIMessageList = ARRAY[1..9] OF MIDIMessage;


   VAR
{variables used by  Real Time MIDI Lab}

      tRect, grfxrect, dataDrawRect: Rect;      {for QuickDraw}
      tabCount: integer;
      textRect, drawRect, dataRect: rect;

      theEvent: EventRecord;
      TheWindow: windowptr;
      TheDialog: DialogPtr;

      anyChanges: boolean;                {flag returns DONE or CANCEL results from DoDlogs}
      Quitting, Finished: boolean;        {flags  to signal shut down}
      DAOpened :boolean;                  {flag tells DoEvent to quit DA}
      ErrorList: ARRAY[dataValueCode..delayValueCode] OF str255;

{global variables for initializing  MIDI routines}

{MIDI Configuration }
      theSCSI, ClockMhz: integer;

{MIDIPascal Filters }
      MPFilters: MPFilterArray;
```

{Note Test}
    theNote, theVelocity: MIDIData;
    theDuration: integer;

{Keyboard test}
    StartNote, EndNote: MIDIData;
    ArpLength, ArpSpeed: integer;

{Send Message }
    SendList: MIDIMessageList;

    MNoteOn, MNoteOff, MCChange, MPChange, MSSelect, MTRqst: MIDIMessage;
    MStart, MStop, MContinue: MIDIMessage;

    theStatus: MIDIStatus;
    theData1: MIDIData;
    theData2: MIDIData;

{Thru Test }
    ThruTestFlag: boolean;
    testByte: MIDIByte;
    repeatCount: integer;

{THRU Routines}

    RunningStatus, theMIDIByte, Transpose, byteCount: integer;
    SkipByte: Boolean;

{Running Status Filters}
    RSFilters: RSFilterArray;

{Channel Mapping}
    ChanMaps: ChannelArray;
    ChanMapOffsetFlag, ChanMapReassignFlag: integer;

{Controller Mapping}
    ControlMaps: MIDIDataArray;
    CntrlInvertFlag, CntrlScaleFlag: integer;
    CntrlOffset: MIDIData;
    CntrlSFactor: integer;

{Program Change Mapping}
    ProgramMaps: MIDIDataArray;

{Velocity Mapping}
    VInvertFlag, VScaleFlag, VFixedFlag: integer;
    VOffset: MIDIData;
    VSFactor: integer;

```
{Transpose}
     HiTransposeNote, LoTransposeNote: MIDIData;
     NoteMap: MIDIDataArray;
     KeyTranspose: integer;

{Auto Harmony}
     HiHarmonyNote, LoHarmonyNote: MIDIData;
     HarmonyMap: ChordArray;
     HarmonySize: ChordLimit;

{ScaleMap}
     ScaleMap: ScaleArray;
     ScaleName: str255;

IMPLEMENTATION

END.
```

```
{FIle name: RTL 01 Menu Globals                              }
{Description:   Menu Globals for Real Time MIDI Lab program  }
{Original Date: 9/16/88        By: SDF                       }

UNIT RTLabMenuGlobals;
INTERFACE

    CONST                                 { these are the globals values for RTL's menus}
      AboutAlertID = 1313;                {alert for About RTL... item}
      DisplayDLOG = 101;                  {dialog window for  Panic & Display Data}
      MenuBottom = 20;                    {height of menu bar}

    {APPLE menu}
      AppleMenuID = 1;                    { resource ID of Apple menu}
      AboutItem = 1;

    {FILE menu}
      FileMenuID = 101;
      QuitItem = 1;

    {MIDI menu}
      MIDIMenuID = 102;
      ConfigureItem = 1;
      MIDIFiltersItem = 2;

    {OUT menu}
      OutMenuID = 103;
      NoteTestItem = 1;
      KeyTestItem = 2;
      SendItem = 4;
      PanicItem = 6;

  {THRU menu}
      ThruMenuID = 104;
      ThruTestItem = 1;
      ThruItem = 3;
      DataDisplayItem = 4;
      RSFilterItem = 5;
      ChanFilterItem = 6;

  {MAPPING menu}
      MapMenuID = 105;
      ChannelMapItem = 1;
      ControlMapItem = 3;
      ProgramMapItem = 4;
      VelocityMapItem = 5;
      TransposeMapItem = 7;
      HarmonyMapItem = 8;

    VAR
      AppleMenu, FileMenu, MIDIMenu, OutMenu, ThruMenu, MapMenu: MenuHandle;

IMPLEMENTATION
END.
```

```
{FIle name:  RTI Dlog Globals}
{Description:   Dialog Globals for Real Time MIDI Lab program}
{Original Date: 9/16/88          By: SDF}

{Resource fille:              <<RTLAB0.rsrc>>}

UNIT RTLResourceIDs;

INTERFACE

  CONST

{MIDI Menu Dialogs}

{     Configure  Resource ID's            }
      MIDISetupDlogID = 104;
      CancelDlogItem = 1;
      DoneDlogItem = 2;
      ModemDlogItem = 3;
      PrinterDlogItem = 4;
      HalfMegDlogItem = 5;
      OneMegDlogItem = 6;
      TwoMegDlogItem = 7;

{     MIDI Pascal Filter  Resource ID's    }
      MPFilterDlogID = 102;
      MPFCancelItem = 1;
      MPFDoneItem = 2;
      MPFActiveOn = 3;
      MPFActiveOff = 4;
      MPFClockOn = 5;
      MPFClockOff = 6;
      MPFClkCmdOn = 7;
      MPFClkCmdOff = 8;
      MPFChangeOn = 9;
      MPFChangeOff = 10;
      MPFAfterTouchOn = 11;
      MPFAfterTouchOff = 12;
      MPFCntrlOn = 13;
      MPFCntrlOff = 14;
      MPFBendOn = 15;
      MPFBendOff = 16;
      MPFSysExOn = 17;
      MPFSysExOff = 18;

{     Panic Resource IDs                }
      PanicDlogID = 101;
```

```
{OUT Menu Dialogs                      }

{      Note Test  Resource IDs         }
       NoteTestDlogID = 200;
       NTestPlayItem = 1;
       NTestCancelItem = 2;
       NTestNoteItem = 3;
       NTestVelocityItem = 4;
       NTestDurationItem = 5;

{      Keyboard Test Resource IDs      }
       KTestDlogID = 201;
       KTestPlayItem = 1;
       KTestCancelItem = 2;
       KTestStartItem = 3;
       KTestEndItem = 4;
       KTestLengthItem = 5;
       KTestSpeedItem = 6;

{      Send ResourceIDs                }
       SendTransmitItem = 1;
       SendCancelItem = 2;
       SendDlogID = 202;
       SendNoteOnItem = 3;
       SendNoteOffItem = 4;
       SendCChangeItem = 5;
       SendPChangeItem = 6;
       SendSSelectItem = 7;
       SendTuneRqstItem = 8;
       SendStartItem = 9;
       SendStopItem = 10;
       SendContinueItem = 11;
       SendStatusItem = 12;
       SendData1Item = 13;
       SendData2Item = 14;

{THRU Menu Dialogs                     }

       DataWindowID = 217; {resource ID of data display window}

{      ThruTest Resource IDs           }
       ThruTestDlogID = 204;
       ThruTestRunItem = 1;
       ThruTestCancelItem = 2;
       ThruTestSendItem = 3;
       ThruTestRepeatItem = 4;
```

```
{     Running Status Filter Resource IDs     }
      RSFilterDlogID = 207;
      RSFilterCancelItem = 1;
      RSFilterDoneItem = 2;
      RSFilterNoteItem = 3;
      RSFilterPPressItem = 4;
      RSFilterCChangeItem = 5;
      RSFilterATouchItem = 6;
      RSFilterPBendItem = 7;


{MIDI MAPPING Menu Dialogs                    }

{     Channel Map ResourceIDs                 }
      ChanMapDlogID = 209;
      ChanMapCancelItem = 1;
      ChanMapDoneItem = 2;
      ChanMapClearItem = 3;
      ChanMapSourceItem = 4;
      ChanMapDestItem = 5;


{     Control Mapping Resource IDs            }
      ControlMapDlogID = 215;
      ControlDoneItem = 1;
      ControlClearItem = 2;
      ControlCancelItem = 3;
      ControlOffsetItem = 4;
      ControlSFactorItem = 5;
      ControlInvertItem = 6;
      ControlScaleItem = 7;
      ControlSourceItem = 8;
      ControlTargetItem = 9;


{     Program Change Map Resource IDs         }
      PChangeMapDlogID = 210;
      PChangeCancelItem = 1;
      PChangeDoneItem = 2;
      PChangeClearItem = 3;
      PChangeMapItem = 4;
      PChangeToItem = 5;


{     Velocity Map Resource IDs               }
      VelocityMapDlogID = 211;
      VCancelItem = 1;
      VDoneItem = 2;
      VInvertItem = 3;
      VScaleItem = 4;
      VFixedItem = 5;
      VOffsetItem = 6;
      VSFactorItem = 7;
```

```
{      Key Transpose Resource IDs             }
       TransposeDlogID = 212;
       TransposeClearItem = 1;
       TransposeCancelItem = 2;
       TransposeDoneItem = 3;
       TransposeHiNoteItem = 4;
       TransposeLoNoteItem = 5;
       TransposeKeyShiftItem = 6;


{      Auto Harmony Resource IDs              }
       HarmonyDlogID = 213;
       HarmonizeItem = 1;
       HarmonyDoneItem = 2;
       HarmonyNewScaleItem = 3;
       HarmonyHiNoteItem = 4;
       HarmonyLoNoteItem = 5;
       HarmonyPolyItem = 6;
       HarmonyScaleMapItem = 7;


{      Scale Map ResourceIDs                  }
       ScaleMapDlogId = 214;
       ScaleMapDoneItem = 1;
       ScaleMapCancelItem = 2;
       ScaleMapClearItem = 3;
       ScaleMapCItem = 4;
       ScaleMapCsItem = 5;
       ScaleMapDItem = 6;
       ScaleMapDsitem = 7;
       ScaleMapEItem = 8;
       ScaleMapFItem = 9;
       ScaleMapFsItem = 10;
       ScaleMapGItem = 11;
       ScaleMapGsItem = 12;
       ScaleMapAItem = 13;
       ScaleMapAsItem = 14;
       ScaleMapBItem = 15;
       ScaleMapNameItem = 16;



IMPLEMENTATION

END.{RTLDlogGlobals}
```

```
{FIle name: RTL 03 Init procs                                                    }
{Description:   Initialization routines for Real Time MIDI Lab }
{Original Date: 9/16/88          By: SDF                                          }


UNIT InitProcedures;

INTERFACE
   USES
      MIDIPascal, RTLabGlobals, RTLabMenuGlobals, MPascalTools;

   PROCEDURE InitRTLab;
   PROCEDURE InitControllerMaps;
   PROCEDURE InitScaleMap;
   PROCEDURE InitTranspose;

IMPLEMENTATION

{————————————————————————————————————————}
PROCEDURE MIDIInit;
   BEGIN
      InitMidi(InSize, OutSize);{initialize MIDIPascal}
      DoActiveSenseFilter;   {filter out Active Sensing}
      SetMIDIPort; {set to theSCSI and ClockMhz, clear and enable buffers}
   END; {MIDIInit}

{————————————————————————————————————————}
PROCEDURE InitErrorList;
   BEGIN
      {error messages for CheckValue function calls}
      ErrorList[dataValueCode] := 'MIDI data values must be between 0 - 127';
      ErrorList[lengthValueCode] := 'Length values must be between 1 - 8';
      ErrorList[speedValueCode] := 'Speed values must be between 1- 15';
      ErrorList[byteValueCode] := 'MIDI byte values must be between 0 - 255';
      ErrorList[polyphonyValueCode] := 'Polyphony values must be between 1-4';
      ErrorList[channelValueCode] := 'Channel values must be between 1-16';
      ErrorList[controlValueCode] := 'Control values must be between 1- 97';
      ErrorList[scaleValueCode] := 'Scale factor values must be ± 10';
      ErrorList[statusValueCode] := 'Status values must between 128 - 255';
      ErrorList[harmonyValueCode] := 'Harmony values must be ± 24';
      ErrorList[durationValueCode] := 'Duration values must be 0 - 100';
      ErrorList[delayValueCode] := 'Delay values must be 0-60';
   END; {InitErrorList}


{————————————————————————————————————————}
   PROCEDURE InitConfiguration;
   BEGIN
{    MIDI Configuration }
      theSCSI := commPort;
      ClockMhz := oneMeg;
   END;


{————————————————————————————————————————}
```

277

```
PROCEDURE InitMPFilters;
  VAR
    count: integer;
BEGIN
{   MIDIPascal Filters }
  FOR count := resetFilters TO filter8 DO
    MPFilters[count] := 0;
  MPFilters[filter1] := 1;                      {set filter1 (Active Sensing) on}
END; {InitMPFilters}

{————————————————————————————————————————}
PROCEDURE InitNoteTest;
BEGIN
{   Note Test }
  theNote := MiddleC;
  theVelocity := Forte;
  theDuration := 1;
END;

{————————————————————————————————————————}
PROCEDURE InitKeyboardTest;
BEGIN
{   Keyboard test}
  StartNote := MiddleC;
  EndNote := MiddleC + 24;
  ArpLength := 4;
  ArpSpeed := 1;
END; {InitKeyboardTest }

{————————————————————————————————————————}
PROCEDURE InitSendMessage;
BEGIN
{   Send Message }
  WITH MNoteOn DO
    BEGIN
      size := 3;
      status := NoteOn;
      data1 := MiddleC;
      data2 := Forte;
    END;
  SendList[1] := MNoteOn;

  WITH MNoteOff DO
    BEGIN
      size := 3;
      status := NoteOff;
      data1 := MiddleC;
      data2 := 0;
    END;
  SendList[2] := MNoteOff;
```

```
WITH MCChange DO
   BEGIN
      size := 3;
      status := ControlChange;
      data1 := ModController;
      data2 := Forte;
   END;
SendList[3] := MCChange;

WITH MPChange DO
   BEGIN
      size := 2;
      status := ProgramChange;
      data1 := 0;
      data2 := -1;
   END;
SendList[4] := MPChange;

WITH MSSelect DO
   BEGIN
      size := 2;
      status := SongSelect;
      data1 := 0;
      data2 := -1;
   END;
SendList[5] := MSSelect;

WITH MTRqst DO
   BEGIN
      size := 1;
      status := TuneRequest;
      data1 := -1;
      data2 := -1;
   END;
SendList[6] := MTRqst;

WITH MStart DO
   BEGIN
      size := 1;
      status := MIDIStart;
      data1 := -1;
      data2 := -1;
   END;
SendList[7] := MStart;

WITH MStop DO
   BEGIN
      size := 1;
      status := MIDIStop;
      data1 := -1;
      data2 := -1;
   END;
SendList[8] := MStop;
```

```
    WITH MContinue DO
      BEGIN
        size := 1;
        status := MIDIContinue;
        data1 := -1;
        data2 := -1;
      END;
    SendList[9] := MContinue;

  END; {InitSendMessage}


{—————————————————————————————}
  PROCEDURE InitThruTest;
  BEGIN
{    Thru Test }
    testByte := EOX;
    repeatCount := 10;
  END; { InitThruTest}


{—————————————————————————————}
  PROCEDURE InitRSFilters;
    VAR
      count: integer;
  BEGIN
{    Running Status Filters}
    FOR count := 1 TO 5 DO
      RSFilters[count] := 0;
  END; {InitRSFilters }


{—————————————————————————————}
  PROCEDURE InitChannelMaps;
    VAR
      count: integer;
  BEGIN
{    Channel Mapping}
    FOR count := Channel1 TO Channel16 DO
      ChanMaps[count] := count;

    ChanMapOffsetFlag := 1;
  END; { InitChannelMaps}


{—————————————————————————————}
  PROCEDURE InitControllerMaps;
    VAR
      count: integer;
  BEGIN
{    Controller Mapping}
    FOR count := ModController TO DataDecrement DO
      ControlMaps[count] := count;

    CntrlInvertFlag := 0;
    CntrlScaleFlag := 0;
    CntrlOffset := 0;
    CntrlSFactor := 1;
  END; {InitChannelMaps }
```

```
{————————————————————————————————}
    PROCEDURE InitPrgrmChangeMaps;
      VAR
        count: integer;
    BEGIN
{     Program Change Mapping}
      FOR count := 0 TO MaxDataValue DO
        ProgramMaps[count] := count;
    END; {InitPrgrmChangeMaps }


{————————————————————————————————}
    PROCEDURE InitVelocity;
    BEGIN
{     Velocity Mapping}
      VInvertFlag := 0;
      VScaleFlag := 0;
      VFixedFlag := 0;
      VOffset := 0;
      VSFactor := 1;
    END; { InitVelocity}


{————————————————————————————————}
    PROCEDURE InitTranspose;
      VAR
        count: integer;
    BEGIN
{     Transpose}
      FOR count := 0 TO MaxDataValue DO
        NoteMap[count] := count;
      HiTransposeNote := MiddleC + twoOctaves;
      LoTransposeNote := MiddleC;
      KeyTranspose := 0;
    END; { InitTranspose}


{————————————————————————————————}
    PROCEDURE InitAutoHarmony;
      VAR
        count: integer;
    BEGIN
{     Auto Harmony}
      FOR count := 1 TO ScaleSize DO
        HarmonyMap[count] := majorThird;

      HiHarmonyNote := MiddleC + twoOctaves;
      LoHarmonyNote := MiddleC;
      HarmonySize := Triad;
    END; { InitAutoHarmony}


{————————————————————————————————}
```

```
   PROCEDURE InitScaleMap;
     VAR
        count: integer;
   BEGIN
{    ScaleMap}
     FOR count := 1 TO ScaleSize DO
        ScaleMap[count] := 4;
     ScaleName := 'Major Thirds';
   END; { }
```

```
{————————————————————————————————}
   PROCEDURE InitParameters;
   BEGIN
     {global variables for initializing  MIDI routines}
     anyChanges := False;
     InitErrorList;
     InitConfiguration;
     InitMPFilters;
     InitNoteTest;
     InitKeyboardTest;
     InitSendMessage;
     InitThruTest;
     InitRSFilters;
     InitChannelMaps;
     InitControllerMaps;
     InitPrgrmChangeMaps;
     InitVelocity;
     InitAutoHarmony;
     InitScaleMap;
     InitTranspose;
   END;{InitParameters}
```

```
{————————————————————————————————}
   PROCEDURE SetUpAppleMenu;
   BEGIN
     AppleMenu := NewMenu(AppleMenuID, Chr(20));
     AppendMenu(AppleMenu, 'About Real Time MIDI Lab... ');
     AppendMenu(AppleMenu, '————————————————');
     AddResMenu(AppleMenu, 'DRVR');              {add DA names to menu}
     InsertMenu(AppleMenu, 0);

   END;{ SetUpAppleMenu }
```

```
{————————————————————————————————}
   PROCEDURE SetUpFileMenu;
   BEGIN
     FileMenu := NewMenu(FileMenuID, 'File');
     AppendMenu(FileMenu, 'Quit');
     InsertMenu(FileMenu, 0);
   END;{SetUpFileMenu}
```

```
{————————————————————————————————}
```

```
  PROCEDURE SetUpMIDIMenu;
  BEGIN
    MIDIMenu := NewMenu(MIDIMenuID, 'MIDI');
    AppendMenu(MIDIMenu, 'Configuration; MIDIFilters');
    InsertMenu(MIDIMenu, 0);
  END;{SetUpMIDIMenu }


{————————————————————————————————————}

  PROCEDURE SetUpOutMenu;
  BEGIN
    OutMenu := NewMenu(OutMenuID, 'Out');
    AppendMenu(OutMenu, 'Note Test;Keyboard Test;(-;Send Message;(-;Panic');
    InsertMenu(OutMenu, 0);
  END;{SetUpOutMenu }


{————————————————————————————————————}

  PROCEDURE SetUpThruMenu;
  BEGIN
    ThruMenu := NewMenu(ThruMenuID, 'Thru');
    AppendMenu(ThruMenu, 'Thru Test;(-;MIDI Thru;Display Data;Running Status Filters');
    InsertMenu(ThruMenu, 0);
  END;{SetUpThruMenu }


{————————————————————————————————————}

  PROCEDURE SetUpMapMenu;
  BEGIN
    MapMenu := NewMenu(MapMenuID, 'Mapping');
    AppendMenu(MapMenu, 'Channel;(-;Controller;Program Change;Velocity;(-;Note Map;Harmony Map ');
    InsertMenu(MapMenu, 0);
  END;{SetUpMapMenu }


{————————————————————————————————————}

  PROCEDURE SetUpMenus;
  BEGIN
    SetUpAppleMenu;
    SetUpFileMenu;
    SetUpMIDIMenu;
    SetUpOutMenu;
    SetUpThruMenu;
    SetUpMapMenu;
    DrawMenuBar;
  END; {SetUpMenus}


{————————————————————————————————————}
```

```
PROCEDURE InitRTLab;
BEGIN
   Quitting := False;
   Finished := False;

   DAOpened := False;

   InitCursor;
   InitParameters;
   MIDIInit;
   SetUpMenus;
END;{InitRTLab}

END.
```

```
{FIle name:  RT Lab Main V 1.0                                    }
{Description:   Real Time MIDI Lab program                        }
{Original Date: 9/16/88     By: Steve De Furia                    }

{This program demonstrates the use of MIDIPascal™ in the          }
{Lightspeed Pascal ™ environment.

{MidiPascal™ is a trademark of ALTECH SYSTEMS                      }
{ Lightspeed Pascal is a trademark of THINK Technologies, Inc.    }

PROGRAM RTLab;
{$I+}
   USES
      InitProcedures, RTEventProcedures, RTLabGlobals;


BEGIN {main RT Lab}

   InitRTLab;                          {initialize RTL program}

   REPEAT

      MainLoop                         {handle events}

   UNTIL Finished;

   DoShutDown;                         {clean up and shut down}
END. {main RT Lab}
```

```
{FIle name:  RTL Event procs                                    }
{Description:   Event handling routines for Real Time MIDI Lab   }
{Original Date: 9/16/88        By: SDF                           }

UNIT RTEventProcedures;

INTERFACE

  USES
    MIDIPascal, RTLabGlobals, RTLabMenuGlobals, DoItemProcedures;

  PROCEDURE MainLoop;
  PROCEDURE DoEvent;
  PROCEDURE DoMouseDown;
  PROCEDURE DoKeysDown;
  PROCEDURE DoShutDown;
  PROCEDURE DoMenuChoice (MenuPick: longint);
  PROCEDURE AppleCmd (ItemID: integer);
  PROCEDURE FileCmd (ItemID: integer);
  PROCEDURE MIDICmd (ItemID: integer);
  PROCEDURE OutCmd (ItemID: integer);
  PROCEDURE ThruCmd (ItemID: integer);
  PROCEDURE MapCmd (ItemID: integer);

IMPLEMENTATION

{the Cmd procedures call the routines for the selected item in each menu}
{ each menu has its own Cmd procedure           }
{------------------------------------------------}
  PROCEDURE AppleCmd (ItemID: integer);
    VAR
      DskAccID: integer;
      DskAccName: str255;
  BEGIN
    CASE ItemID OF
      AboutItem:
        DoAbout;
      OTHERWISE
        BEGIN
          GetItem(AppleMenu, itemID, DskAccName);
          DskAccID := OpenDeskAcc(DskAccName);
          DAOpened := True;
        END;
    END {case}
  END; {AppleCmd }
{------------------------------------------------}
  PROCEDURE FileCmd (ItemID: integer);
  BEGIN
    CASE ItemID OF
      QuitItem:
        DoQuit
    END {case}
  END; {FileCmd }
```

```
{─────────────────────────────────────}
    PROCEDURE MIDICmd (ItemID: integer);
    BEGIN
        CASE ItemID OF
            ConfigureItem:
                DoConfigure;

            MIDIFiltersItem:
                DoMIDIFilters

        END {case}
    END; {MIDICmd }
{─────────────────────────────────────}
    PROCEDURE OutCmd (ItemID: integer);
    BEGIN
        CASE ItemID OF
            NoteTestItem:
                DoNoteTest;

            KeyTestItem:
                DoKeyTest;

            SendItem:
                DoSend;

            PanicItem:
                DoPanic

        END {case}
    END; {OutCmd }
{─────────────────────────────────────}
    PROCEDURE ThruCmd (ItemID: integer);
    BEGIN
        CASE ItemID OF
            ThruTestItem:
                DoThrutest;

            ThruItem:
                DoThru;

            DataDisplayItem:
                DoDataDisplay;

            RSFilterItem:
                DoRSFilter;

        END {case}
    END; { ThruCmd}
{─────────────────────────────────────}
```

```
PROCEDURE MapCmd (ItemID: integer);
BEGIN
   CASE ItemID OF
      ChannelMapItem:
         DoChannelMap;

      ControlMapItem:
         DoControlMap;

      ProgramMapItem:
         DoProgramMap;

      VelocityMapItem:
         DoVelocityMap;

      TransposeMapItem:
         DoTransposeMap;

      HarmonyMapItem:
         DoHarmonyMap

   END {case}
END; { MapCmd}
{───────────────────────────────────────}


PROCEDURE DoMenuChoice; {(MenuPick:longint)}
{ find out which menu and which item where picked}
{then call the appropriate Cmd procedure      }

   CONST
      noSelection = 0;

   VAR
      MenuID, ItemID: integer;

BEGIN
   MenuID := HiWord(MenuPick);
   ItemID := LoWord(MenuPick);

   CASE MenuID OF
      noSelection:
         ;{no action taken}

      AppleMenuID:
         AppleCmd(ItemID);

      FileMenuID:
         FileCmd(ItemID);

      MIDIMenuID:
         MIDICmd(ItemID);
```

```
        OutMenuID:
          OutCmd(ItemID);

        ThruMenuID:
          ThruCmd(ItemID);

        MapMenuID:
          MapCmd(ItemID)
      END; {Case MenuID}

      HiliteMenu(0)

    END; {DoMenuChoice}
{————————————————————————————}
    PROCEDURE DoMenuHit;
    {respond to mouse down in menu bar}
      VAR
        MenuPick: longint;

    BEGIN
      MenuPick := MenuSelect(theEvent.where);
      DoMenuChoice(MenuPick);
    END; {DoMenuHit}


{————————————————————————————}
    PROCEDURE DoMouseDown;
    {find out where mouse down occurred   }
      VAR
        whichWindow: WindowPtr;
        thePart: integer;

    BEGIN
      thePart := FindWindow(theEvent.where, whichWindow);
      CASE thePart OF
        InDesk:
          ; {Don't do anything}
        InMenuBar:
          DoMenuHit;
        InSysWindow:                        {takes care of click in DA window}
          SystemClick(theEvent, whichWindow);
        OTHERWISE
          {don't do anything}
      END {case thePart}
    END; { DoMenuHit}


{————————————————————————————}
    PROCEDURE DoKeysDown;
    BEGIN

                                    {  this is where your program would}
                                    {  handle key down events}

    END; { DoKeysDown}


{————————————————————————————}
```

289

```
PROCEDURE ShutDownDskAcc;
{close opened DA is "quit" is selected from the File menu }
   VAR
      whichWindow: WindowPeek;
      DskAccID: integer;

BEGIN
   DAOpened := false;
   quitting := false;
   whichWindow := WindowPeek(FrontWindow);
   DskAccID := whichWindow^.windowKind;
   CloseDeskAcc(DskAccID);
END;{ShutDownDskAcc }
```

{————————————————————————————}

```
PROCEDURE DoShutDown;
BEGIN
   QuitMIDI;
END; { DoShutDown}
```

{————————————————————————————}

```
PROCEDURE DoEvent;
{handle events}
BEGIN
   IF GetNextEvent(EveryEvent, theEvent) THEN
      CASE theEvent.what OF
         MouseDown:
            IF NOT Quitting THEN
               DoMouseDown;

         KeyDown, AutoKey:
            IF NOT Quitting THEN
               DoKeysDown;

         OTHERWISE
         {don't do anything}
         END {Case theEvent}

   ELSE IF quitting THEN

      IF DAOpened = True THEN
         ShutDownDskAcc
      ELSE
         Finished := True

END; {do event}
```

{————————————————————————————}

```
PROCEDURE MainLoop;
BEGIN
   DoEvent;
END;{MainLoop}
END.{RTEventProcedures }
```

```
{FIle name:  RTL DoItem procs                                    }
{Description:   DoItem procedures Real Time MIDI Lab program      }
{Original Date: 9/16/88         By: SDF                           }

UNIT DoItemProcedures;

INTERFACE

   USES
     MIDIPascal, RTLabGlobals, RTLabMenuGlobals, RTDLogProcedures, RTLDlogUtilities, MPascalTools;


   PROCEDURE DoAbout;
   PROCEDURE DoQuit;
   PROCEDURE DoConfigure;
   PROCEDURE DoMIDIFilters;
   PROCEDURE DoNoteTest;
   PROCEDURE DoKeyTest;
   PROCEDURE DoSend;
   PROCEDURE DoPanic;
   PROCEDURE DoThruTest;
   PROCEDURE DoThru;
   PROCEDURE DoDataDisplay;
   PROCEDURE DoRSFilter;
   PROCEDURE DoChannelMap;
   PROCEDURE DoControlMap;
   PROCEDURE DoProgramMap;
   PROCEDURE DoVelocityMap;
   PROCEDURE DoTransposeMap;
   PROCEDURE DoHarmonyMap;

IMPLEMENTATION

{These "DoItem"  procedures are called from the menu Cmd procedures.}
{They were originally installed as "dummy" procedures, which just displayed}
{ an alert with the procedure name.}
{We've left the alert statement in each procedure - commented out - so  }
{ you could see how this was done.}

{————————————————————————————————}
   PROCEDURE DoAbout;
   BEGIN
      TellUser(AboutAlertID, 'Real Time MIDI Lab by Steve De Furia');
   END; {DoAbout}


   {————————————————————————————————}
PROCEDURE DoQuit;
   BEGIN
      Quitting := True;
   END; {DoQuit }


{————————————————————————————————}
```

```
   PROCEDURE DoConfigure;
   BEGIN
{TellUser(AboutAlertID, 'Configure is not implemented.');}
      DoConfigureDLog;
      IF anyChanges THEN
         SetMIDIPort;
   END; {Configure}


{——————————————————————}

   PROCEDURE DoMIDIFilters;
   BEGIN
{TellUser(AboutAlertID, 'MIDI Filters are not implemented.');}
      DoMPFilterDlog;
      IF anyChanges THEN
        BEGIN
           SetMPFilters;
           MIDI(resetMIDI);
        END;
   END; {MIDIFilters }

{——————————————————————}

   PROCEDURE DoNoteTest;
   BEGIN
{TellUser(AboutAlertID, 'Note Test is not implemented.');}
      DoNoteTestDlog;
      MIDI(ResetMIDI);
   END; { NoteTest}

{——————————————————————}

   PROCEDURE DoKeyTest;
   BEGIN
{TellUser(AboutAlertID, 'Keyboard Test is not implemented.');}

      DoKeyTestDlog;
      MIDI(resetMIDI);
   END; {KeyTest }

{——————————————————————}

   PROCEDURE DoSend;
   BEGIN
{   TellUser(AboutAlertID, 'Send Message is not implemented.');}
      DoSendDlog;
      MIDI(resetMIDI);
   END; {Send }

{——————————————————————}

   PROCEDURE DoPanic;
   BEGIN
{TellUser(AboutAlertID, 'Panic is not implemented.');}
      DoPanicDlog;
   END; {Panic }

{——————————————————————}
```

```
    PROCEDURE DoThruTest;
    BEGIN
{TellUser(AboutAlertID, 'Thru Test is not implemented.');}
        DoThruTestDlog;
    END; {ThruTest}


{————————————————————————————————}
    PROCEDURE DoThru;
    BEGIN
{TellUser(AboutAlertID, 'MIDI Thru is not implemented.');}
        DoMIDIThru;
    END; {Thru}


{————————————————————————————————}
    PROCEDURE DoDataDisplay;
    BEGIN
{TellUser(AboutAlertID, 'Data Display is not implemented.');}
        DoThruDlog;
    END; { DataDisplay}


{————————————————————————————————}
    PROCEDURE DoRSFilter;
    BEGIN
{TellUser(AboutAlertID, 'Running Status Filters are not implemented.');}
        DoRSFilterDlog;
    END; { RSFilter}


{————————————————————————————————}
    PROCEDURE DoChannelMap;
    BEGIN
{TellUser(AboutAlertID, 'Channel Mapping is not implemented.');}
        DoChannelMapDlog;
    END; {Channel }


{————————————————————————————————}
    PROCEDURE DoControlMap;
    BEGIN
{TellUser(AboutAlertID, 'Controller Mapping is not implemented.');}
        DoControlMapDlog;
    END; { ControlMap}


{————————————————————————————————}
    PROCEDURE DoProgramMap;
    BEGIN
{TellUser(AboutAlertID, 'Program Change Mapping is not implemented.');}
        DoProgramMapDlog;
    END; { ProgramMap}


{————————————————————————————————}
```

```
    PROCEDURE DoVelocityMap;
    BEGIN
{TellUser(AboutAlertID, 'Velocity Mapping is not implemented.');}
        DoVelocityMapDlog;
    END; {VelocityMap }

{————————————————————————————}
    PROCEDURE DoTransposeMap;
    BEGIN
{TellUser(AboutAlertID, 'Note mapping is not implemented.');}
        DoTransposeDlog;
    END; { TransposeMap}

{————————————————————————————}
    PROCEDURE DoHarmonyMap;
    BEGIN
{TellUser(AboutAlertID, 'Harmony Mapping is not implemented.');}
        DoHarmonyMapDlog;

    END; {Harmony Map }


END. {DoItemProcedures}
```

```
{FIle name:  RTL Dlog Utility procs                                          }
{Description:     Utility Functions and Procedures for DoDialog routines}
{                 in Real Time MIDI Lab program          ------------        }
{Original Date: 9/16/88        By: SDF                                       }

UNIT RTLDlogUtilities;

INTERFACE

  USES
    MIDIPascal, RTLabMenuGlobals, RTLabGlobals, RTLResourceIDs;

  FUNCTION ToggleFlag (flag: integer): integer;
  FUNCTION NumberFromItem (theDialog: DialogPtr; DlogItem: Integer): integer;
  FUNCTION InDataRange (dataValue, lowLimit, hiLimit: integer): boolean;
  FUNCTION CheckValue (theItem, oldValue, valueCode: integer): integer;
  PROCEDURE TellUser (AlertID: integer; message: str255);
  PROCEDURE ShowResDialog (DlogID: integer; defaultState: boolean);
  PROCEDURE NumberToItem (theDialog: DialogPtr; DlogItem, theNumber: Integer);
  PROCEDURE ResetDlogCntrl (theDlogItem, theParameter, theValue: integer);
  PROCEDURE ResetCheckBox (selectedBox: integer);
  PROCEDURE ResetRadioList (lowButton, hiButton, selectedButton: integer);


IMPLEMENTATION

{------------------------------------------------------}
  FUNCTION ToggleFlag (flag: integer): integer;
  BEGIN
    flag := ABS(Flag - 1);  {reverse 1 to 0 or 0 to1}
    ToggleFlag := flag;
  END;{ToggleFlag}


{------------------------------------------------------}
  FUNCTION NumberFromItem (theDialog: DialogPtr; DlogItem: Integer): integer;
    VAR
      DlogType: integer;
      DlogRect: rect;
      DlogHandle: handle;
      thetext: str255;
      theNumber: Longint;

  BEGIN
    GetDItem(theDialog, DlogItem, Dlogtype, DlogHandle, DlogRect);
    GetIText(DlogHandle, thetext);
    StringToNum(theText, theNumber);
    NumberFromItem := theNumber;
  END;{NumberFromItem}


{------------------------------------------------------}
```

```
FUNCTION InDataRange (dataValue, lowLimit, hiLimit: integer): boolean;
BEGIN
   IF (dataValue < lowLimit) OR (dataValue > hiLimit) THEN
      InDataRange := FALSE
   ELSE
      InDataRange := TRUE;
END;{InDataRange}

{————————————————————————————————}
   FUNCTION CheckValue (theItem, oldValue, valueCode: integer): integer;
     VAR
        newValue, loLimit, hiLimit: integer;
        theMessage: str255;

BEGIN
   CASE valueCode OF
     dataValueCode:
        BEGIN
           theMessage := ErrorList[valueCode];
           loLimit := 0;
           hiLimit := maxDataValue;
        END;

     lengthValueCode:
        BEGIN
           theMessage := ErrorList[valueCode];
           loLimit := 1;
           hiLimit := 8;
        END;

     speedValueCode:
        BEGIN
           theMessage := ErrorList[valueCode];
           loLimit := 1;
           hiLimit := 15;
        END;

     byteValueCode:
        BEGIN
           theMessage := ErrorList[valueCode];
           loLimit := 0;
           hiLimit := SystemReset;
        END;

     polyphonyValueCode:
        BEGIN
           theMessage := ErrorList[valueCode];
           loLimit := 1;
           hiLimit := polyphony;
        END;
```

```
channelValueCode:
  BEGIN
    theMessage := ErrorList[valueCode];
    loLimit := Channel1;
    hiLimit := Channel16;
  END;

controlValueCode:
  BEGIN
    theMessage := ErrorList[valueCode];
    loLimit := ModController;
    hiLimit := DataDecrement;
  END;

scaleValueCode:
  BEGIN
    theMessage := ErrorList[valueCode];
    loLimit := -10;
    hiLimit := 10;
  END;

statusValueCode:
  BEGIN
    theMessage := ErrorList[valueCode];
    loLimit := NoteOff;
    hiLimit := SystemReset;
  END;

harmonyValueCode:
  BEGIN
    theMessage := ErrorList[valueCode];
    loLimit := -24;
    hiLimit := 24;
  END;

durationValueCode:
  BEGIN
    theMessage := ErrorList[valueCode];
    loLimit := 0;
    hiLimit := 100;
  END;

delayValueCode:
  BEGIN
    theMessage := ErrorList[valueCode];
    loLimit := 0;
    hiLimit := 60;
  END;
```

```
      OTHERWISE
        BEGIN
          {check Value code with debugger if you have problems here}
          TellUser(AboutAlertID, 'undefined value code passed to CheckData');
          disposDialog(theDialog);
          loLimit := 999;
          hiLimit := -999;
        END;

    END;{case valueCode}
    newValue := NumberFromItem(theDialog, theItem);

    IF NOT InDataRange(newValue, loLimit, hiLimit) THEN
      BEGIN
        TellUser(AboutAlertID, theMessage);
        newValue := oldValue;
        NumberToItem(theDialog, theItem, newValue);
      END;
    CheckValue := newValue;
  END; {CheckValue}

{————————————————————————————————}
PROCEDURE NumberToItem (theDialog: DialogPtr; DlogItem, theNumber: Integer);
    VAR
        DlogType: integer;
        DlogRect: rect;
        DlogHandle: handle;
        thetext: str255;

  BEGIN
    GetDItem(theDialog, DlogItem, Dlogtype, DlogHandle, DlogRect);
    NumToString(theNumber, theText);
    SetIText(DlogHandle, thetext);
  END;{NumberToItem}

{————————————————————————————————}
  PROCEDURE TellUser; {(AlertID: integer; message: str255)}
    VAR
      dontCare: integer;

  BEGIN
    ParamText(message, '', '', '');
    dontCare := Alert(AlertID, NIL);
  END; {TellUser}

{————————————————————————————————}
```

```
PROCEDURE BoldOKButton;
  VAR
    DlogType: integer;
    dispRect: rect;
    DlogHandle: handle;
    cntrlHandle: controlHandle;
    curState: PenState;

BEGIN
  GetPenState(curState);
  GetDItem(theDialog, OK, Dlogtype, DlogHandle, dispRect);
  PenSize(3, 3);
  InsetRect(dispRect, -4, -4);
  FrameRoundRect(dispRect, 16, 16);
  SetPenState(curState);
END;{Bold OKButton}
```

{————————————————————————————————————}

```
PROCEDURE ShowResDialog;{DLOGID,defaultState}
BEGIN
  TheDialog := GetNewDialog(DLOGID, NIL, WindowPtr(-1));
  SetPort(TheDialog);
  IF defaultState = On THEN
    BoldOKButton;
  DrawDialog(TheDialog);
END; {ShowResDialog}
```

{————————————————————————————————————}

```
PROCEDURE ResetDlogCntrl (theDlogItem, theParameter, theValue: integer);
  VAR
    DlogType: integer;
    DlogRect: rect;
    DlogHandle: handle;
    cntrlHandle: controlHandle;

BEGIN
  GetDItem(theDialog, theDlogItem, Dlogtype, DlogHandle, DlogRect);
  cntrlHandle := ControlHandle(DlogHandle);
  IF theParameter = theValue THEN
    SetCtlValue(cntrlHandle, 1)
  ELSE
    SetCtlValue(cntrlHandle, 0);
END; {ResetDlogCntrl}
```

{————————————————————————————————————}

```
PROCEDURE ResetCheckBox (selectedBox: integer);
    VAR
        DlogType, boxFlag: integer;
        DlogRect: rect;
        DlogHandle: handle;
        cntrlHandle: controlHandle;
BEGIN
    GetDItem(theDialog, selectedBox, Dlogtype, DlogHandle, DlogRect);
    cntrlHandle := ControlHandle(DlogHandle);
    boxFlag := GetCtlValue(cntrlHandle);
    boxFlag := ToggleFlag(boxFlag);
    SetCtlValue(cntrlHandle, boxFlag);
END; {ResetCheckBox}


{—————————————————————————————————}
PROCEDURE ResetRadioList (lowButton, hiButton, selectedButton: integer);
    VAR
        DlogSelection, DlogType, theButton: integer;
        DlogRect: rect;
        DlogHandle: handle;
        cntrlHandle: controlHandle;
BEGIN
    DlogSelection := selectedButton;
    FOR theButton := lowButton TO hiButton DO
        BEGIN
            GetDItem(theDialog, theButton, Dlogtype, DlogHandle, DlogRect);
            cntrlHandle := ControlHandle(DlogHandle);
            IF theButton = selectedButton THEN
                SetCtlValue(cntrlHandle, 1)
            ELSE
                SetCtlValue(cntrlHandle, 0);
        END;{for count}
END; {ResetRadioList}

END. {unit RTLDlogUtilities}
```

```
{FIle name: RTL Dlog procs                                                      }
{Description:Procedures for display and update of dialogs      }
{Description:   used by  Real Time MIDI Lab program                              }
{Original Date: 9/16/88        By: SDF                                           }
{Resource File:      <<<<<<RTLAB0.resc>>>>>>                                     }

UNIT RTDLogProcedures;

INTERFACE

  USES
MIDIPascal,RTLabMenuGlobals,RTLabGlobals,RTLResourceIDs,RTLDlogUtilities,InitProcedures,
MPascalTools;

    PROCEDURE DoConfigureDlog;
    PROCEDURE DoMPFilterDlog;

    PROCEDURE DoNoteTestDlog;
    PROCEDURE DoKeyTestDlog;
    PROCEDURE DoSendDlog;
    PROCEDURE DoPanicDlog;

    PROCEDURE DoThruTestDlog;
    PROCEDURE DoThruDlog;
    PROCEDURE DoRSFilterDlog;

    PROCEDURE DoChannelMapDlog;
    PROCEDURE DoControlMapDlog;
    PROCEDURE DoProgramMapDlog;
    PROCEDURE DoVelocityMapDlog;
    PROCEDURE DoTransposeDlog;
    PROCEDURE DoHarmonyMapDlog;

IMPLEMENTATION


{----------------------------------------------------------------}
  PROCEDURE DoConfigureDlog;
    VAR
      DlogItem, DlogType, whichSCSI, clockRate, ItemListOffset: integer;
      DlogRect: rect;
      DlogHandle: handle;
  BEGIN
    ItemListOffset := 5;
    whichSCSI := theSCSI;
    clockRate := clockMhz;
    ShowResDialog(MIDISetupDlogID, On);

    ResetDlogCntrl(ModemDlogItem, theSCSI, commPort);
    ResetDlogCntrl(PrinterDlogItem, theSCSI, printerPort);
    ResetDlogCntrl(halfMegDlogItem, clockMhz, halfMeg);
    ResetDlogCntrl(oneMegDlogItem, clockMhz, oneMeg);
    ResetDlogCntrl(twoMegDlogItem, clockMhz, twoMeg);
```

```
REPEAT
  BEGIN
    ModalDialog(NIL, DlogItem);
    CASE DlogItem OF
      ModemDlogItem, PrinterDlogItem:
        BEGIN
          ResetRadioList(ModemDlogItem, PrinterDlogItem, DlogItem);
          whichSCSI := DlogItem;
        END;
      HalfMegDlogItem, OneMegDlogItem, TwoMegDlogItem:
        BEGIN
          ResetRadioList(HalfMegDlogItem, TwoMegDlogItem, DlogItem);
          clockRate := DlogItem - ItemListOffset;
        END;
      OTHERWISE
        {do nothing}
    END {CaseDlogItem}
  END; {repeat}
UNTIL (DlogItem = DoneDlogItem) OR (DlogItem = CancelDlogItem);
IF DlogItem = DoneDlogItem THEN
  BEGIN
    anyChanges := TRUE; {return Done result update global variables}
    theSCSI := whichSCSI;
    ClockMhz := clockRate;
  END
ELSE
  anyChanges := False;{ return Cancel result, don't change global variables}
  DisposDialog(TheDialog);
END;{DoConfigureDlog}


{─────────────────────────────────────────────}
PROCEDURE DoMPFilterDlog;
  VAR
    DlogItem, DlogType: integer;
    DlogRect: rect;
    DlogHandle: handle;
    theMPFilter: MPFilterArray;
    count, theDlogItem: integer;
BEGIN
  ShowResDialog(MPFilterDlogID, On);

  theDlogItem := MPFActiveOn;                              {the first item in the filter radio list}
  FOR count := 1 TO 8 DO                                   {for each of the filters…}
    BEGIN
      theMPFilter[count] := MPFilters[count];              {set local array to current global values}
      ResetDlogCntrl(theDlogItem, MPFilters[count], 1);
      ResetDlogCntrl(theDlogItem + 1, MPFilters[count], 0); theDlogItem := theDlogItem + 2;
        {increment to next filter}
    END;
```

```
REPEAT
 BEGIN
  ModalDialog(NIL, DlogItem);
  CASE DlogItem OF

   MPFActiveOn, MPFActiveOff:
    BEGIN
     ResetRadioList(MPFActiveOn, MPFActiveOff, DlogItem);
     IF DlogItem = MPFActiveOn THEN
       theMPFilter[1] := 1
     ELSE
       theMPFilter[1] := 0;
    END;

   MPFClockOn, MPFClockOff:
    BEGIN
     ResetRadioList(MPFClockOn, MPFClockOff, DlogItem);
     IF DlogItem = MPFClockOn THEN
       theMPFilter[2] := 1
     ELSE
       theMPFilter[2] := 0;
    END;

   MPFClkCmdOn, MPFClkCmdOff:
    BEGIN
     ResetRadioList(MPFClkCmdOn, MPFClkCmdOff, DlogItem);
     IF DlogItem = MPFClkCmdOn THEN
       theMPFilter[3] := 1
     ELSE
       theMPFilter[3] := 0;
    END;

   MPFChangeOn, MPFChangeOff:
    BEGIN
     ResetRadioList(MPFChangeOn, MPFChangeOff, DlogItem);
     IF DlogItem = MPFChangeOn THEN
       theMPFilter[4] := 1
     ELSE
       theMPFilter[4] := 0;
    END;

   MPFAfterTouchOn, MPFAfterTouchOff:
    BEGIN
     ResetRadioList(MPFAfterTouchOn, MPFAfterTouchOff, DlogItem);
     IF DlogItem = MPFAfterTouchOn THEN
       theMPFilter[5] := 1
     ELSE
       theMPFilter[5] := 0;
    END;
```

```
      MPFCntrlOn, MPFCntrlOff:
        BEGIN
          ResetRadioList(MPFCntrlOn, MPFCntrlOff, DlogItem);
          IF DlogItem = MPFCntrlOn THEN
            theMPFilter[6] := 1
          ELSE
            theMPFilter[6] := 0;
        END;

      MPFBendOn, MPFBendOff:
        BEGIN
          ResetRadioList(MPFBendOn, MPFBendOff, DlogItem);
          IF DlogItem = MPFBendOn THEN
            theMPFilter[7] := 1
          ELSE
            theMPFilter[7] := 0;
        END;

      MPFSysExOn, MPFSysExOff:
        BEGIN
          ResetRadioList(MPFSysExOn, MPFSysExOff, DlogItem);
          IF DlogItem = MPFSysExOn THEN
            theMPFilter[8] := 1
          ELSE
            theMPFilter[8] := 0;
        END;
      OTHERWISE
        {do nothing}
     END {CaseDlogItem}
   END; {repeat}
UNTIL (DlogItem = MPFDoneItem) OR (DlogItem = MPFCancelItem);
IF DlogItem = MPFDoneItem THEN
   BEGIN
     anyChanges := True;
     FOR count := 1 TO 8 DO{relplace the global values with the local array values}
        MPFilters[count] := theMPFilter[count];
   END
ELSE
   anyChanges := False;{Cancel: don't change anything}
DisposDialog(TheDialog);
END;{DoMPFilterDisplay}
```

```
{————————————————————————————}
```

```
PROCEDURE DoNoteTestDlog;
   VAR
      DlogItem, DlogType, thisNote, thisVelocity, thisDuration: integer;
      DlogRect: rect;
      DlogHandle: handle;
BEGIN
   thisNote := theNote;
   thisVelocity := theVelocity;
   thisduration := theDuration;

   ShowResDialog(NoteTestDlogID, On);
   NumberToItem(theDialog, NTestNoteItem, thisNote);
   NumberToItem(theDialog, NTestVelocityItem, thisVelocity);
   NumberToItem(theDialog, NTestDurationItem, thisDuration);

   REPEAT
      BEGIN
         ModalDialog(NIL, DlogItem);
         CASE DlogItem OF
            NTestNoteItem:
               BEGIN
                  thisNote := CheckValue(DlogItem, MiddleC, dataValueCode);
               END;
            NTestVelocityItem:
               BEGIN
                  thisVelocity := CheckValue(DlogItem, Forte, dataValueCode);
               END;
            NTestDurationItem:
               thisDuration := CheckValue(DlogItem, 0, durationValueCode);
            NTestPlayItem:
               BEGIN
                  theNote := thisNote;      {pass local to global}
                  theVelocity := thisVelocity;
                  theDuration := thisDuration;
                  PlayTestNote;             {play global}
               END;
            OTHERWISE
               ;{do nothing}
         END {CaseDlogItem}
      END; {repeat}
   UNTIL DlogItem = NTestCancelItem;
   DisposDialog(TheDialog);
   ;
END;{DoNoteTestDlog}
```

{————————————————————————————————}

```
PROCEDURE DoKeyTestDlog;
  VAR
    DlogItem, DlogType: integer;
    DlogRect: rect;
    DlogHandle: handle;

    thisStart, thisEnd, thisLength, thisSpeed: integer;

BEGIN
  thisStart := StartNote;
  thisEnd := EndNote;
  thisLength := ArpLength;
  thisSpeed := ArpSpeed;

  ShowResDialog(KTestDlogID, On);
  NumberToItem(theDialog, KTestStartItem, thisStart);
  NumberToItem(theDialog, KTestEndItem, thisEnd);
  NumberToItem(theDialog, KTestLengthItem, thisLength);
  NumberToItem(theDialog, KTestSpeedItem, thisSpeed);

  REPEAT
    BEGIN
      ModalDialog(NIL, DlogItem);
      CASE DlogItem OF
        KTestStartItem:
          BEGIN
            thisStart := CheckValue(DlogItem, MiddleC, dataValueCode);
          END;
        KTestEndItem:
          BEGIN
            thisEnd := CheckValue(DlogItem, MiddleC + 24, dataValueCode);
          END;
        KTestLengthItem:
          BEGIN
            thisLength := CheckValue(DlogItem, 4, lengthValueCode);
          END;
        KTestSpeedItem:
          BEGIN
            thisSpeed := CheckValue(DlogItem, 50, speedValueCode);
          END;
        KTestPlayItem:
          BEGIN
            StartNote := thisStart;     {local to global}
            EndNote := thisEnd;
            ArpLength := thisLength;
            ArpSpeed := thisSpeed;
            PlayKeyTest;
          END;
        OTHERWISE
          ;{do nothing}
      END {Case DlogItem}
    END; {repeat}
```

```
      UNTIL DlogItem = KTestCancelItem;
      StartNote := thisStart;
      EndNote := thisEnd;
      ArpLength := thisLength;
      ArpSpeed := thisSpeed;

      DisposDialog(TheDialog);
   END;{DoKeyTestDlog}


{————————————————————————————}
   PROCEDURE DoSendDlog;
      VAR
         DlogItem, DlogType, ItemListOffset: integer;
         DlogRect: rect;
         DlogHandle: handle;
         count: integer;
         thisMessage: MIDIMessageList;
         Send: MIDIMessage;
         thisSize, thisStatus, thisData1, thisData2: integer;

   BEGIN
      ItemListOffset := 2;
      FOR count := 1 TO 9 DO
         thisMessage[count] := SendList[count];
      Send := thisMessage[1];

      ShowResDialog(SendDlogID, On);

      ResetDlogCntrl(SendNoteOnItem, 1, 1); {light button for NoteOn Status}
      NumberToItem(theDialog, SendStatusItem, Send.status);
      NumberToItem(theDialog, SendData1Item, Send.data1);
      NumberToItem(theDialog, SendData2Item, Send.Data2);

      REPEAT
         BEGIN
            ModalDialog(NIL, DlogItem);
            IF (DlogItem >= SendNoteOnItem) AND (DlogItem <= SendContinueItem) THEN
               BEGIN
                  ResetRadioList(SendNoteOnItem, SendContinueItem, DlogItem);
                  Send := thisMessage[DlogItem - ItemListOffset];

                  IF Send.size = 1 THEN
                     BEGIN
                        HideDItem(theDialog, SendData1Item); {hide and show routines Mac Plus and above!}
                        HideDItem(theDialog, SendData2Item)
                     END

                  ELSE IF send.size = 2 THEN
                     BEGIN
                        ShowDItem(theDialog, SendData1Item);
                        HideDItem(theDialog, SendData2Item)
                     END
```

```
            ELSE
              BEGIN
                ShowDItem(theDialog, SendData1Item);
                ShowDItem(theDialog, SendData2Item);
              END;

            NumberToItem(theDialog, SendStatusItem, Send.status);
            NumberToItem(theDialog, SendData1Item, Send.data1);
            NumberToItem(theDialog, SendData2Item, Send.Data2);
          END

        ELSE
          CASE DlogItem OF
            SendStatusItem:
              BEGIN
                Send.status := CheckValue(DlogItem, NoteOn, statusValueCode);
              END;
            SendData1Item:
              BEGIN
                Send.data1 := CheckValue(DlogItem, MiddleC, dataValueCode);
              END;
            SendData2Item:
              BEGIN
                Send.data2 := CheckValue(DlogItem, Forte, dataValueCode);
              END;
            SendTransmitItem:
              BEGIN
                PlayMessage(Send);
              END;
            OTHERWISE
              {do nothing}
          END {CaseDlogItem}
      END; {repeat}
    UNTIL DlogItem = SendCancelItem;
    DisposDialog(TheDialog);
END;{DoSendDlog}


{————————————————————————————————————}
PROCEDURE DoPanicDlog;
  CONST
    PanicDlogID = 101;
  VAR
    oldDialog: DialogPtr;
    DlogItem: integer;
BEGIN
  oldDialog := theDialog;
  ShowResDialog(PanicDlogID, OFF);
  REPEAT
    KillAllNotes;
  UNTIL button;
  DisposDialog(TheDialog);
  theDialog := oldDialog;
END;{ DoPanicDlog}
```

```
{————————————————————————————————————}
  PROCEDURE RunTheTest;
    VAR
       count, InByte: integer;
       delayFactor, dontCare: longint;
  BEGIN
    textFont(geneva);
    textSize(9);

    delayFactor := repeatCount;

    MIDIOut(testByte);
    delay(delayFactor, dontCare);
    MIDIIn(InByte);

    moveTo(50, 60);
    writeDraw('Test byte ');
    moveTo(100, 60);
    WriteDraw(testByte);

    moveTo(50, 70);
    writeDraw('Result byte');
    moveTo(100, 70);
    WriteDraw(inByte);

    IF testByte <> InByte THEN
      BEGIN
        textSize(12);
        moveTo(30, 85);
        WriteDraw('Error detected');
        textSize(9);
        delay(60, dontCare);
      END;
  END;{ RunTheTest}


{————————————————————————————————————}
  PROCEDURE DoTest;
    VAR
       oldDialog: DialogPtr;
       DlogItem, DlogType: integer;
       dlogRect: rect;
       displayRect: rect;
       DlogHandle: handle;
       thetext: str255;
  BEGIN
    oldDialog := theDialog;
    DlogItem := 1;
    theText := 'Testing MIDI Thru';

    TheDialog := GetNewDialog(PanicDlogID, NIL, WindowPtr(-1));
    SetPort(TheDialog);
    GetDItem(theDialog, DlogItem, Dlogtype, DlogHandle, DlogRect);
    SetIText(DlogHandle, thetext);
    DrawDialog(TheDialog);
```

```
WITH displayRect DO
  BEGIN
    top := 40;
    left := 15;
    bottom := 100;
    right := 200;
  END;
frameRect(displayRect);
insetRect(displayRect, 5, 5);
REPEAT
  BEGIN
    RunTheTest;
    eraseRect(displayRect);
  END;
UNTIL button;
DisposDialog(TheDialog);
theDialog := oldDialog;
setPort(theDialog);
END;{ DoTest}


{─────────────────────────────────────────────}

PROCEDURE DoThruTestDlog;
  VAR
    DlogItem, DlogType: integer;
    DlogRect: rect;
    DlogHandle: handle;
    thisByte, thisRepeat: integer;

    dontCare: longint;
BEGIN
  ThruTestFlag := FALSE;
  thisByte := testByte;
  thisRepeat := repeatCount;

  ShowResDialog(ThruTestDlogID, On);

  NumberToItem(theDialog, ThruTestSendItem, thisByte);
  NumberToItem(theDialog, ThruTestRepeatItem, thisRepeat);

  REPEAT
    BEGIN
      ModalDialog(NIL, DlogItem);
      CASE DlogItem OF
        ThruTestSendItem:
          BEGIN
            thisByte := CheckValue(DlogItem, EOX, byteValueCode);
          END;
        ThruTestRepeatItem:
          BEGIN
            thisRepeat := CheckValue(DlogItem, 1, delayValueCode);
          END;
        ThruTestRunItem:
          BEGIN
```

```
                    repeatCount := thisRepeat;
                    testByte := thisByte;
                    ThruTestFlag := TRUE;
                    DoTest;
                END;
            OTHERWISE
                ;{        do nothing}
          END {CaseDlogItem}
        END; {repeat}
    UNTIL (DlogItem = ThruTestCancelItem);
    DisposDialog(TheDialog);
  END;{ThruTestDlog}
{─────────────────────────────────────────}
  PROCEDURE DoThruDlog;
    VAR
        oldDialog: DialogPtr;
        DlogItem, DlogType: integer;
        dlogRect: rect;
        displayRect: rect;
        DlogHandle: handle;
        thetext: str255;
  BEGIN
    oldDialog := theDialog;
    DlogItem := 1;
    theText := 'MIDI Thru Display';

    TheDialog := GetNewDialog(PanicDlogID, NIL, WindowPtr(-1));
    SetPort(TheDialog);
    GetDItem(theDialog, DlogItem, Dlogtype, DlogHandle, DlogRect);
    SetIText(DlogHandle, thetext);
    DrawDialog(TheDialog);

    WITH displayRect DO
      BEGIN
        top := 25;        {set dimensions of text display}
        bottom := 100;
        left := 10;
        right := 275;
      END;
    frameRect(displayRect);
    insetRect(displayRect, 5, 5);
    resetPen;
    MIDI(ClearInput);          {clear buffers}
    MIDI(ClearOutput);
    REPEAT
      BEGIN
        MIDIThruDisplay;
      END;
    UNTIL button;
    DisposDialog(TheDialog);
    theDialog := oldDialog;
    setPort(theDialog);
  END;{ DoThruDlog}
```

```
{—————————————————————————————————————}
PROCEDURE DoRSFilterDlog;
  VAR
    DlogItem, DlogType, ItemListOffset: integer;
    DlogRect: rect;
    DlogHandle: handle;
    thisRSFilter: RSFilterArray;
    FilterID: integer;
    count: integer;

BEGIN

  ItemListOffset := 2;
  FOR count := 1 TO 5 DO
{set local array to global values}
    thisRSFilter[count] := RSFilters[count];

  ShowResDialog(RSFilterDlogID, On);

  FOR count := RSFilterNoteItem TO RSFilterPBendItem DO        {set dialog controls to local settings}
    ResetDlogCntrl(count, thisRSFilter[count - ItemListOffset], 1); {check box if flag is one}

  REPEAT
    BEGIN
      ModalDialog(NIL, DlogItem);
      CASE DlogItem OF
        RSFilterNoteItem:
          BEGIN
            FilterID := DlogItem - ItemListOffset;
            ResetCheckBox(DlogItem);
            thisRSFilter[FilterID] := ToggleFlag(thisRSFilter[FilterID]);
          END;
        RSFilterPPressItem:
          BEGIN
            FilterID := DlogItem - ItemListOffset;
            ResetCheckBox(DlogItem);
            thisRSFilter[FilterID] := ToggleFlag(thisRSFilter[FilterID]);
          END;
        RSFilterCChangeItem:
          BEGIN
            FilterID := DlogItem - ItemListOffset;
            ResetCheckBox(DlogItem);
            thisRSFilter[FilterID] := ToggleFlag(thisRSFilter[FilterID]);
          END;
        RSFilterATouchItem:
          BEGIN
            FilterID := DlogItem - ItemListOffset;
            ResetCheckBox(DlogItem);
            thisRSFilter[FilterID] := ToggleFlag(thisRSFilter[FilterID]);
          END;
        RSFilterPBendItem:
```

```
          BEGIN
            FilterID := DlogItem - ItemListOffset;
            ResetCheckBox(DlogItem);
            thisRSFilter[FilterID] := ToggleFlag(thisRSFilter[FilterID]);
          END;
        OTHERWISE
          ;{      do nothing}
      END {Case DlogItem}
    END; {repeat}
  UNTIL (DlogItem = RSFilterDoneItem) OR (DlogItem = RSFilterCancelItem);
  IF DlogItem = RSFilterDoneItem THEN
    BEGIN
      FOR count := 1 TO 5 DO    {set global array to new values}
        RSFilters[count] := thisRSFilter[count];
    END
  ELSE
    ;{Cancel: don't change anything}
  DisposDialog(TheDialog);
END;{DoRSFilterDlog}


{----------------------------------------------------}

PROCEDURE DoChannelMapDlog;
  VAR
    DlogItem, DlogType: integer;
    DlogRect: rect;
    DlogHandle: handle;

    thisChannel: ChannelArray;
    count, thisSourceChannel, thisTargetChannel: integer;
    thisOffsetFlag, thisReassignFlag: integer;

BEGIN
  thisSourceChannel := Channel1;
  thisTargetChannel := ChanMaps[Channel1];

  FOR count := Channel1 TO Channel16 DO
    thisChannel[count] := ChanMaps[count];

  ShowResDialog(ChanMapDlogID, On);

  NumberToItem(theDialog, ChanMapSourceItem, thisSourceChannel);
  NumberToItem(theDialog, ChanMapDestItem, thisTargetChannel);

  REPEAT
    BEGIN
      ModalDialog(NIL, DlogItem);
      CASE DlogItem OF
        ChanMapSourceItem:
          BEGIN
            thisSourceChannel := CheckValue(DlogItem, Channel1, channelValueCode);
            NumberToItem(theDialog, ChanMapDestItem, thisChannel[thisSourceChannel]);
          END;
```

```
          ChanMapDestItem:
             BEGIN
                thisTargetChannel := CheckValue(DlogItem, Channel1, channelValueCode);
                thisChannel[thisSourceChannel] := thisTargetChannel;
             END;
          ChanMapClearItem:
             BEGIN
                FOR count := Channel1 TO Channel16 DO
                   thisChannel[count] := count;
                NumberToItem(theDialog, ChanMapSourceItem, Channel1);
                NumberToItem(theDialog, ChanMapDestItem, thisChannel[Channel1]);
             END;
          OTHERWISE
             {do nothing}
        END {CaseDlogItem}
     END; {repeat}
  UNTIL (DlogItem = ChanMapDoneItem) OR (DlogItem = ChanMapCancelItem);
  IF DlogItem = ChanMapDoneItem THEN
     FOR count := Channel1 TO Channel16 DO
        ChanMaps[count] := thisChannel[count]
  ELSE
     ;{Cancel: don't change anything}
  DisposDialog(TheDialog);
END;{DoChannelMapDlog}


{————————————————————————————————————}

PROCEDURE DoVelocityMapDlog;
  VAR
     DlogItem, DlogType, VelocityOffset: integer;
     DlogRect: rect;
     DlogHandle: handle;

     thisInvertFlag, thisScaleFlag, thisFixedFlag: integer;
     thisVOffset, thisVSFactor: integer;

BEGIN
  thisInvertFlag := VInvertFlag;
  thisFixedFlag := VFixedFlag;
  thisScaleFlag := VScaleFlag;
  thisVOffset := VOffset;
  thisVSFactor := VSFactor;
  ShowResDialog(VelocityMapDlogID, On);

  ResetDlogCntrl(VInvertItem, thisInvertFlag, 1); {check box if flag is one}
  ResetDlogCntrl(VScaleItem, thisScaleFlag, 1);{check box if flag is one }
  ResetDlogCntrl(VFixedItem, thisFixedFlag, 1);{check box if flag is one }
  NumberToItem(theDialog, VOffsetItem, thisVOffset);
  NumberToItem(theDialog, VSFactorItem, thisVSFactor);
```

```
REPEAT
   BEGIN
      ModalDialog(NIL, DlogItem);
      CASE DlogItem OF
         VInvertItem:
            BEGIN
               ResetCheckBox(DlogItem);
               thisInvertFlag := ToggleFlag(thisInvertFlag);         {toggle the flag from 1 to 0 or 0 to 1}
            END;
         VScaleItem:
            BEGIN
               ResetCheckBox(DlogItem);
               thisScaleFlag := ToggleFlag(thisScaleFlag);          {toggle the flag from 1 to 0 or 0 to 1}
            END;
         VFixedItem:
            BEGIN
               ResetCheckBox(DlogItem);
               thisFixedFlag := ToggleFlag(thisFixedFlag);          {toggle the flag from 1 to 0 or 0 to 1}
            END;
         VOffsetItem:
            thisVOffset := CheckValue(DlogItem, Forte, dataValueCode);
         VSFactorItem:
            thisVSFactor := CheckValue(DlogItem, 1, scaleValueCode);
         OTHERWISE
            ;{        do nothing}
      END {CaseDlogItem}
   END; {repeat}
UNTIL (DlogItem = VDoneItem) OR (DlogItem = VCancelItem);
IF DlogItem = VDoneItem THEN
   BEGIN
      VInvertFlag := thisInvertFlag;
      VScaleFlag := thisScaleFlag;
      VFixedFlag := thisFixedFlag;
      VOffset := thisVOffset;
      VSFactor := thisVSFactor;
   END
ELSE
   ;{Cancel: don't change anything}
DisposDialog(TheDialog);
END;{DoVelocityMap}
```

```
{─────────────────────────────────────────────────}
  PROCEDURE DoControlMapDlog;
    VAR
      DlogItem, DlogType: integer;
      DlogRect: rect;
      DlogHandle: handle;

      thisControl: MIDIDataArray;
      count, thisSourceCntrl, thisTargetCntrl: integer;
      thisInvertFlag, thisScaleFlag: integer;
      thisCntrlOffset, thisCntrlSFactor: integer;

BEGIN
  thisSourceCntrl := 1;
  thisCntrlOffset := CntrlOffset;
  thisCntrlSFactor := CntrlSFactor;
  thisTargetCntrl := ControlMaps[thisSourceCntrl];
  thisInvertFlag := CntrlInvertFlag;
  thisScaleFlag := CntrlScaleFlag;
  ShowResDialog(ControlMapDlogID, On);

  FOR count := ModController TO DataDecrement DO
    thisControl[count] := ControlMaps[count];

  ResetDlogCntrl(ControlInvertItem, thisInvertFlag, 1); {check box if flag is one}
  ResetDlogCntrl(ControlScaleItem, thisScaleFlag, 1);{light box if flag is one }
  NumberToItem(theDialog, ControlOffsetItem, thisCntrlOffset);
  NumberToItem(theDialog, ControlSFactorItem, thisCntrlSFactor);
  NumberToItem(theDialog, ControlSourceItem, thisSourceCntrl);
  NumberToItem(theDialog, ControlTargetItem, thisControl[thisSourceCntrl]);


  REPEAT
    BEGIN
      ModalDialog(NIL, DlogItem);
      CASE DlogItem OF
        ControlOffsetItem:
          thisCntrlOffset := CheckValue(DlogItem, MiddleC, dataValueCode);
        ControlSFactorItem:
          thisCntrlSFactor := CheckValue(DlogItem, 1, scaleValueCode);
        ControlInvertItem:
          BEGIN
            ResetCheckBox(DlogItem);
            thisInvertFlag := ToggleFlag(thisInvertFlag);          {toggle the flag from 1 to 0 or 0 to 1}
          END;
        ControlScaleItem:
          BEGIN
            ResetCheckBox(DlogItem);
            thisScaleFlag := ToggleFlag(thisScaleFlag);          {toggle the flag from 1 to 0 or 0 to 1}
          END;
        ControlSourceItem:
```

```
            BEGIN
                thisSourceCntrl := CheckValue(DlogItem, ModController, controlValueCode);
                NumberToItem(theDialog, ControlTargetItem, thisControl[thisSourceCntrl]);
            END;
        ControlTargetItem:
            BEGIN
                thisTargetCntrl := CheckValue(DlogItem, ModController, controlValueCode);
                thisControl[thisSourceCntrl] := thisTargetCntrl;
            END;
        ControlClearItem:
            BEGIN
                InitControllerMaps;
                FOR count := ModController TO DataDecrement DO
                    thisControl[count] := ControlMaps[count];
                NumberToItem(theDialog, ControlSourceItem, thisSourceCntrl);
                NumberToItem(theDialog, ControlTargetItem, thisControl[thisSourceCntrl]);
            END;
        OTHERWISE
            ;{      do nothing}
    END {CaseDlogItem}
  END; {repeat}
UNTIL (DlogItem = ControlDoneItem) OR (DlogItem = ControlCancelItem);
IF DlogItem = ControlDoneItem THEN
    BEGIN
        CntrlInvertFlag := thisInvertFlag;
        CntrlScaleFlag := thisScaleFlag;
        CntrlOffset := thisCntrlOffset;
        CntrlSFactor := thisCntrlSFactor;
        FOR count := ModController TO DataDecrement DO
            ControlMaps[count] := thisControl[count];
    END
ELSE
    ;{Cancel: don't change anything}
    DisposDialog(TheDialog);
END;{DoControlMapDlog}



{———————————————————————————————}
PROCEDURE DoProgramMapDlog;
    VAR
        DlogItem, DlogType: integer;
        DlogRect: rect;
        DlogHandle: handle;

        thisMap: MIDIDataArray;
        count, SourceProgram, TargetProgram: integer;
```

```
BEGIN
   SourceProgram := 1;
   TargetProgram := 1;
   FOR count := 0 TO MaxDataValue DO
     thisMap[count] := ProgramMaps[count];

   ShowResDialog(PChangeMapDlogID, On);

   NumberToItem(theDialog, PchangeMapItem, SourceProgram);
   NumberToItem(theDialog, PChangeToItem, thisMap[SourceProgram]);

   REPEAT
     BEGIN
        ModalDialog(NIL, DlogItem);
        CASE DlogItem OF
          PChangeMapItem:
            BEGIN
               SourceProgram := CheckValue(DlogItem, 1, dataValueCode);
               NumberToItem(theDialog, PChangeToItem, thisMap[SourceProgram]);
            END;
          PChangeToItem:
            BEGIN
               TargetProgram := CheckValue(DlogItem, 1, dataValueCode);
               thisMap[SourceProgram] := TargetProgram;
            END;
          PChangeClearItem:
            BEGIN
               FOR count := 0 TO MaxDataValue DO
                  thisMap[count] := count;
               NumberToItem(theDialog, PchangeMapItem, SourceProgram);
               NumberToItem(theDialog, PChangeToItem, thisMap[SourceProgram]);

            END;
          OTHERWISE
             ;{do nothing}
        END {CaseDlogItem}
     END; {repeat}
   UNTIL (DlogItem = PChangeDoneItem) OR (DlogItem = PChangeCancelItem);
   IF DlogItem = PChangeDoneItem THEN
     BEGIN
        FOR count := 0 TO MaxDataValue DO
           ProgramMaps[count] := thisMap[count];
     END
   ELSE
     ;{Cancel: don't change anything}
   DisposDialog(TheDialog);
END;{ DoProgramMapDlog}
```

```
{────────────────────────────────────────────────}
PROCEDURE DoTransposeDlog;
   VAR
      DlogItem, DlogType: integer;
      DlogRect: rect;
      DlogHandle: handle;
      thisHiNote, thisLoNote, thisShift, count: integer;
BEGIN

   thisHiNote := HiTransposeNote;
   thisLoNote := LoTransposeNote;
   thisShift := KeyTranspose;

   ShowResDialog(TransposeDlogID, On);
   NumberToItem(theDialog, TransposeHiNoteItem, thisHiNote);
   NumberToItem(theDialog, TransposeLoNoteItem, thisLoNote);
   NumberToItem(theDialog, TransposeKeyShiftItem, thisShift);

   REPEAT
      BEGIN
         ModalDialog(NIL, DlogItem);
         CASE DlogItem OF

            TransposeHiNoteItem:
               BEGIN
                  thisHiNote := CheckValue(DlogItem, MiddleC + 24, dataValueCode);
                  IF thisHiNote + thisShift > maxDataValue THEN
                     BEGIN          {reset KeyTranspose so it works with this hi note value}
                        thisShift := maxDataValue - thisHiNote;
                        NumberToItem(theDialog, TransposeKeyShiftItem, thisShift);
                     END;
               END;

            TransposeLoNoteItem:
               BEGIN          {reset KeyTranspose so it works with this lo note value}
                  thisLoNote := CheckValue(DlogItem, MiddleC, dataValueCode);
                  IF thisLoNote + thisShift < 0 THEN
                     BEGIN
                        thisShift := -thisLoNote;
                        NumberToItem(theDialog, TransposeKeyShiftItem, thisShift);
                     END
               END;
```

```
TransposeKeyShiftItem:
   BEGIN
      thisShift := CheckValue(DlogItem, 0, harmonyValueCode);
      IF thisLoNote + thisShift < 0 THEN
         BEGIN          {reset lo note to work with this key shift value}
            thisLoNote := -thisShift;
            NumberToItem(theDialog, TransposeLoNoteItem, thisLoNote);
         END
      ELSE IF thisHiNote + thisShift > maxDataValue THEN
         BEGIN          {reset hi note to work with this key shift value}
            thisHiNote := maxDataValue - thisShift;
            NumberToItem(theDialog, TransposeHiNoteItem, thisHiNote);
         END;
   END;

TransposeClearItem:
   BEGIN
      InitTranspose;
      thisHiNote := HiTransposeNote;
      thisLoNote := LoTransposeNote;
      thisShift := KeyTranspose;
      NumberToItem(theDialog, TransposeHiNoteItem, thisHiNote);
      NumberToItem(theDialog, TransposeLoNoteItem, thisLoNote);
      NumberToItem(theDialog, TransposeKeyShiftItem, thisShift);
   END;


OTHERWISE
   ;{        do nothing}
   END {CaseDlogItem}
   END; {repeat}


UNTIL (DlogItem = TransposeDoneItem) OR (DlogItem = TransposeCancelItem);

IF DlogItem = TransposeDoneItem THEN
   BEGIN
      FOR count := thisLoNote TO thisHiNote DO
         NoteMap[count] := NoteMap[count] + thisShift;  {add KeyTranspose value to note numbers}
      HiTransposeNote := thisHiNote;
      LoTransposeNote := thisLoNote;
      KeyTranspose := thisShift;
   END
ELSE
   ;{Cancel: don't change anything}

   DisposDialog(TheDialog);
END;{DoTransposeDlog}
```

```
{————————————————————————————————————————————}
  PROCEDURE DoScaleMapNoteItem (thisScale: ScaleArray; theDlogItem, scaleNumber: integer);
  BEGIN
     thisScale[scaleNumber] := NumberFromItem(theDialog, theDlogItem);
     IF NOT InDataRange(thisScale[scaleNumber], -24, 24) THEN
        BEGIN
           TellUser(AboutAlertID, 'Harmony value must be  ± 2 octaves');
           thisScale[scaleNumber] := ScaleMap[scaleNumber];
           NumberToItem(theDialog, theDlogItem, thisScale[scaleNumber]);
        END;
  END;


{————————————————————————————————————————————}
  PROCEDURE DoScaleMapDlog;
     VAR
        DlogItem, DlogType, ItemListOffset: integer;
        DlogRect: rect;
        DlogHandle: handle;

        thisScale: ScaleArray;
        count, theScaleItem, ScaleID: integer;
        thisScaleName: str255;

  BEGIN
     ItemListOffset := 3;
     ShowResDialog(ScaleMapDlogID, On);
     theScaleItem := ScaleMapCItem;

     FOR count := 1 TO ScaleSize DO
        BEGIN
           thisScale[count] := ScaleMap[count];
           NumberToItem(theDialog, theScaleItem, thisScale[count]);
           theScaleItem := theScaleItem + 1;
        END;

     thisScaleName := ScaleName;
     GetDItem(theDialog, ScaleMapNameItem, Dlogtype, DlogHandle, DlogRect);
     SetIText(DlogHandle, thisScaleName);

     REPEAT
        BEGIN
           ModalDialog(NIL, DlogItem);
           CASE DlogItem OF
              ScaleMapCItem:
                 BEGIN
                    ScaleID := DlogItem - ItemListOffset;
                    thisScale[ScaleID] := CheckValue(DlogItem, majorThird, harmonyValueCode);
                 END;
```

```
ScaleMapCsItem:
  BEGIN
    ScaleID := DlogItem - ItemListOffset;
    thisScale[ScaleID] := CheckValue(DlogItem, majorThird, harmonyValueCode);
  END;
ScaleMapDItem:
  BEGIN
    ScaleID := DlogItem - ItemListOffset;
    thisScale[ScaleID] := CheckValue(DlogItem, majorThird, harmonyValueCode);
  END;
ScaleMapDsItem:
  BEGIN
    ScaleID := DlogItem - ItemListOffset;
    thisScale[ScaleID] := CheckValue(DlogItem, majorThird, harmonyValueCode);
  END;
ScaleMapEItem:
  BEGIN
    ScaleID := DlogItem - ItemListOffset;
    thisScale[ScaleID] := CheckValue(DlogItem, majorThird, harmonyValueCode);
  END;
ScaleMapFItem:
  BEGIN
    ScaleID := DlogItem - ItemListOffset;
    thisScale[ScaleID] := CheckValue(DlogItem, majorThird, harmonyValueCode);
  END;
ScaleMapFsItem:
  BEGIN
    ScaleID := DlogItem - ItemListOffset;
    thisScale[ScaleID] := CheckValue(DlogItem, majorThird, harmonyValueCode);
  END;
ScaleMapGItem:
  BEGIN
    ScaleID := DlogItem - ItemListOffset;
    thisScale[ScaleID] := CheckValue(DlogItem, majorThird, harmonyValueCode);
  END;
ScaleMapGsItem:
  BEGIN
    ScaleID := DlogItem - ItemListOffset;
    thisScale[ScaleID] := CheckValue(DlogItem, majorThird, harmonyValueCode);
  END;
ScaleMapAItem:
  BEGIN
    ScaleID := DlogItem - ItemListOffset;
    thisScale[ScaleID] := CheckValue(DlogItem, majorThird, harmonyValueCode);
  END;
ScaleMapAsItem:
  BEGIN
    ScaleID := DlogItem - ItemListOffset;
    thisScale[ScaleID] := CheckValue(DlogItem, majorThird, harmonyValueCode);
  END;
```

```
         ScaleMapBItem:
           BEGIN
             ScaleID := DlogItem - ItemListOffset;
             thisScale[ScaleID] := CheckValue(DlogItem, majorThird, harmonyValueCode);
           END;
         ScaleMapNameItem:

           ;
         ScaleMapClearItem:
           BEGIN
             InitScaleMap;
             theScaleItem := ScaleMapCItem;
             FOR count := 1 TO ScaleSize DO
               BEGIN
                 thisScale[count] := ScaleMap[count];
                 NumberToItem(theDialog, theScaleItem, thisScale[count]);
                 theScaleItem := theScaleItem + 1;
               END;

             thisScaleName := ScaleName;
             GetDItem(theDialog, ScaleMapNameItem, Dlogtype, DlogHandle, DlogRect);
             SetIText(DlogHandle, thisScaleName);
           END;
         OTHERWISE
           ;{        do nothing}
       END {CaseDlogItem}
     END; {repeat}
  UNTIL (DlogItem = ScaleMapDoneItem) OR (DlogItem = ScaleMapCancelItem);
  IF DlogItem = ScaleMapDoneItem THEN
     BEGIN
       FOR count := 1 TO ScaleSize DO
         ScaleMap[count] := thisScale[count];

       GetDItem(theDialog, ScaleMapNameItem, Dlogtype, DlogHandle, DlogRect);
       getIText(DlogHandle, thisScaleName);
       ScaleName := thisScaleName;
     END
  ELSE
     ;{Cancel: don't change anything}
  DisposDialog(TheDialog);
END;{DoScaleMapDlog}

{—————————————————————————————}

PROCEDURE DoHarmonyMapDlog;
  VAR
     DlogItem, DlogType: integer;
     DlogRect: rect;
     DlogHandle: handle;

     HarmonyDialog: DialogPtr;

     thisHiNote, thisLoNote, thisSize: integer;
     thisScaleName: str255;
```

323

```
BEGIN
  thisHiNote := HiHarmonyNote;
  thisLoNote := LoHarmonyNote;
  thisSize := HarmonySize;
  thisScaleName := ScaleName;

  ShowResDialog(HarmonyDlogID, On);
  HarmonyDialog := theDialog; {store the pointer to the Harmony dialog }

  NumberToItem(theDialog, HarmonyHiNoteItem, thisHiNote);
  NumberToItem(theDialog, HarmonyLoNoteItem, thisLoNote);
  NumberToItem(theDialog, HarmonyPolyItem, thisSize);

  GetDItem(theDialog, HarmonyScaleMapItem, Dlogtype, DlogHandle, DlogRect);
  SetIText(DlogHandle, thisScaleName);

  REPEAT
    BEGIN
      ModalDialog(NIL, DlogItem);
      CASE DlogItem OF
        HarmonyHiNoteItem:
          BEGIN
            thisHiNote := CheckValue(DlogItem, MiddleC + 24, dataValueCode);
          END;
        HarmonyLoNoteItem:
          BEGIN
            thisLoNote := CheckValue(DlogItem, MiddleC, dataValueCode);
          END;
        HarmonyPolyItem:
          BEGIN
            thisSize := CheckValue(DlogItem, HarmonySize, polyphonyValueCode);
          END;
        HarmonyScaleMapItem:
          BEGIN
            GetDItem(theDialog, HarmonyScaleMapItem, Dlogtype, DlogHandle, DlogRect);
            GetIText(DlogHandle, thisScaleName);
          END;
        HarmonyNewScaleItem:
          BEGIN
            DoScaleMapDlog;
            theDialog := HarmonyDialog;
            GetDItem(theDialog, HarmonyScaleMapItem, Dlogtype, DlogHandle, DlogRect);
            SetIText(DlogHandle, ScaleName);
          END;
        HarmonizeItem:
          BEGIN
            HarmonySize := thisSize;
            HiHarmonyNote := thisHiNote;
            LoHarmonyNote := thisLoNote;
            PlayHarmony;
          END;
```

```
        OTHERWISE
            ;{        do nothing}
        END {CaseDlogItem}
      END; {repeat}
    UNTIL DlogItem = HarmonyDoneItem;
    DisposDialog(TheDialog);
  END;{DoHarmonyMapDlog}


END.
```

```
{FIle name:  MIDI Tools 0                                            }
{Description:    MIDI procedures and functions for                   }
{                    Real Time MIDI Lab program                      }

{ uses MIDIPascal  code library                                      }

{Original Date: 9/16/88          By: SDF                ...............}

{MidiPascal™ is a trademark of ALTECH SYSTEMS                        }
{ Lightspeed Pascal is a trademark of THINK Technologies, Inc.       }


UNIT MPascalTools;

INTERFACE

  USES
    RTLabGlobals, MidiPascal;

    PROCEDURE SetMIDIPort;
    PROCEDURE SetMPFilters;
    PROCEDURE DoActiveSenseFilter;
    PROCEDURE DoMClockFilter;
    PROCEDURE DoMClockCmdsFilter;
    PROCEDURE DoSystemFilter;
    PROCEDURE DoAfterTouchFilter;
    PROCEDURE DoControllerFilter;
    PROCEDURE DoPChangeFilter;
    PROCEDURE DoBenderFilter;
    PROCEDURE PlayTestNote;
    PROCEDURE PlayMessage (theMessage: MIDIMessage);
    PROCEDURE PlayKeyTest;
    PROCEDURE PlayNote (keyNumber, velocityData: MIDIData);
    PROCEDURE DoMIDIStartUp;
    PROCEDURE KillAllNotes;
    PROCEDURE RunThruTest;
    PROCEDURE resetPen;
    PROCEDURE MIDIThruDisplay;
    PROCEDURE PlayHarmony;
    PROCEDURE DoMIDIThru;

    PROCEDURE TextDrawInit;
IMPLEMENTATION

{─────────────────────────────────────────────}
  FUNCTION InvertData (byte: integer): integer;
    VAR
        x: integer;
  BEGIN
    x := maxDataValue - byte;
    InvertData := x;
  END;
```

```
{————————————————————————————}
   FUNCTION WaitForMIDI: integer;
      VAR
         x: integer;
   BEGIN
      MIDIIn(x);
      WHILE x = -1 DO
         MIDIIn(x);
      WaitForMIDI := x;
   END;{WaitForMIDI}

{————————————————————————————}
   FUNCTION MIDIorMouse: integer;
      VAR
         x: integer;
   BEGIN
      MIDIIn(x);
      WHILE (x = -1) AND (button = false) DO
         BEGIN
            MIDIIn(x);
         END;
      MIDIorMouse := x;
   END; {MIDIorMouse}

{————————————————————————————}
   FUNCTION GetChannel (byte: integer): integer;
      VAR
         x: integer;
   BEGIN
      x := bitAnd(byte, channelMask);
      GetChannel := x;
   END;{GetChannel}

{————————————————————————————}
   FUNCTION GetStatus (byte: integer): integer;
      VAR
         X: integer;
   BEGIN
      x := bitAnd(byte, statusMask);
      GetStatus := x;
   END; {GetStatus}

{————————————————————————————}
   FUNCTION GetSemitone (key: integer): integer;
      VAR
         x: integer;

   BEGIN
      x := (key MOD 12) + 1;
      GetSemitone := x;
   END;{GetSemitone}

{————————————————————————————}
```

```
PROCEDURE SetMIDIPort;
BEGIN
   MidiPort(ClockMhz);
   MidiPort(theSCSI);
   MIDI(resetMIDI);
END;
```

{————————————————————————}

```
PROCEDURE DoActiveSenseFilter;
BEGIN
   IF MPFilters[filter1] = 1 THEN
      MidiFilter(Filter1, ActiveSense, ActiveSense, 0)
   ELSE
      MidiFilter(Filter1, 0, 1, 0);
END; {DoActiveSenseFilter}
```

{————————————————————————}

```
PROCEDURE DoMClockFilter;
BEGIN
   IF MPFilters[filter2] = 1 THEN
      MidiFilter(Filter2, MIDIClock, MIDIClock, 0)
   ELSE
      MidiFilter(Filter2, 0, 1, 0);
END;
```

{————————————————————————}

```
PROCEDURE DoMClockCmdsFilter;
BEGIN
   IF MPFilters[filter3] = 1 THEN
      MidiFilter(Filter3, MIDIClock, MIDIStop, 0)
   ELSE
      MidiFilter(Filter3, 0, 1, 0);
END;
```

{————————————————————————}

```
PROCEDURE DoPChangeFilter;
BEGIN
   IF MPFilters[filter4] = 1 THEN
      MidiFilter(Filter4, ProgramChange, ProgramChange, 1)
   ELSE
      MidiFilter(Filter4, 0, 1, 0);
END;
```

{————————————————————————}

```
PROCEDURE DoAfterTouchFilter;
BEGIN
   IF MPFilters[filter5] = 1 THEN
      MidiFilter(Filter5, ChannelPressure, ChannelPressure, 2)
   ELSE
      MidiFilter(Filter5, 0, 1, 0);
END;
```

{————————————————————————}

```
    PROCEDURE DoControllerFilter;
    BEGIN
      IF MPFilters[filter6] = 1 THEN
        MidiFilter(Filter6, ControlChange, ControlChange, 2)
      ELSE
        MidiFilter(Filter6, 0, 1, 0);
    END;
```

{——————————————————————————————}

```
    PROCEDURE DoBenderFilter;
    BEGIN
      IF MPFilters[filter7] = 1 THEN
        MidiFilter(Filter7, PitchBend, PitchBend, 2)
      ELSE
        MidiFilter(Filter7, 0, 1, 0);
    END;
```

{——————————————————————————————}

```
    PROCEDURE DoSystemFilter;
    BEGIN
      IF MPFilters[filter8] = 1 THEN
        MidiFilter(Filter8, SystemMessage, SystemMessage, 0)
      ELSE
        MidiFilter(Filter8, 0, 1, 0);
    END;
```

{——————————————————————————————}

```
    PROCEDURE SetMPFilters;
    BEGIN
      DoActiveSenseFilter;
      DoMClockFilter;
      DoMClockCmdsFilter;
      DoSystemFilter;
      DoAfterTouchFilter;
      DoControllerFilter;
      DoPChangeFilter;
      DoBenderFilter;
    END;{SetMPFilters }
```

```
{————————————————————————————————}
PROCEDURE PlayTestNote;
  VAR
    level1count, level2count: integer;
BEGIN
  MIDIOut(NoteOn);
  MIDIOut(theNote);
  MIDIOut(theVelocity);

  IF theDuration > 0 THEN
    BEGIN
      FOR level1count := 1 TO 10 * theduration DO
        FOR level2count := 1 TO 500 DO
                                              {wait for a while...}

      MIDIOut(NoteOff);                       { then send note off}
      MIDIOut(theNote);
      MIDIOut(OffVelocity);
    END;
END;{ PlayTestNote}


{————————————————————————————————}
PROCEDURE PlayMessage (theMessage: MIDIMessage);
BEGIN
  CASE theMessage.size OF
    1:   {1 byte message format}
       MIDIOut(theMessage.status);


    2:   {2 byte message format}
       BEGIN
         MIDIOut(theMessage.status);
         MIDIOut(theMessage.data1);
       END;

    3:   {3 byte message format}
       BEGIN
         MIDIOut(theMessage.status);
         MIDIOut(theMessage.data1);
         MIDIOut(theMessage.data2);
       END;
  END; {case theMessage.size}

END;{ PlayMessage}
```

```
{─────────────────────────────────────────────────}
  PROCEDURE RunThruTest;
    VAR
      displayRect: rect;
      count, InByte: integer;
      dontCare: longint;
  BEGIN
    WITH displayRect DO
      BEGIN
        top := 40;
        left := 20;
        bottom := 80;
        right := 80;
      END;
    frameRect(displayRect);
    insetRect(displayRect, 5, 5);
    TextFont(geneva);
    textSize(9);
    FOR count := 1 TO repeatCount DO
      BEGIN
        MIDIOut(testByte);
        delay(1, dontCare);
        MIDIIn(InByte);
        IF testByte <> InByte THEN
          BEGIN
            moveTo(50, 50);
            writeDraw(InByte);
            moveTo(50, 100);
            writeDraw(testByte);
          END;
      END;

  END;{ RunThruTest}
```

```
{————————————————————————————————}
PROCEDURE KillAllNotes;
   VAR
      tabCount, channel, keyNumber: integer;
      row, column: integer;
      displayRect: rect;
BEGIN
   WITH displayRect DO
      BEGIN
         top := 50;
         left := 50;
         bottom := 80;
         right := 215;
      END;
   frameRect(displayRect);
   row := 30;
   column := 35;
   tabCount := 1;
   moveTo(column, row);

   textFont(Geneva);
   textSize(9);
   WriteDraw(' Turning off all notes for channel: ');
   row := row + 30;
   moveTo(column, row);
   FOR channel := 0 TO 15 DO
      BEGIN
         MIDIOut(ControlChange + channel);
         MIDIOut(AllNotesData);
         MIDIOut(0);
         MIDIOut(NoteOff + channel);
         IF tabCount = 9 THEN
            BEGIN
               tabCount := 1;
               row := row + 10;
            END; {if tabCount}
         tabCount := tabCount + 1;
         moveTo((column - 15) * tabCount, row);
         WriteDraw(channel + 1);
         FOR keyNumber := 0 TO 127 DO                    {running status transmission}
            BEGIN
               MIDIOut(KeyNumber);
               MIDIOut(0);
            END; {for KeyNumber}
      END; {for channel}
   EraseRect(displayRect);
END;{KillAllNotes}
```

```
{------------------------------------------------------------}
  PROCEDURE PlayNote (keyNumber, velocityData: MIDIData);
  BEGIN
    MIDIOut(NoteOn);
    MIDIOut(keyNumber);
    MIDIOut(velocityData);
  END;{ PlayNote (keyNumber, velocityData)}

{------------------------------------------------------------}
  PROCEDURE DoOneNote (keyNumber, velocityData: MIDIData; ticks: longint);
    VAR
        time: longint;
  BEGIN
    PlayNote(keyNumber, theVelocity);
    delay(ticks, time);
    PlayNote(keyNumber, OffVelocity);
  END;{doOneNote}

{------------------------------------------------------------}
  PROCEDURE PlayKeyTest;
    VAR
        firstNote, lastNote, count1, count2, loopSize: integer;
        ticks, time: longint;
        hiLimit, lolimit, swing: integer;
        interval1, interval2: integer;
  BEGIN
    hiLimit := maxDataValue;
    loLimit := minDataValue;
    ticks := ArpSpeed;
    swing := (ticks * 1);
    interval1 := minorThird;
    interval2 := majorThird;
    lastNote := startNote;
    loopSize := EndNote - StartNote;
{Start Loop}
    FOR count2 := 1 TO loopSize DO
      BEGIN
        firstNote := lastNote;
        BEGIN
          FOR count1 := 1 TO ArpLength DO
            BEGIN
              DoOneNote(firstNote, Forte, swing);
              firstNote := FirstNote + interval1;
```

```
            IF FirstNote > hiLimit THEN
               BEGIN
                  firstNote := StartNote;
                  leave;
               END; {leave check}
            DoOneNote(firstNote, Forte, ticks);
            firstNote := FirstNote + interval2;

            IF FirstNote > hiLimit THEN
               BEGIN
                  firstNote := endNote;                    {don'tgo over end note}
                  leave;
               END;
         END;


         FOR count1 := 1 TO ArpLength - 1 DO
            BEGIN
               DoOneNote(firstNote, Forte, ticks);
               firstNote := FirstNote + interval2;

               IF FirstNote < loLimit THEN
                  BEGIN
                     firstNote := StartNote;
                     leave;
                  END; {leave check}
               DoOneNote(firstNote, Forte, swing);
               firstNote := FirstNote - (interval1 + interval2);

               IF FirstNote < loLimit THEN
                  BEGIN
                     firstNote := StartNote;               {don't go under start note}
                     leave;
                  END;
            END;


         lastNote := lastNote + 1;
{End of Loop}
        END;
      END;
   END; {PlayKeyTest}


{-------------------------------------------------}
   PROCEDURE ResetPen;
   BEGIN
      MoveTo(20, 40);
   END;{ResetPen}
```

```
{—————————————————————————————————}
  PROCEDURE DrawData (inByte: integer);
    VAR
       thePoint: point;
       displayRect: rect;
       column, row, line: integer;
       leftEdge, bottomEdge: integer;
BEGIN
    leftEdge := 220;
    bottomEdge := 90;
    column := 20;
    line := 10;
    row := 40;
    WITH displayRect DO
       BEGIN
          top := 25;                              {set dimensions of text display}
          bottom := 100;
          left := 10;
          right := 275;
       END;
    insetRect(displayRect, 5, 5);

    GetPen(thePoint);
    textFont(geneva);
    textSize(9);
    IF thePoint.h > leftEdge THEN
       BEGIN
          thePoint.h := column;
          thePoint.v := thePoint.V + line;
          IF thePoint.v > bottomEdge THEN
             BEGIN
                thePoint.v := row;
                EraseRect(displayRect);
             END;
          MoveTo(thePoint.h, thePoint.v);
       END;
    WriteDraw('   ', inByte);
END;{draw data}
```

```
{————————————————————————————————————}
    PROCEDURE TextDrawInit;                    {set up dimensions of text and draw windows}
    BEGIN
      tRect.top := 40;                         {set dimensions of text display}
      tRect.bottom := 115;
      tRect.left := 25;
      tRect.right := 475;
      SetTextRect(tRect);                       {draw text display on screen}
      ShowText;                                 {enable text drawing}

      grfxRect.top := 135;                      {set global dimensions of text draw display}
      grfxRect.bottom := 325;
      grfxRect.left := 25;
      grfxRect.right := 475;
      SetDrawingrect(grfxRect);
      ShowDrawing;

      dataDrawRect.top := 0;                    {set local dimensions of draw display}
      dataDrawRect.bottom := 190;
      dataDrawRect.left := 0;
      dataDrawRect.right := 450;
    END;{TextDrawInit}
{————————————————————————————————————}
    PROCEDURE DrawDataByte (inByte: integer); {display data value}
    BEGIN
      WriteDraw(inByte);
    END;{draw data}
{————————————————————————————————————}
    PROCEDURE DrawStatusByte (InByte: integer); {display MIDI status type}
      VAR
        status: integer;
    BEGIN
      status := BitAnd(Inbyte, $f0);
      CASE status OF
        NoteOff:
          WriteDraw('NoteOff');
        NoteOn:
          WriteDraw('NoteOn');
        PolyPressure:
          WriteDraw('Poly Pressure');
        ControlChange:
          WriteDraw('Controller');
        ProgramChange:
          WriteDraw('Prgrm Change');
        ChannelPressure:
          WriteDraw('After Touch');
        PitchBend:
          WriteDraw('Pitch Bend');
        SystemMessage:
          WriteDraw('System Message');
        OTHERWISE
          WriteDraw('UNKNOWN STATUS !!')
      END {case status}
    END; {DrawStatus}
```

336

```
{──────────────────────────────────────────}
  PROCEDURE SetUpStatusDraw;                {move pen to start of next line}
    VAR
       thePoint: point;
  BEGIN
    tabCount := 1;
    GetPen(thePoint);
    thePoint.v := thePoint.v + vertOffset;   {move position down one line}
    IF thePoint.v > 90 THEN {VerticalLimit}
    {check vertical position}
       BEGIN
          thePoint.v := Row1;               {position of  top od display}
          EraseRect(dataDrawRect);
       END;
    MoveTo(Column1, thePoint.v);            {move pen}
  END;{SetUpStatusDraw}
     {──────────────────────────────────────}
PROCEDURE SetUpDataDraw;                    {move pen to next column}
    VAR
       thePoint: point;
  BEGIN
    tabCount := tabCount + 1;
    GetPen(thePoint);
    thePoint.h := tabCount * horzOffset;
    IF thePoint.h > 220 THEN {HorizontalLimit}
    {check horizontal position}
       BEGIN
          thePoint.h := horzOffset;         {position of left side of display}
          tabCount := 1;
          thePoint.v := thePoint.v + vertOffset;  {move pen down one line}
       END;
    IF thePoint.v > 90 THEN {VerticalLimit}
    {check vertical position}
       BEGIN
          thePoint.v := Row1;               {position of top of display}
          EraseRect(dataDrawRect);          {erase previous display}
       END;
    MoveTo(thePoint.h, thePoint.v);         {move pen to new position}
  END;{SetUpDataDraw}


  {──────────────────────────────────────────}
PROCEDURE DoStatusByte (InByte: integer);  {process status byte}
  BEGIN
    SetUpStatusDraw;
    DrawStatusByte(InByte);
  END;{DoStatusByte}


{──────────────────────────────────────────}
  PROCEDURE DoDataByte (InByte: integer); {process data byte}
  BEGIN
    SetUpDataDraw;
    DrawDataByte(InByte);
  END;{DoDataByte}
```

```
{———————————————————}
  PROCEDURE ProcessMIDI (InByte: integer);    {parse MIDI status and data}
  BEGIN
     textFont(geneva);
     textSize(9);
     WITH dataDrawRect DO
        BEGIN
           top := 25;                          {set dimensions of text display}
           bottom := 100;
           left := 10;
           right := 275;
        END;
     insetRect(dataDrawRect, 5, 5);

     IF InByte > maxDataValue THEN
        DoStatusByte(InByte)
     ELSE
        DoDataByte(InByte);
  END;{ProcessMIDI}

{———————————————————}
  PROCEDURE MIDIThruDisplay;
     VAR
        inByte: integer;                       {these variables hold MIDI data}
  BEGIN
     MIDIIn(InByte);                           {check In port for data (Inbyte holds result)}
     IF InByte <> -1 THEN                      {this is only true when Inbyte is valid MIDI data }
        BEGIN
           MIDIOut(InByte);                     {send the data to the Out port}
           ProcessMIDI(InByte);
        END; {if <>-1}
        MIDI(resetMIDI);}
  END; {MIDIThruDisplay}

{———————————————————}
  PROCEDURE DoUpdateStatus;
     VAR
        status: integer;
  BEGIN
     SkipByte := False;                        {when this is false bytes are Xmitted by MIDIThru }
     byteCount := 1;                           {new status, so reset byte counter to 1}

     status := GetStatus(theMIDIByte);
     CASE Status OF
        NoteOn, NoteOff:
           BEGIN
              IF RSFilters[1] = 1 THEN         {if the RSFilter box is checked}
                 BEGIN
                    SkipByte := True;          {bytes with this status won't be sent out}
                 END
              ELSE
                 RunningStatus := Status;      {updated to new running status}
           END;
```

338

```
    PolyPressure:
      BEGIN
        IF RSFilters[2] = 1 THEN
          BEGIN
            SkipByte := True;
          END
        ELSE
          RunningStatus := Status;
      END;

    ControlChange:
      BEGIN
        IF RSFilters[3] = 1 THEN
          BEGIN
            SkipByte := True;
          END
        ELSE
          RunningStatus := Status;
      END;

    ProgramChange:
      RunningStatus := Status;

    ChannelPressure:
      BEGIN
        IF RSFilters[4] = 1 THEN
          BEGIN
            SkipByte := True;
          END
        ELSE
          RunningStatus := Status;
      END;

    PitchBend:
      BEGIN
        IF RSFilters[5] = 1 THEN
          BEGIN
            SkipByte := True;
          END
        ELSE
          RunningStatus := Status;
      END;

    OTHERWISE                                    {take care of System Common and SysEx status bytes}
      IF Status < MIDIClock THEN                 {ignore System  Real Time bytes      }
        RunningStatus := Status;
  END; {Case Status }
END;{DoUpdateStatus }
```

```
{─────────────────────────────────────}
  PROCEDURE ChannelizeStatus;
    VAR
        inputChannel: integer;
  BEGIN
    inputChannel := GetChannel(theMIDIByte) + 1;
    theMIDIByte := RunningStatus + ChanMaps[inputChannel] - 1;
  END;{ChannelizeStatus }

{─────────────────────────────────────}
  PROCEDURE ProcessNoteData;
  BEGIN
    CASE ByteCount OF
        1: {process note number }
          BEGIN
            byteCount := 2;
            theMIDIByte := NoteMap[theMIDIByte];
          END;

        2: {process velocity data}
          BEGIN
            byteCount := 1;
            IF theMIDIByte > minOnVelocity THEN
              BEGIN
                IF VFixedFlag = 1 THEN
                  theMIDIByte := VOffset

                ELSE IF VScaleFlag = 1 THEN
                  BEGIN
                    theMIDIByte := (theMIDIByte + VOffset) * VSFactor;

                    IF theMIDIByte > maxDataValue THEN
                      theMIDIByte := maxDataValue

                    ELSE IF theMIDIByte < MinOnVelocity THEN
                      theMIDIByte := minOnVelocity;
                  END;
                IF VInvertFlag = 1 THEN
                  theMIDIByte := InvertData(theMIDIByte);
              END;
          END;

        OTHERWISE
            ;{do nothing}
    END;
  END;{ ProcessNoteData }
```

```
{——————————————————————————————}
  PROCEDURE SendHarmony (key, velocity: integer);
    VAR
       i, scaleNumber: integer;

  BEGIN{SendChord}
     FOR i := 1 TO HarmonySize DO
        BEGIN
           scaleNumber := GetSemitone(key);
           key := key + ScaleMap[scaleNumber];
           MIDIOut(key);
           MIDIOut(velocity);
        END; {for i}
  END;{SendChord}


{——————————————————————————————}
  PROCEDURE ProcessControlData;
  BEGIN
     CASE byteCount OF
       1:  {first data byte (controller ID}
          BEGIN
             byteCount := 2;                              {increment byte counter}
             theMIDIByte := ControlMaps[theMIDIByte];     {re-assign control ID to mapped value}
          END;

       2: {second data byte (controller value}
          BEGIN
             byteCount := 1;                              {reset Byte counter}
             IF CntrlScaleFlag = 1 THEN
                BEGIN
                   theMIDIByte := theMIDIByte + CntrlOffset;
                   IF theMIDIByte > maxDataValue THEN
                      theMIDIByte := maxDatavalue;
                END;
             IF CntrlInvertFlag = 1 THEN
                theMIDIByte := InvertData(theMIDIByte);
          END;

       OTHERWISE
          ;{do nothing}
     END;
  END;{ProcessControlData }
```

```
{——————————————————————————————}
 PROCEDURE DoMIDIThru;
   VAR
      inChannel: integer;

BEGIN
  REPEAT
    MIDIIn(theMIDIByte);
    IF theMIDIByte <> -1 THEN
      BEGIN
        IF theMIDIByte >= NoteOff THEN
          DoUpdateStatus;

        IF (theMIDIByte >= NoteOff) AND (theMIDIByte < SysEx) THEN
          ChannelizeStatus;

        IF theMIDIByte <= maxDataValue THEN
          CASE RunningStatus OF
            NoteOn, NoteOff:
              ProcessNoteData;

            PolyPressure:
              ;

            ControlChange:
              ProcessControlData;

            ProgramChange: {re-assign program number to mapped value}
              theMIDIByte := ProgramMaps[theMIDIByte];

            ChannelPressure:
              ;

            PitchBend:
              ;

            OTHERWISE
              ;

          END; {Case RunningStatus}

        IF SkipByte = False THEN
          MIDIOut(theMIDIByte);
      END; {if byte ,.-1}

  UNTIL Button;
END;{DoMIDIThru }


{——————————————————————————————}
```

```
PROCEDURE PlayHarmony;
   VAR
      byte1, keyData, velocityData, status: integer;
BEGIN {PlayHarmony}
   MIDI(ClearInput);
   MIDI(ClearOutput);

   REPEAT
     BEGIN
        MIDIIn(byte1);
        IF byte1 <> -1 THEN
          BEGIN
            IF byte1 >= NoteOff THEN
              status := GetStatus(byte1);

            CASE status OF
               NoteOff, NoteOn:
                 BEGIN

                    CASE GetStatus(byte1) OF
                       NoteOn:
                         BEGIN
                            MIDIOut(byte1);
                            keyData := WaitForMIDI;
                            velocityData := WaitForMIDI;
                            MIDIOut(keyData);
                            MIDIOut(velocityData);
                            IF (keyData > LoHarmonyNote) AND (Keydata < HiHarmonyNote) THEN
                               SendHarmony(keyData, velocityData);
                         END;{byte1=NoteOff,NoteOn}

                       OTHERWISE
                         BEGIN
                            keyData := byte1;
                            velocityData := WaitForMIDI;
                            MIDIOut(keyData);
                            MIDIOut(velocityData);
                            IF (keyData > LoHarmonyNote) AND (Keydata < HiHarmonyNote) THEN
                               SendHarmony(keyData, velocityData);
                         END;{otherwise byte1 = runningstatus data}

                    END;{case GetStatus(byte1)}
                 END;{ status = NoteOff,NoteOn}

               OTHERWISE
                    MIDIout(byte1);
            END;{Case Status}

          END;{byte1<> -1}
     END; {repeat loop}
   UNTIL button;
END;{PlayHarmony}

END.
```

Appendix B

Subroutine Listing for SysEx MIDI Lab

```
'File name:  SysEx Lab V1.0
'{Description:  System Exclusive  MIDI Lab program
'{Original Date: 10/1/88    By: Steve De Furia

'This program demonstrates the use of MIDIBASIC™ in the
'QuickBASIC ™ environment.

'MIDIBASIC™ is a trademark of ALTECH SYSTEMS
'QuickBASIC is a trademark of MICROSOFT Corporation
```

```
' If you compile this program,  you must install the CODE resources from
' MIDIBASIC into the compiled version of the program.
' Use ResEdit to copy the CODEs from MIDIBASIC and paste them into
' SysEx MIDI Lab's  Code resources.

' This program  is a System Exclusive "lab".  It will send request messages for:
'    DX7 II & TX802 voice edit buffers
'    CZ 1, 101, 230s, 5000, 1000, and  3000  single timbre data
'    MSB+ dumps
'    JamBox4 dumps
'    LXP-1 all parameters dumps

' It demonstrates sending and receiving one way and two way (handshaking)
' SysEx messages
'It also shows how to write and read MIDI data to disk, and  serves as a good
' example for a non-Toolbox version of a Macintosh event driven program
```
'---
```
'          Initialize BASIC
CLEAR ,90000!,5000

compiled% = 0                               'Toggle for compiled/interpreted versions (1 = compiler)
   FOR i%=1 TO PEEK(&H910)
     libname$=libname$+CHR$(PEEK(&H910+i%))
   NEXT
   IF compiled% THEN LIBRARY libname$ ELSE LIBRARY "MIDIBASIC"

   'Use ResEdit to install MIDIBASIC Code resources,
   'otherwise, the program will compile but not run.

DEFLNG a-Z
OPTION BASE 1
```

```
'_____

                                            'MIDIBASIC Variables
    halfMeg% = 0
    oneMeg% = 1
    twoMeg%= 2
    modem% = 3
    printer% = 4
    ClearIn% = 5
    ClearOut% = 6
    mode% = 0
    count%= 0
    result% = 0
    loHiMode% = 1
    maxBufferSize% = 5000
    TempBufferSize = 8500
    CheckOn = 2
    CheckOff = 1
    port% = modem%
    clockRate% = oneMeg%

    MSBFlag = 1                                 'flags for file type
    JamFlag = 2
    DX7Flag = 3
    LXPFlag = 4
    CZ1Flag = 5
    CZ32Flag =6
    noDataFlag = 0
    DumpFlag=noDataFlag


' SyxEx  Format Variables
' string buffer variable

    temp1$ = SPACE$(1)


'_____

'   MSB Formats

    MSBSize% = 1029                             'size of the MSB edit full dump (in bytes)
    MSB$ = SPACE$(MSBSize%)                     'this string will hold the MSB+ Data
    MSBRequestSize% = 5                         'size of MSB+ Full Dump SysEx request

DIM MSBRequest(MSBRequestSize%)                 'Array to hold 5 byte MSB+ request
    MSBRequest(1) = &HF0                        'SysEx
    MSBRequest(2) = &H15                        'JL Cooper ID
    MSBRequest(3) = &HB                         'MSB+ ID Code
    MSBRequest(4) = &H1                         'Full dump request
    MSBRequest(5) = &HF7                        'Last byte: EOX
```

```
'_____

'   JamBox4 formats

    JamSize% = 304                              'size of the Jam Box edit full dump (in bytes)
    Jam$ = SPACE$(JamSize%)                     'this string will hold the Jam Box Data
    JamRequestSize% = 5                         'size of Jam Box Full Dump SysEx request

DIM JamRequest(JamRequestSize%)                 'Array to hold 5 byte MSB+ request
    JamRequest(1) = &HF0                        'SysEx  status
    JamRequest(2) = &H28                        'Southworth ID
    JamRequest(3) = &H17                        'Message Request
    JamRequest(4) = &H18                        'Full dump request
    JamRequest(5) = &HF7                        'Last byte: EOX

'_____ DX7  Formats  _____

    DX7RequestSize% = 5
    DX7Size% = 163                              'size of voice edit buffer dump
    DX7$ = SPACE$(DX7Size%)

    DIM DX7DumpRequest(DX7RequestSize%)         'array to hold DX7 II edit request
    DX7DumpRequest(1) = &HF0                    'SysEx status
    DX7DumpRequest(2) = &H43                    'Yamaha ID
    DX7DumpRequest(3) = &H20                    'sub status/ channel 1
    DX7DumpRequest(4) = &H0                     'voice edit buffer
    DX7DumpRequest(5) = &HF7                    'EOX

'_____

'   LXP-1 Formats

    LXPRequestSize% = 7
    LXPSize% = 7176                             'size of an LXP's "all parameters" dump
    LXP$ = SPACE$(LXPSize%)

    DIM LXPRequest(LXPRequestSize%)             'array for LXP-1 all registers request
    LXPRequest(1) = &HF0                        'SysEx
    LXPRequest(2) = &H6                         'Lexicon ID
    LXPRequest(3) = &H2                         'LXP-1 ID
    LXPRequest(4) = &H30                        'channel 1
    LXPRequest(5) = &H64                        'event code = "all registers"
    LXPRequest(6) = &H0                         'ignored for "all register" request
    LXPRequest(7) = &HF7                        'EOX
```

```
'_____

'   CZ1 Formats

    CZTimbre1Size% = 129                       'size in byte of one CZ timbre
    TimbresPerVoice% = 100                     'number of voices in a bank.
                                               'There are 100 (0-99) for a CZ-230s

    BankSize% = (CZTimbre1Size% * TimbresPerVoice%)
    CZBank$ =SPACE$(BankSize%)                 'buffer used to hold CZ voices
    CZRequest1Size% = 7                        'size of Request message
    CZReadySize% = 6                           'size of Ready message
    CZReady$ = SPACE$(CZReadySize%)            'buffer to hold Readt message
    RawTimbre1Size% =257                       'size of nibblized data dump
    CZTimbre1$ = SPACE$(CZTimbre1Size%)        'buffer to hold de-nibblized data dump

    DIM CZRequest1(CZRequest1Size%)            'array for CZ  requests
    CZRequest1(1) = &HF0                       'SysEx
    CZRequest1(2) = &H44                       'CasioID
    CZRequest1(3) = &H0                        'Sub ID1
    CZRequest1(4) = &H0                        'Sub ID 2
    CZRequest1(5) = &H70                       'channel 1
    CZRequest1(6) = &H10                       'op code send rqst H10, receive rqst H20
    CZRequest1(7) = &H0                        'internal  voice number 1

    CZBank1% = 0                               'start and stop voice numbers
    CZBank32% = 3                              'set to four for sends to CZ-230s


'_____

'   initialization main window

screenW%=SYSTEM(5)                             'screen height
screenH%=SYSTEM(6)                             'screen width
menuBarH%=PEEKW(&HBAA)                          'menu bar height
TitleH%=20                                     'height of window type 1 title bar
height%=screenH%-(menuBarH%+TitleH%+10)
centerWindow 1,"SysEx Lab",height%,screenW%-10,1,1/2

IF compiled% THEN
    PRINT "Use ResEdit to install MIDIBasic Code resources!"
END IF

GOSUB SetUpMenus
GOSUB INITMIDI
```

```
'_____
'_____
'   main loop
WHILE 1
  ON MENU   GOSUB DoMenu    :MENU ON
  ON BREAK  GOSUB DoBreak   :BREAK ON
WEND
'_____
'_____
DoMenu:
  MenuID= MENU(0)
  MenuItem= MENU(1)
  CLS
  SELECT CASE MenuID
     CASE 1   :GOSUB FileCmd                  'File menu
     CASE 2   :GOSUB UploadCmd                'Upload menu
     CASE 3   :GOSUB DownloadCmd              'Download menu
     CASE 4   :GOSUB MIDICmd                  'MIDI menu
     CASE ELSE                                'ignore any other menu
        PRINT "Unknown menuID:" MenuID
  END SELECT
  MENU                                        'restore unhighlighted state
RETURN
'_____
FileCmd:
  SELECT CASE MenuItem
     CASE 1   :GOSUB DoSave
     CASE 3                                   'quit
     LIBRARY CLOSE
     END
     CASE ELSE
     PRINT "Undefined menu item."
     END SELECT
RETURN
'_____
'
UploadCmd:
  MOUSE ON                                    'look for mouse clicks during these routines
  SELECT CASE MenuItem
     CASE 1   :GOSUB DoDX7
     CASE 2   :GOSUB DoCZ1
     CASE 3   :GOSUB DoCZ32
     CASE 4   :GOSUB DoJamBox
     CASE 5   :GOSUB DoMSB
     CASE 6   :GOSUB DoLXP
     CASE ELSE
        PRINT "Undefined menu item."
  END SELECT
  MOUSE OFF
RETURN
```

```
DownloadCmd:
   SELECT CASE MenuItem
      CASE 1   :GOSUB DoOneWay
      CASE 3   :GOSUB DoHandShake
      CASE ELSE
         PRINT "Undefined menu item."
      END SELECT
RETURN

'_____
'
MIDICmd:
   SELECT CASE MenuItem
      CASE 1   :GOSUB DoModem
      CASE 2   :GOSUB DoPrinter
      CASE 4   :GOSUB DoHalfMeg
      CASE 5   :GOSUB DoOneMeg
      CASE 6   :GOSUB DoTwoMeg
      CASE ELSE
         PRINT "Undefined menu item."
      END SELECT
      PRINT "Reseting Interface"
      CALL MIDIPort(clockRate%)              'reset the MIDI clock rate
      CALL MIDIPort(port%)                   'reset the MIDI port
RETURN

'_____

DoBreak:
   PRINT "Leaving SysEx Lab"
   LIBRARY CLOSE
   END

'_____

DoSave:
   IF DumpFlag = noData THEN
      PRINT "There is no data in the buffer to save."
      RETURN
   END IF
      FileName$=FILES$(0,"File to save:")
   IF FileName$="" THEN
      RETURN 'Cancel was selected
   END IF
   SELECT CASE DumpFlag
      CASE 1      :GOSUB SaveMSBData
      CASE 2      :GOSUB SaveJamData
      CASE 3      :GOSUB SaveDX7Data
      CASE 4      :GOSUB SaveLXPData
      CASE 5,6 :GOSUB SaveCZ1Data
      CASE ELSE
         PRINT "Unknown Dump type" DumpFlag
      END SELECT
RETURN
```

```
'_____
SaveMSBData:
  'PRINT "Can't save " FileName$
  ' PRINT "Save routine for dump type" DumpFlag "is not implemented"
  FileSize% =MSBSize%
  PRINT"Saving" FileSize% "bytes…"
  PRINT "length of MSB$is " LEN(MSB$)
  OPEN FileName$ FOR OUTPUT AS #1
  FOR J = 1  TO FileSize%
    LOCATE 3,1
    WRITE #1,ASC(MID$(MSB$,J,1))
    PRINT "Byte :" J,"Hex Value:"HEX$(ASC(MID$(MSB$,J,1)))
  NEXT J
  CLOSE #1
  PRINT
  NAME FileName$ AS FileName$,"sXI1 " 'types file as one way data
RETURN


'_____
SaveJamData:
  ' PRINT "Can't save " FileName$
  ' PRINT "Save routine for dump type" DumpFlag "is not implemented"
  FileSize% =JamSize%
  PRINT"Saving" FileSize% "bytes…"
  PRINT "length of Jam$ is " LEN(Jam$)
  OPEN FileName$ FOR OUTPUT AS #1
  FOR J = 1  TO FileSize%
    LOCATE 3,1
    WRITE #1,ASC(MID$(Jam$,J,1))
    PRINT "Byte :" J,"Hex Value:"HEX$(ASC(MID$(Jam$,J,1)))
  NEXT J
  CLOSE #1
  PRINT
  NAME FileName$ AS FileName$,"sXI1" 'types file as one way data
RETURN


'_____
SaveDX7Data:
  FileSize% =DX7Size%
  PRINT"Saving" FileSize% "bytes…"
  OPEN FileName$ FOR OUTPUT AS #1
  FOR J = 1  TO FileSize%
  LOCATE 3,1
    WRITE #1,ASC(MID$(DX7$,J,1))
    PRINT "Byte :" J,"Hex Value:"HEX$(ASC(MID$(DX7$,J,1)))
    NEXT J
  CLOSE #1
  PRINT
  NAME FileName$ AS FileName$,"sXI1"                    'types file as one way data
RETURN
```

```
SaveLXPData:
   PRINT "Can't save " FileName$
   PRINT "Save routine for dump type" DumpFlag "is not implemented"
   FileSize% =LXPSize%
'  PRINT"Saving" FileSize% "bytes…"
'  PRINT "length of LXP$ is " LEN(LXP$)
'  OPEN FileName$ FOR OUTPUT AS #1
'  FOR J = 1  TO FileSize%
'     LOCATE 3,1
'     WRITE #1,ASC(MID$(LXP$,J,1))
'     PRINT "Byte :" J,"Hex Value:"HEX$(ASC(MID$(LXP$,J,1)))
'  NEXT J
'  CLOSE #1
'  PRINT
'  NAME FileName$ AS FileName$,"sXl1" 'types file as one way data
RETURN
```

```
SaveCZ1Data:
   FileSize% = (startPoint% + CZTimbre1Size%)-1
   PRINT"Saving" FileSize% "bytes…"
   PRINT "length of CZBank$is " LEN(CZBank$)
   OPEN FileName$ FOR OUTPUT AS #1
   FOR J = 1  TO FileSize%
      LOCATE 3,1
      WRITE #1,ASC(MID$(CZBank$,J,1))
      PRINT "Byte :" J,"Hex Value:"HEX$(ASC(MID$(CZBank$,J,1)))
   NEXT J
   CLOSE #1
   PRINT
   NAME FileName$ AS FileName$,"sXl2" 'types file as CZ Timbre data
RETURN
```

```
'

SetUpMenus:
   GOSUB SetupFileMenu
   GOSUB SetupUploadMenu
   GOSUB SetupDownloadMenu
   GOSUB SetUpMIDIMenu
RETURN
```

```
'

SetupFileMenu:
   MENU 1,0,1,"File"
   MENU 1,1,1,"Save"          :cmdKey 1,1,"S"
   MENU 1,2,0,"-"
   MENU 1,3,1,"Quit"          :cmdKey 1,3,"Q"
RETURN
```

```
'_____
'
SetupUploadMenu:
    MENU 2,0,1,"Upload"
    MENU 2,1,1,"DX7"          :cmdKey 2,1,"D"
    MENU 2,2,1,"CZ Voice"     :cmdKey 2,2,"Z"
    MENU 2,3,1,"CZ Bank"      :cmdKey 2,3,"B"
    MENU 2,4,1,"JamBox4"      :cmdKey 2,4,"J"
    MENU 2,5,1,"MSB+"         :cmdKey 2,5,"M"
    MENU 2,6,1,"LXP-1"        :cmdKey 2,6,"L"
RETURN


'_____
'
SetupDownloadMenu:
    MENU 3,0,1, "Download"
    MENU 3,1,1,"One Way "     :cmdKey 3,1,"O"
    MENU 3,2,0,"-"
    MENU 3,3,1,"Handshake"    :cmdKey 3,3,"H"
RETURN


'_____
'
SetUpMIDIMenu:
    ModemCheck = 2
    PrinterCheck = 1
    halfMegCheck = 1
    oneMegCheck =2
    twoMegCheck = 3
    MENU 4,0,1, "MIDI"
    MENU 4,1,2,"Modem"        :cmdKey 4,1,"M"
    MENU 4,2,1,  "Printer"    :cmdKey 4,2,"R"
    MENU 4,3,0,"-"
    MENU 4,4,1, ".5 MHz"      :cmdKey 4,4,"5"
    MENU 4,5,2,"1 MHz"        :cmdKey 4,5,"1"
    MENU 4,6,1, "2MHz"        :cmdKey 4,6,"2"
RETURN


'_____
'
'SysEx DoItem Sub Routines

'_____
'
'Upload Menu Item Subroutines

EndIt:
    result% = 1
RETURN


'_____
'
'   DX7 Upload Sub Routines
```

```
DoDX7:
  ' PRINT "DX7  is not implemented"
    DumpFlag = DX7Flag
    GOSUB DX7Up
RETURN
```

```
DX7Up:
    PRINT ,"Sending DX7 II (TX 802) Edit Buffer Dump Request"
    GOSUB ClearMIDI
    ByteCount = DX7RequestSize%
    FOR J = 1 TO ByteCount
      X% = DX7DumpRequest(J)
      MIDIOut X%
      PRINT " " HEX$(X%);
    NEXT J
    PRINT
    result% =-1
    click% = 0
    PRINT "Hit mouse to stop transfer"
    WHILE result% = -1
      ON MOUSE GOSUB EndIt
      CALL GetMIDI(DX7$,0,count%,result%)
    WEND
    IF result% = 1 THEN
      PRINT "Time out error.  Edit buffer data not received."
      DumpFlag = noData 'reset dump flag on error
      RETURN
    END IF
    PRINT "Retrieved"count% "bytes of 'DX7 II Edit Buffer Data."
RETURN    'DX7up
```

```
'   CZ Upload Sub Routines
```

```
DoCZ1:
  'PRINT "CZ Voice is not implemented"
    DumpFlag = CZ1Flag
    voiceCount% = 1
    PRINT "What is the number of the voice you want to request";
    INPUT voice%
    CZRequest1(7) = voice%
    GOSUB CZ1Up
RETURN
```

```
DoCZ32:
  DumpFlag = CZ32Flag
  voiceCount% = 1
  FOR voice% = CZBank1% TO CZBank32%
    CZRequest1(7) = voiceCount% 'put the voice number into the request
    GOSUB CZ1Up                                    ' go get the timbre data fo the voice
    IF result% = 1 THEN
      LOCATE 12,1
      PRINT "Bank dump has stopped after receiving voice number" voice%-1
      RETURN
    END IF
    voiceCount% = voiceCount%+1 'increment the voice being requested
    PRINT "Received voice number :"CZRequest1(7)
  NEXT voice%
RETURN
```

```
LoadBank:
  startPoint% = (voiceCount% * CZTimbre1Size%)-(CZTimbre1Size%-1)
  PRINT "loading bank buffer starting at point number" startPoint%
  MID$(CZBank$,startPoint%) = CZTimbre1$
RETURN
```

```
GetTimbreData:
  WHILE count% < RawTimbre1Size%     'wait for input buffer to fill with 257 bytes (the size of a voice dump)
    CALL InCount(count%)
  WEND
  PRINT "There are" count% "bytes of 'nibblized' data waiting in the buffer."
  DumpFlag = CZ1Flag    'set dump type to Jambox
  CALL GetMIDI(CZTimbre1$,loHiMode%,count%,result%)              'get the voice dump from the buffer
  PRINT "Retrieved"count% "bytes of 'de-nibblized' CZ Timbre Data."
RETURN
```

```
CZ1Up:   'Upload CZ1 Voice Bulk data
  LOCATE 2,1
  CZRequest1(6) = &H10                             'op code for send1 request
  PRINT "Sending CZ1 Send Request 1for voice number :" CZRequest1(7)
  GOSUB ClearMIDI
  GOSUB DoSend1
  GOSUB GetReady1
  IF result% = 1 THEN
    PRINT "Request unsuccessful, no response from CZ."
    DumpFlag = noData
    RETURN                                      'do not continue with the rest of the routine
  END IF
  GOSUB DoContinue
  GOSUB GetTimbreData
  GOSUB LoadBank
RETURN   'CZ1up
```

```
DoSend1:
  ByteCount = CZRequest1Size%
  FOR J = 1 TO ByteCount
    X% = CZRequest1(J)
    MIDIOut X%
    PRINT " " HEX$(X%);
  NEXT J
  PRINT
RETURN
```

```
GetReady1:
Test% = -1
  WHILE Test% = -1                              'wait for CZ to handshake with a ready1 message
    CALL GetMIDI(temp1$, mode%,count%, result%)
    IF temp1$ = CHR$(&HF0) OR result% = 1 THEN
      Test% = 0
    END IF
  WEND
  IF result% = 1 THEN
    LOCATE 10,1
  PRINT "Time out error.   $F0 never received"
  ELSE
    WHILE Test% = 0
      CALL GetMIDI(temp1$, mode%,count%, result%)
      IF temp1$ = CHR$(&H30) OR result% = 1 THEN
        Test% = -1
      END IF
    WEND
    IF result% = 1 THEN
      PRINT "Time out error. $30 never received"
    END IF
  END IF
RETURN
```

```
DoContinue:
'send a continue handshake back to the CZ
  X% = &H70
  CALL MIDIOut(X%)
  X% = &H31
  CALL MIDIOut(X%)
RETURN
```

```
'    JamBox 4 upload routines


'_____

 DoJamBox:
' PRINT "JamBox 4 is not implemented"
    DumpFlag = JamFlag
    GOSUB JamUp
RETURN


'_____
'

JamUp:    'Upload Jam Box Bulk data
    PRINT ,"Sending JamBox4+ Full Dump Request"
    GOSUB ClearMIDI
    ByteCount = JamRequestSize%
    FOR J = 1 TO ByteCount
       X% = JamRequest(J)
       MIDIOut X%
       PRINT " " HEX$(X%);
    NEXT J
    PRINT
    result% =-1
    click% = 0
    PRINT "Hit mouse to stop transfer"
    WHILE result% = -1 AND click% = 0
       ON MOUSE GOSUB EndIt
       CALL getMIDI(Jam$,0,count%,result%)
    WEND
    IF result% = 1 THEN
       PRINT "Time out error.  JamBox 4 data not received."
       DumpFlag = noData 'reset dump flag on error
       RETURN
    END IF
RETURN    'JamUp


'_____

DoMSB:
    'PRINT "MSB+  is not implemented"
     DumpFlag = MSBFlag
     GOSUB MSBUp
RETURN


'_____
```

```
'    MSB + Upload Sub Routines

'_____

MSBUp:    'Upload MSB+ bulk dump data
    PRINT, "Sending MSB+ Full Dump Request
    GOSUB ClearMIDI
    ByteCount = MSBRequestSize%
    FOR J = 1 TO ByteCount
        X% = MSBRequest(J)
         MIDIOut X%
        PRINT " " HEX$(X%);
    NEXT J
    PRINT
    result% =-1
    click% = 0
    PRINT "Hit mouse to stop transfer"
    WHILE result% = -1 AND click% = 0
        ON MOUSE GOSUB EndIt
        CALL getMIDI(MSB$,0,count%,result%)
    WEND
    IF result% = 1 THEN
        PRINT "Time out error.  MSB+ data not received."
        DumpFlag = noData 'reset dump flag on error
        RETURN
    END IF
RETURN    'MSBUp


'_____

'   LXP Upload Sub Routines

'_____

DoLXP:
    'PRINT "LXP-1 is not implemented"
    DumpFlag = LXPFlag
    GOSUB LXPUp
RETURN

'_____
```

```
LXPUp:    'Upload "all registers" from LXP-1
   DumpFlag = LXPFlag
   PRINT ,"Sending LXP-1 All Register Dump Request"
   GOSUB ClearMIDI
   ByteCount = LXPRequestSize%
   FOR J = 1 TO ByteCount
      X% = LXPRequest(J)
      MIDIOut X%
      PRINT " " HEX$(X%);
   NEXT J
   PRINT
   result% =-1
   click% = 0
   PRINT "Hit mouse to stop transfer"
   WHILE result% = -1 AND click% = 0
      ON MOUSE GOSUB EndIt
      CALL getMIDI(LXP$,0,count%,result%)
   WEND
   IF result% = 1 THEN
      PRINT "Time out error.  LXP-1 All Parameters data not received."
      DumpFlag = noData 'reset dump flag on error
      RETURN
   END IF
RETURN    'LXPup


'_____

'Download Menu Item Subroutines

'_____

' One way download routines - for devices that do not use handshaking
'_____

DoOneWay:
   FileName$=FILES$(1,"sXl1")
   IF FileName$="" THEN
      RETURN
   END IF
   PRINT FileName$ " is being transmitted."
   ByteCount% = 1
   OPEN FileName$ FOR INPUT AS#1
   WHILE NOT EOF(1)
      INPUT #1, X%
      LOCATE 3,1
      PRINT "Byte :" ByteCount%,"Hex Value:"HEX$(X%)
      ByteCount% = ByteCount% +1
      CALL MIDIOut(X%)
   WEND
   CLOSE #1
RETURN


'_____
```

```
' Two way Download routines for devices that require handshaking


'_____

TransmitCZData:
   startPoint% = 1
   CZRequest1(6) = &H20                              'op code for receive1 request
   CZRequest1(7) = 96                                'first programmable voice on CZ-230S
   FOR Z = 1 TO voiceCount%
      CZTimbre1$=MID$(CZBank$,startPoint%,CZTimbre1Size%)
      LOCATE 2,1
      PRINT "Sending CZ1 Receive  Request 1for voice number :" CZRequest1(7)
      GOSUB ClearMIDI
      GOSUB DoSend1
      GOSUB GetReady1
      IF result% = 1 THEN
         PRINT "Request unsuccessful, no response from CZ."
         RETURN                                      'dont continue with the rest of the routine
      END IF
      CALL SendMIDI(CZTimbre1$,loHiMode%)
      X% = &HF7                                      'be sure to complete the handshake!
      CALL MIDIOut(X%)
      startPoint% = startPoint% + CZTimbre1Size%
      PRINT "transmitted voice number" CZRequest1(7)
      CZRequest1(7) = CZRequest1(7)+1
   NEXT Z
RETURN


'_____

FillBank:
   startPoint% = 1
   OPEN FileName$ FOR INPUT AS #1
   WHILE NOT EOF(1)
      INPUT#1, X%
      MID$(CZBank$,startPoint%,1)=CHR$(X%)
      startPoint% = startPoint%+1
   WEND
   CLOSE #1
   FileSize% = startPoint%-1
   voiceCount% = FileSize%/CZTimbre1Size%
   LOCATE 5,1
   PRINT "There are " voiceCount% "voices in the file."
RETURN


'_____
```

```
DoHandShake:
  voiceCount% = 0
  FileName$=FILES$(1,"sXl2")
  IF FileName$="" THEN
      RETURN
  END IF
  GOSUB FillBank
  PRINT "This file is "FileSize% "bytes long."
  GOSUB TransmitCZData
RETURN


'_____

'MIDI MENU Item Subroutines

'_____

'
DoModem:
  MENU 4,1,CheckOn                        'reset modem item check mark
  MENU 4,2, CheckOff                      'reset printer item check mark
  port% = modem%
RETURN


'_____

'
DoPrinter:
  MENU 4,1,CheckOff                       'reset modem item check mark
  MENU 4,2, CheckOn                       'reset printer item check mark
  port% = printer%
RETURN

'_____

'
DoHalfMeg:
  MENU 4,4,CheckOn                        'reset .5 MHz item check mark
  MENU 4,5, CheckOff                      'reset 1 MHz item check mark
  MENU 4,6, CheckOff                      'reset 2 MHz item check mark
  clockRate% = halfMeg%
RETURN


'_____

'
DoOneMeg:
  MENU 4,4,CheckOff                       'reset .5 MHz item check mark
  MENU 4,5, CheckOn                       'reset 1 MHz item check mark
  MENU 4,6, CheckOff                      'reset 2 MHz item check mark
  clockRate% = oneMeg%
RETURN

'_____
```

```
DoTwoMeg:
  MENU 4,4,CheckOff                              'reset .5 MHz item check mark
  MENU 4,5, CheckOff                             'reset 1 MHz item check mark
  MENU 4,6, CheckOn                              'reset 2 MHz item check mark
  clockRate% = twoMeg%
RETURN

INITMIDI:
  CALL MIDIopen(maxBufferSize%,maxBufferSize%)
  CALL MIDIFilter(1,254,254,0)                   'Filter out active sensing !!
  CALL MIDIPort(clockRate%)
  CALL MIDIPort(port%)
  GOSUB ClearMIDI
RETURN

ClearMIDI:
  CALL MIDI(ClearIn%)
  CALL MIDI(ClearOut%)
RETURN

'_____

' window routine
SUB centerWindow(id%,title$,high%,wide%,type%,fract!)STATIC
  SELECT CASE ABS(type%)
     CASE 1 :overt%=18 :overb%=2
     CASE 2 :overt%=8 :overb%=8
     CASE ELSE :overt%=0 :overb%=0
  END SELECT
  left%=(SYSTEM(5)-(wide%))/2
  top%=PEEKW(&HBAA)+overt%*fract!+(SYSTEM(6)-(PEEKW(&HBAA)+high%+overb%))*fract!
  WINDOW id%,title$,(left%,top%)-(left%+wide%,top%+high%),type%
END SUB
```

About the Authors

Steve De Furia

Joe Scacciaferro

Steve De Furia is a columnist for *Keyboard* magazine and is an active studio musician and synthesist with numerous album, film, and session credits. He got his start as a computer programmer by writing music composition software for Frank Zappa.

Joe Scacciaferro is president of Triple S Electronics, a leading design and service facility for computer-based musical equipment. He is a MIDI expert specializing in digital systems design and is a featured columnist for *Music, Computers and Software* magazine.

Index

More Programming Tools
from M&T Books

Programming Languages

C

Graphics Programming in C
Roger T. Stevens
Item #019-2 $39.95 (book/disk)
Item #018-4 $24.95 (book)
Details the fundamentals of graphics processes for the IBM PC family and its clones. All the information needed to program graphics in C, including source code, is presented. The provided source code will enable the user to easily modify graphics functions to suit specific needs. Both Turbo C and Microsoft C are supported.

C Chest and Other C Treasures from *Dr. Dobb's Journal*
Edited by Allen Holub
Item #40-2 $24.95 (book)
Item #49-6 $39.95 (book/disk)
This comprehensive anthology contains the popular "C Chest" columns from *Dr. Dobb's Journal of Software Tools*, along with the lively philosophical and practical discussions they inspired, in addition to other information-packed articles by C experts. The software in the book is also available on disk with full source code. MS-DOS format.

Turbo C: The Art of Advanced Program Design, Optimization, and Debugging
Stephen R. Davis
Item #38-0 $24.95 (book)
Item #45-3 $39.95 (book/disk)
Overflowing with example programs, this book fully describes the techniques necessary to skillfully program, optimize, and debug in Turbo C. All programs are also available on disk with full source code. MS-DOS format.

A Small C Compiler: Language, Usage, Theory, and Design
James E. Hendrix
Item #88-7 $23.95 (book)
Item #97-6 $38.95 (book/disk)
A full presentation of the design and theory of the Small C compiler (including source code) and programming language. The author has implemented many features in this compiler that make it an excellent example for learning basic compiler theory. Some of these features are: recursive descent parsing, one-pass compilation, and the generation of assembly language. Here is a look into a real compiler with the opportunity for hands-on experience in designing one.

Dr. Dobb's Toolbook of C
Editors of *Dr. Dobb's Journal*
Item #89303-615-3 $29.95
From *Dr. Dobb's Journal of Software Tools* and Brady Communications, this book contains a comprehensive library of valuable C code. *Dr. Dobb's Journal of Software Tools'* most popular articles on C are updated and reprinted here, along with new C programming tools. Also included is a complete C compiler, an assembler, text processing programs, and more!

The Small-C Handbook
James E. Hendrix
Item #8359-7012-4 $17.95 (book)
Item #67-4 $37.90 (book and CP/M disk)
Also from *Dr. Dobb's Journal of Software Tools* and Brady Communications, the handbook is a valuable companion to the Small-C compiler, described below. The book explains the language and the compiler, and contains entire source listings of the compiler and its library of arithmetic and logical routines.

Forth

Dr. Dobb's Toolbook of Forth
Edited by Marlin Ouverson
Item #10-0 $22.95 (book)
Item #57-7 $39.95 (book/disk)
This comprehensive collection of useful Forth programs and tutorials contains expanded versions of *Dr. Dobb's Journal of Software Tools'* best Forth articles and other material, including practical code and in-depth discussions of advanced Forth topics. The screens in the book are also available on

disk as ASCII files in the following formats: MS/PC-DOS, Apple II, Macintosh, or CP/M: Osborne or 8" SS/SD.

Dr. Dobb's Toolbook of Forth, Volume II
Editors of *Dr. Dobb's Journal*
Item #41-0 $29.95 (book)
Item #51-8 $45.95 (book/disk)
This complete anthology of Forth programming techniques and developments picks up where the Toolbook of Forth, First Edition left off. Included are the best articles on Forth from *Dr. Dobb's Journal of Software Tools*, along with the latest material from other Forth experts. The screens in the book are available on disk as ASCII files in the following formats: MS-DOS, Macintosh, and CP/M: Osborne or 8" SS/SD.

BASIC

QuickBASIC: Programming Techniques and Library Development
Namir Clement Shammas
Item #004-4 $34.95 (book/disk)
Item #003-6 $19.95 (book)
This book provides the reader with the opportunity to learn the details of creating subroutines, functions, and libraries to permit more structured coding. The remainder of the book is dedicated to an in-depth discussion of building original libraries and functions to fulfill individual programming needs. Programs and subroutines are available on disk with full source code.

Turbo BASIC: Programming Techniques and Library Development
Namir Clement Shammas
Item #016-8 $34.95 (book/disk)
Item #015-X $19.95 (book)
Advanced programmers will be introduced to the flexible Turbo BASIC environment, programming framework, data types, and the use of libraries, functions and subroutines to permit more structured coding. As with the QuickBASIC book, the techniques discussed in this volume are then put to use building a selection of useful libraries. All programs and subroutines are also available on disk with full source code.

HyperTalk

Dr. Dobb's Essential HyperTalk Handbook
Michael Swaine
Item #99-5 $39.95 (book/disk)
Item #99-0 $24.95 (book)
Well-known columnist Michael Swaine provides a complete analyses of HyperTalk in this new book. Complete coverage of topics such as the move from authoring to scripting, concepts and components of the language, programming style considerations, full language exposition and discussion, and more, are presented. Programs available on disk.

MIDI

C Programming for MIDI
Jim Conger
Item #86-0 $22.95 (book)
Item #90-9 $37.95 (book/disk)
For musicians and programmers alike, here is the source that will help you write programs for music applications. The author begins by outlining the features of MIDI (Musical Instrument Digital Interface) and its support of real-time access to musical devices. An introduction to C programming fundamentals as they relate to MIDI is also provided. The author fully demonstrates these concepts with two MIDI applications: a patch librarian and a simple sequencer.

MIDI Programming for the Macintosh
Steve De Furia and Joe Scacciaferro, Ferro Technologies
Item #022-2 $37.95 (book/disk)
Item #021-4 $22.95 (book)
This book equips the musician and programmer alike with the background necessary to program music applications and to take advantage of all the Macintosh and the MIDI interface have to offer. Specific examples are presented and all source code is available on disk.

Business

PC Accounting Solutions
Editors of *PC Accounting* (formerly *Business Software*)
Item #008-7 $37.95 (book/disk)
Item #009-5 $22.95 (book)
This anthology serves as a well-rounded source of expert information for managers who want to implement a PC-based accounting system or to gain better control of their existing system. From choosing and maximizing your accounting systems and software to building better spreadsheets and budgets, this book is an immensely valuable source that will improve your ability to analyze the information that is critical to the success of your business.

Public-Domain Software and Shareware: Untapped Resources for the PC User, Second Edition
Rusel DeMaria and George R. Fontaine
Item #011-7 $19.95 (book)
Item #014-1 $34.95 (book/disk)
Organized into a comprehensive reference, this book introduces the novice and guides the experienced user to a source of often overlooked software—public domain and Shareware. This book will tell you where it is, how to get it, what to look for, and why it's for you. The sample programs and some of the software reviewed is available on disk in MS-DOS format. Includes information on how to obtain $15 worth of free access time on CompuServe, and other special offers.

Time and Task Management with dBASE III
Timothy Berry
Item #09-7 $49.95 (manual/MS-DOS disk)
Like an accounting system for time and tasks, this package helps users organize hours, budgets, activities, and resources. Providing both a useful time-management system and a library of dBASE III code and macros, this package has practical as well as educational value. To be used with dBASE III. Source code and documentation is included. MS-DOS disk format.

Sales Management with dBASE III
Timothy Berry
Item #15-1 $49.95 (manual/MS-DOS disk)
Sales management works with dBASE III to provide a powerful information system that will help you to keep track of clients, names, addresses,

follow-ups, pending dates, and account data. This system organizes all the day-to-day activities of selling and includes program files, format files, report files, index files, and data bases. Documentation and full source code is included.

Programming Tools and Source Code Libraries

C

Small-Windows: A Library of Windowing Functions for the C Language
James E. Hendrix
Item #35-X $29.95
Small-Windows is a complete windowing library for C. The package includes video functions, menu functions, window functions, and more. The package is available for MS-DOS systems for the following compilers: Microsoft C Version 4.0 and 5.0; Small-C; Turbo C 1.0 and 1.5; and Lattice C 3.1. Documentation and full C source code is included.

Tools

Small Tools: Programs for Text Processing
James E. Hendrix
Item #78-X $29.95 (manual/disk)
This package of text-processing programs written in Small-C is designed to perform specific, modular functions on text files. Source code is included. Small Tools is available in both CP/M and MS/PC-DOS versions and includes complete documentation.

Small Assembler: A Macro Assembler Written in Small C
James E. Hendrix
MS-DOS version: Item #024-9 $29.95 (manual/disk)
CP/M version: Item #77-1 $29.95 (manual/disk)
Here is a full macro assembler which was developed primarily for use with the Small-C compiler. It provides an excellent example for learning the basics of how assembler works. The manual provides an overview of the Small Assembler, documents the command lines that invoke programs, and more. The accompanying disk includes both the executable assembler and full source code.

NR: An Implementation of the UNIX NROFF Word Processor
Allen Holub
Item #33-X $29.95
NR is a text formatter that is written in C and compatible with UNIX's NROFF. *NR* comes configured for any Diablo-compatible printer, as well as Hewlett Packard's ThinkJet and LaserJet. Both the ready-to-use program and full source code are included. For PC compatibles.

Turbo Pascal

Statistical Toolbox for Turbo Pascal
Namir Clement Shammas
Item #22-4 $39.95 (manuals/disks)
Two statistical packages in one! A library disk and reference manual that includes statistical distribution functions, random number generation, basic descriptive statistics, parametric and nonparametric statistical testing, bivariate linear regression, and multiple and polynomial regression. The demonstration disk and manual incorporate these library routines into a fully functioning statistical program. For IBM PCs and compatibles.

Turbo Advantage
Lauer and Wallwitz
Item #26-7 $29.95
A library of more than 200 routines, with source code sample programs and documentation. Routines are organized and documented under the following categories: bit manipulation, file management, MS-DOS support, string operations, arithmetic calculations, data compression, differential equations, Fourier analysis and synthesis, and much more! For MS/PC-DOS systems.

Turbo Advantage: Complex
Lauer and Wallwitz
Item #27-5 $39.95
This library provides the Turbo Pascal code for digital filters, boundary-value solutions, vector and matrix calculations with complex integers and variables, Fourier transforms, and calculations of convolution and correlation functions. Some of the *Turbo Advantage: Complex* routines are most effectively used with Turbo Advantage. Source code and documentation included.

Turbo Advantage: Display
Lauer and Wallwitz
Item #28-3 $39.95
Turbo Advantage: Display includes an easy-to-use form processor and thirty Turbo Pascal procedures and functions to facilitate linking created forms to your program. Full source code and documentation are included. Some of the *Turbo Advantage* routines are necessary to compile *Turbo Advantage: Display.*

Operating Systems

OS/2

The Programmer's Essential OS/2 Handbook
David E. Cortesi
Item #82-8 $24.95 (book)
Item #89-5 $39.95 (book/disk)
Here is a resource no developer can afford to be without! Cortesi succinctly organizes the many features of OS/2 into related topics and illuminates their uses. Detailed indexes and a web of cross referencing provide easy access to all OS/2 topic areas. Equal support for Pascal and C programmers is provided. *The* essential reference for programmers developing in the OS/2 environment.

UNIX

UNIX Programming on the 80286/80386
Alan Deikman
Item #83-6 $24.95 (book)
Item #91-9 $39.95 (book/disk)
A complete professional-level tutorial and reference for programming UNIX and XENIX on 80286/80386-based computers. Succinct coverage of the UNIX program environment, UNIX file system, shells, utilities, and C programming under UNIX are covered. The author also delves into the development of device drivers; some examples of these are video displays, tape cartridges, terminals, and networks.

On Command: Writing a UNIX-Like Shell for MS-DOS
Allen Holub
Item #29-1 $39.95

Learn how to write shells applicable to MS-DOS, as well as to most other programming environments. This book and disk include a full description of a UNIX-like shell, complete C source code, a thorough discussion of low-level DOS interfacing, and significant examples of C programming at the system level. All source code is included on disk.

/util: A UNIX-Like Utility Package for MS-DOS
Allen Holub
Item #12-7 $29.95

This collection of utilities is intended to be accessed through SH but can be used separately. It contains programs and subroutines that, when coupled with SH, create a fully functional UNIX-like environment. The package includes a disk with full C source code and documentation in a UNIX-style manual.

MS-DOS

Taming MS-DOS, Second Edition
Thom Hogan
Item #87-9 $19.95
Item #92-5 $34.95

Described by reviewers as "small in size, large on content," and "fun." The second edition promises to be just as readable and is updated to cover MS-DOS 3.3. Some of the more perplexing elements of MS-DOS are succinctly described here with time-saving tricks to help customize any MS-DOS system. Each trick is easily implemented into your existing tools and for programmers, Hogan includes many complete source code files that provide very useful utilities. All source code is written in BASIC.

Program Interfacing to MS-DOS
William G. Wong
Item #34-8 $29.95

Program Interfacing to MS-DOS will orient any experienced programmer to the MS-DOS environment. The package includes a ten-part manual with sample program files and a detailed description of how to build device drivers, along with the device driver for a memory disk and a character device driver on disk with macro assembly source code.

Other

Tele Operating System Toolkit
Ken Berry

This task-scheduling algorithm drives the Tele Operating System and is composed of several components. When integrated, they form an independent operating system for any 8086-based machine. Tele has also been designed for compatibility with MS-DOS, UNIX, and the MOSI standard.

SK: THE SYSTEM KERNEL
Item #30-5 $49.95 (manual/disk)

The System Kernel contains an initialization module, general-purpose utility functions, and a real-time task management system. The kernel provides MS-DOS applications with multitasking capabilities. The System Kernel is required by all other components. All source code is included on disk in MS-DOS format.

DS: WINDOW DISPLAY
Item #32-1 $39.95 (manual/disk)

This component contains BIOS level drivers for a memory-mapped display, window management support and communication coordination between the operator and tasks in a multitasking environment. All source code is included on disk in MS-DOS format.

FS: THE FILE SYSTEM
Item #65-8 $39.95 (manual/disk)

The File System supports MS-DOS disk file structures and serial communication channels. All source code is included on disk in MS-DOS format.

XS: THE INDEX SYSTEM
Item #66-6 $39.95 (manual/disk)

The Index System implements a tree-structured free-form database. All source code is included on disk in MS-DOS format.

Chips

Dr. Dobb's Toolbook of 80286/80386 Programming
Edited by Phillip Robinson
Item #42-9 $24.95 (book)
Item #53-4 $39.95 (book/disk)
This toolbook is a comprehensive discussion of the powerful 80X86 family of microprocessors. Editor Phillip Robinson has gathered the best articles from numerous key programming publications to create this valuable resource for all 80X86 programmers. All programs are available on disk with full source code.

Dr. Dobb's Z80 Toolbook
David E. Cortesi
Item #07-0 $25.00 (book)
Item #55-0 $40.00 (book/disk)
This book contains everything users need to write their own Z80 assembly-language programs, including a method of designing programs and coding them in assembly language and a complete, integrated toolkit of subroutines. All the software in the book is available on disk in the following formats: 8" SS/SD, Apple, Osborne, or Kaypro.

Dr. Dobb's Toolbook of 68000 Programming
Editors of *Dr. Dobb's Journal*
Item #13-216649-6 $29.95 (book)
Item #75-5 $49.95 (book/disk)
From *Dr. Dobb's Journal of Software Tools* and Brady Communications, this collection of practical programming tips and tools for the 68000 family contains the best 68000 articles reprinted from *Dr. Dobb's Journal of Software Tools*, along with much new material. The book contains many useful applications and examples. The software in the book is also available on disk in the following formats: MS/PC-DOS, Macintosh, CP/M 8", Osborne, Amiga, and Atari 520ST.

X68000 Cross Assembler
Brian R. Anderson
Item #71-2 $25.00
This manual and disk contain an executable version of the 68000 Cross Assembler discussed in *Dr. Dobb's Toolbook of 68000 Programming*, complete with source code and documentation. The Cross-Assembler requires CP/M 2.2 with 64K or MS-DOS with 128K. The disk is available in the following formats: MS-DOS, 8" SS/SD, and Osborne.

General Interest

DESQview: A Guide to Programming the DESQview Multitasking Environment
Stephen R. Davis
Item #06-0 $39.95 (book/disk)
Item #28-1 $24.95 (book)
Fully endorsed by Quarterdeck Office Systems, publisher of DESQview, this book provides users with the information they need to get the most out of DESQview. Contents include the object-oriented DESQview 2.0 API (Application Program Interface) and multitasking concepts necessary to program the DESQview environment, example programs that control and interact with DESQview's API, and demonstrations of such concepts as windowing, intertask communication, and subtask control.

Interfacing to S-100/IEEE 696 Microcomputers
Mark Garetz and Sol Libes
Item #85-2 $24.95
This book helps S-100 bus users expand the utility and power of their systems. It describes the S-100 bus with unmatched precision. Various chapters describe its mechanical and functional design, logical and electrical relationships, bus interconnections, and busing techniques.

Building Local Area Networks
Patrick H. Corrigan and Scott Herndon
Item #025-7 $39.95 (book/disk)
Item #010-9 $24.95 (book)
The specifics of building and maintaining PC LANs, including hardware configurations, software development, cabling, selection criteria, installation, and on-going management, are described in a detailed, "how-to" manner with numerous illustrations and sample LAN management forms.

Dr. Dobb's Journal Bound Volume Series

Each volume in this series contains a full year's worth of useful code and fascinating history from *Dr. Dobb's Journal of Software Tools*. Each volume contains every issue of *DDJ* for a given year, reprinted and combined into one comprehensive reference.

Volume	1: 1976	*Item #13-5*	*$30.75*
Volume	2: 1977	*Item #16-X*	*$30.75*
Volume	3: 1978	*Item #17-8*	*$30.75*
Volume	4: 1979	*Item #14-3*	*$30.75*
Volume	5: 1980	*Item #18-6*	*$30.75*
Volume	6: 1981	*Item #19-4*	*$30.75*
Volume	7: 1982	*Item #20-8*	*$35.75*
Volume	8: 1983	*Item #00-3*	*$35.75*
Volume	9: 1984	*Item #08-9*	*$35.75*
Volume	10: 1985	*Item #21-6*	*$35.75*
Volume	11: 1986	*Item #72-0*	*$35.75*
Volume	12: 1987	*Item #84-4*	*$39.95*
Volume	13: 1988	*Item #27-3*	*$39.95*

To order any of these products send your payment, along with $2.95 per item for shipping, to M&T Books, 501 Galveston Drive, Redwood City, California 94063. California residents, please include the appropriate sales tax. Or, call toll-free 800-533-4372 (in California 800-356-2002) Monday through Friday between 8 A.M. and 5 P.M. Pacific Standard Time. When ordering disks, please indicate format.